Advance praise for *Paradise Besieged*:

"Get ready for an extraordinary adventure—a journey that challenges the mind as well as the spirit. Richard Friedlander has written a thoughtful, honest, thrilling and insightful book that allows us not merely to imagine, but indirectly experience monastic life in all its complexity, profundity and richness. Fascinating from start to finish."
—**Ken Cloke**, author of *Mediating Dangerously: The Frontiers of Conflict Resolution*

"R. J. Friedlander—an American Jew—becomes a Greek Orthodox monk. He writes autobiographically with refreshing candor, joyous humor and good taste."
—**James Steve Counelis**, author of *Higher Learning and Orthodox Christianity* and *Inheritance and Change in Orthodox Christianity*

"This book is a nearly unparalleled opportunity to be the proverbial fly on the wall in the male-only, Orthodox confines of a skete in Greece—a place most readers could never enter.... Friedlander's endearingly irreverent memoir of an extraordinary decade in his life deserves many readers. Highly recommended."
—**Graham Christian**, Andover-Harvard Theological Library

"A fascinating description of how two worlds—inner and outer, temporal and eternal, archaic and hi-tech—collide, or more accurately slither in and out and around each other. If you are curious as to how ignorance can be laced with wisdom, and how feet that scarcely touch the ground can get mired in the world's muck, this book will not allay your curiosity, but it will circle it engagingly."
—**Huston Smith**, author of *Tales of Wonder: Adventures Chasing the Divine, an Autobiography* and *The World's Religions*

PARADISE BESIEGED

To Anna & John,
Hope this gives you
lots of fun and food
for thought!
All the best,
[signature]

PARADISE
BESIEGED

A Journey to Medieval
Mount Athos at the Dawn of the
Information Age

Richard John Friedlander

REVISED EDITION

Flying High Press
Berkeley

PARADISE BESIEGED:
A Journey to Medieval Mount Athos at the Dawn of the Information Age

First published 2007 by iUniverse.com

Revised Edition

Copyright © 2009 by Richard Friedlander

Flying High Press books may be ordered through booksellers or by contacting:

Flying High Press
3051 Buena Vista Way
Berkeley, CA 94708
1-510-701-3423
RAFmed@juno.com

ISBN: 978-0-578-04192-6

Printed in the United States of America

To my mother and Father James Williams—as unlikely and unwitting collaborators as it would be possible to find on God's fractured earth

TABLE OF CONTENTS

PREFACE

In my junior year at Yale, as I was trying to figure out why I was there, I took a course in American Colonial History from the brilliant Professor Edmund S. Morgan. Professor Morgan lived his subject so thoroughly, he came to look like a 17th century Thanksgiving Pilgrim, needing only a tall, wide-brimmed hat with a silver buckle, a turkey, and a blunderbuss to complete the picture. His worn, Harris Tweed jacket seemed more time machine than garment.

I am deeply indebted to Professor Morgan. Not only did he get me out of having to attend any classes in my senior year by recommending me for the Scholar of the House program of independent study, but he let me know how little I knew about Christianity. At the top of a short research paper on which he had bestowed the unusual grade of "100 minus 5" – the five points the price of my habitual reluctance to meet deadlines – he scribbled that from my description of Roger Williams' hasty flight from persecution in Massachusetts to persecutor in Rhode Island, it was clear I knew nothing about the sacrament of communion. The generous grade did not encourage me to seek a cure for my ignorance. Fifteen years later, Holy Communion became the center of my life. And it was I who had become the pilgrim.

Professor Morgan had faith in my ability to write. He also planted the seed that eventually produced this book. In his classic exposition of the spiritual and earthly trials of John Winthrop, governor of the Massachusetts Bay Colony, my teacher summarized *The Puritan Dilemma* as "the paradox that required a man to live in the world without being of it." To Calvinist Puritans believing in predestination, this was indeed a daunting task. Their beliefs required them to try to live a godly life in a world where they were foredoomed to do evil, while uncertain of their reward in the world to come. For most of us, this is a 'so what?' conundrum, and yet we confront a comparable dilemma every day. Allowing for all the changes that have occurred in the last four hundred years, the brain that allows us to love others whom we have no reason to love is still the same brain is able to justify our killing others when our survival is not at stake. We might pose our own moral predicament as this: How can we render unto Darwin the things that are Darwin's and to something else the rest?

Our answer to this question, in any of its guises, determines what we experience in our brief stay on earth, both as individuals and as a species – whether it is progress or destruction, conservatism or reaction, liberty or license, zeal or bigotry, sanctity or fanaticism. The contraction of space and time, driven by unprecedented material progress, makes this even more of a challenge. It has hauled even Mount Athos, the remote epicenter of Orthodox Christian monasticism, out of a thousand years of torpor and into the 21st century by the seat of its pants.

In ancient days, when I began this piece, it was fourteen years since I had been to the Holy Mountain of Athos and two years before the reunion that is my Epilogue. At any other time in its thousand-year history, this would be irrelevant. Time simply stopped at the borders of the wild monastic fiefdom. But physical isolation can no more deny the transformative power of modern technology than stone walls forty feet high could save Constantinople from the conquering horsemen of Muhammad II. The journey on which we are about to embark draws on my experience of life on Mount Athos in the years between 1975 and 1984, when scouts were just beginning to appear on the surrounding hilltops and to probe its defenses; when a possibility entered the consciousness that eventually would become fact; when monks, if they ever thought about it at all, still believed "it can't happen here."

PREFACE TO THE REVISED EDITION

*S*chindler's List ends with Schindler kicking himself for not doing more to help the Jews in his employ, lamenting his inability to rewrite history. Writers have neither the humility nor limitation. Samuel Johnson said that some people have one book in them, while others have a whole library; but some can make that one book into a library, while some libraries actually contain only one book. I have not rewritten *Paradise Besieged*. But I have made corrections, filled in the pot-holes, expanded or cut what was already there, reexamined stale opinions, and untangled comments that had even me saying "What could I possibly have meant by that!?" And most of all, for the sake of readers, including myself, I have rearranged the order of the chapters in Part One, so that my digressions will not have all of us wondering if we ever will get to Mount Athos.

ACKNOWLEDGMENTS

After reading the introduction to my first draft, Dr. Matthias Meier, of Limassol, Cyprus, son-in-law of my friend, the marvelous pediatrician-turned-iconographer, Dr. Takis Aristides and his late wife, Lukia, made an observation without which I would forever have been up to my cross in quicksand or worse. "What is this book about?" he asked. "You or Mount Athos?" For this one comment, he has my deepest thanks. Funny. Until then, despite the difference in our ages, I had thought the Holy Mountain and I were synonymous. I spent a good part of ten years believing I would live out my days there, while I avoided vows and secretly back-pocketed the world. Thirty pages of noxious egotism immediately went into the shredder.

Within the Orthodox Church, I want to thank Father Tom Paris of the Ascension Cathedral in Oakland for eleven years of invigorating friendship, and the Ascension community for being just that. My thanks, also, to Fathers Anthony Coniaris and John Chryssavgis for reading my manuscript and for their delighted encouragement. I want to thank Huston Smith, Dr. James Counelis, Ken Cloke, and Graham Christian for their kind advance notices. I also want to thank Kevin Starr for his faith in my writing ability, and Howard Junker, for putting his printer where his mouth is by publishing an excerpt from the book in his magazine, ZYZZYVA. Thanks, too, to Jeff Kunkel, Cathy Luchetti, Sally Small, and Sandy Bails for their timely contributions, and to Miriam Leigh for her help with the cover. Also, all of the readers from all walks of life, inside and outside the Orthodox Church, clergy and laity, men and women, who have told me they found *Paradise Besieged* entertaining, useful, and yes, even "necessary."

Most of all, I want to thank my sister, Jane Treacy, my cousin, Joanne Marx, and especially my darling wife, Pamela, who insists I have written something far better than good, but what does she know? After all, look who she married. But it is ironic, no? That these three are women, and the book over which they pored and about which they made such useful comments is about a place they could never visit just because they are? But perhaps that sets the proper tone for what follows.

LIST OF MAPS AND ILLUSTRATIONS

*M*y thanks to Suki Hill for the photo of the author and his wife – one of many beautiful shots she took at their wedding. All of the photos of Mt. Athos, Paros, and Cyprus were taken by the author. I have no idea who took the magnificent shots of "Father Hierotheos" and "The Beast of the East" and no way of finding out, but I am deeply grateful for them. The archival photos of the author were taken by commercial photographers long forgotten and friends.

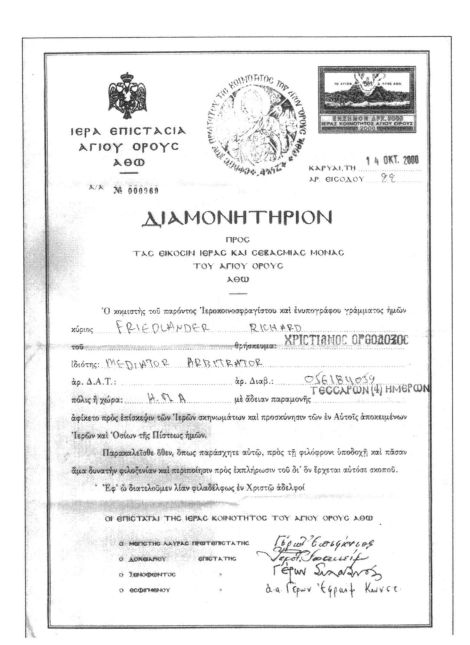

ΙΕΡΑ ΕΠΙCΤΑCΙΑ
ΑΓΙΟΥ ΟΡΟΥC
ΑΘΩ

Λ/Κ № 000969

ΚΑΡΥΑΙ ΤΗ .... 1 4 ΟΚΤ. 2000
ΑΡ. ΕΙCΟΔΟΥ 88

ΔΙΑΜΟΝΗΤΗΡΙΟΝ

ΠΡΟC

ΤΑC ΕΙΚΟCΙΝ ΙΕΡΑC ΚΑΙ CΕΒΑCΜΙΑC ΜΟΝΑC
ΤΟΥ ΑΓΙΟΥ ΟΡΟΥC
ΑΘΩ

Ὁ κομιστὴς τοῦ παρόντος Ἱεροκοινοσφραγίστου καὶ ἐνυπογράφου γράμματος ἡμῶν

κύριος   FRIEDLANDER   RICHARD

τοῦ ....   θρήσκευμα: ΧΡΙCΤΙΑΝΟC ΟΡΘΟΔΟΞΟC

ἰδιότης: MEDIATOR   ARBITRATOR

ἀρ. Δ.Α.Τ.: ....   ἀρ. Διαβ.: 056184059

πόλις ἢ χώρα: ..... Η.Π.Α ....   μὲ ἄδειαν παραμονῆς ΤΕCCΑΡΩΝ (4) ΗΜΕΡΩΝ

ἀφίκετο πρὸς ἐπίσκεψιν τῶν Ἱερῶν σκηνωμάτων καὶ προσκύνησιν τῶν ἐν Αὐτοῖς ἀποκειμένων

Ἱερῶν καὶ Ὁσίων τῆς Πίστεως ἡμῶν.

Παρακαλεῖσθε ὅθεν, ὅπως παράσχητε αὐτῷ, πρὸς τῇ φιλόφρονι ὑποδοχῇ καὶ πᾶσαν

ἅμα δυνατὴν φιλοξενίαν καὶ περιποίησιν πρὸς ἐκπλήρωσιν τοῦ δι' ὃν ἔρχεται αὐτόσε σκοποῦ.

Ἐφ' ᾧ διατελοῦμεν λίαν φιλαδέλφως ἐν Χριστῷ ἀδελφοί

ΟΙ ΕΠΙCΤΑΤΑΙ ΤΗC ΙΕΡΑC ΚΟΙΝΟΤΗΤΟC ΤΟΥ ΑΓΙΟΥ ΟΡΟΥC ΑΘΩ

Ο ΜΕΓΙCΤΗC ΛΑΥΡΑC ΠΡΩΤΕΠΙCΤΑΤΗC
Ο ΔΟΧΕΙΑΡΙΟΥ   ΕΠΙCΤΑΤΗC
Ο ΞΕΝΟΦΩΝΤΟC   »
Ο ΕCΦΙΓΜΕΝΟΥ   »

Literally, your passport into the Holy Mountain. The four signatures are those of the four members of the *Epistasia*. All four must sign for the passport to be valid.

o Ierissos
Tripoli
o

Hilandar +   + Esphigmenou

Ouranopolis

Vatopedi +

+ Zographou   * Prophet Elias
Konstamonitou +   + Dochiariou   + Pantokrator
Xenophontas +   + Stavronikita
                    St. Andrew * Karyes
                Panteleimon +   + Koutloumousi

MOUNT ATHOS   Bourazerei *   + Iveron
AND   Daphni   +Xeropotamou
ITS LOCATION   + Philotheou
IN   Simonopetra +   Karakallou +
GREECE   Grigoriou +
                    Dionysiou +
+ Major monastery   St. Paul +   Great Lavra +
* Skete   Timion Prodromos *
o Town

Δ

INTRODUCTION

A TRAVELER'S ADVISORY

Man is a rope connecting animal and superman—a rope over a precipice…. What is great in man is that he is a bridge and not a goal.

Friedrich Nietzsche, *Thus Spake Zarathustra*

Midnight in one of the most beautiful places on earth. The massive stone buildings loom sinister against the ebony sky. No smudges mar the canopy of stars; no lamplight stakes a competing claim. It is cat quiet. At the end of a stone corridor, a black-shrouded figure stands absolutely still, shouldering a long piece of wood, a mallet in his hand. Somewhere below a clock softly tolls the hour. He moves forward. Mallet strikes wood, and the message shatters the stillness like a jackhammer on a New York street. Faster and faster, it increases in volume until the hallways are hollow with noise and the pounding flat-lines into frenzy. A final thump and then silence. On a pallet of straw in a cramped, dark cell, a monk opens his eyes and remembers he is going to die. It might be today.

"Why in hell should I care about men who think it is a holy act to give up meat, who never wash, and who abstain from women and every other form of human intercourse?" That has to be the first question asked by anyone confronting this book and unfamiliar with its subject. Relax. You are not alone. Up to my chance run-in with Greek Orthodox Christianity, whatever I knew about religion and ballroom dancing I had learned at the very reformed Jewish Temple Beth Elohim, in Brooklyn, New York.

In the Eastern confession of the Christian way, Sacred Tradition rules theology and practice the way the Pope directs the Catholic Church and the Bible sets the bounds for Protestants. In this Tradition, monasteries are beautiful places and monks are holy men. Ask any Greek, and he will piously explain that, if he could, he too would live the monastic life, "but...." —and he throws up his hands, obedient to the will of God and dumbfounded by its judgments and leaving it to the hearer to imagine the best. With choleric face, and a voice stinking with indignation, he will anathematize the utterly rational Englishman, Edward Gibbon, whose *Decline and Fall of the Roman Empire* describes Eastern Christian monks as ignorant, filthy, crazy, and dangerous—a disgrace to the rest of humanity. Make of his performance what you will. A Greek friend assured me, "Greeks have such a profound respect for the truth, they never show it to strangers." But inquire among Greeks with whom you have found acceptance, and you will almost certainly hear that many believe that their holy monks are lazy, crazy, or homosexual, and, not dangerous, perhaps, but definitely maladjusted.

It is not so strange that Greeks themselves can't make up their minds about monks, because where you are going is one of the most confusingly simple places on this planet. Its wild beauty will take your breath away, and you will find every path you take lined with exotic and fragrant berries and fruits that appear to have been placed there purely for your benefit. You will find impenetrable ignorance and ineffable wisdom. You will attend church services that devour sixteen hours at a gulp, and expend other hours trying to find a monastery that looked to be half a mile away. You will be awed, confounded, amused, insulted and angered, humbled by hospitality, offended by exclusion and boorishness, puzzled by the mix of consideration and selfishness, and perplexed by the respect for God's creation and the disrespect for nature. For women it is a journey you could in reality make only over the dead bodies of the men amongst whom I once lived. But if you believe that every one of us contains something of the entire world, and that every individual experience or way of thinking or living throws a little more light on who we are; if you believe that it is essential to search for meaning even if there is none; if you can sympathize where it is impossible to empathize, then, by reading what follows, you just might find you do care about these men and the future of their way of life.

And what gives me the impudence to lead this expedition into the past as present and future? A quarter of a century ago, I took my first sip of the strange and compelling brew that is Orthodox Christianity—the westernmost of the Eastern religions. On a day late in May when I had panted my own feckless way up a mountain on the island of Paros under a brutal Aegean sun; and Longovarda, the white-washed Greek Orthodox monastery before me represented only a likely glass of water; and Christianity of any brand was my tribal enemy, a powerfully-built, gray-bearded monk—an English expatriate dressed in shabby black—shyly offered me a book to keep me busy while he hurried away to make cheese. The book was *The Way of a Pilgrim*. I did not accept his offer immediately since I suspected he was out to make me one of "them." "Read the first paragraph," he added, demolishing my reluctance with a calm sophistication that I soon learned was not in his everyday nature. "If you like it, continue. If you don't, find something else in our cell."

"Our?!..." "Cell?!..." Was it even worse than I suspected? Nevertheless, I opened the book. In my rudderless state, how could I not like *The Way of a Pilgrim*? The hero spends his life walking this way and that all

4

over 19th century Russia. People don't just not hassle him—they love him! Peasants and princes alike. What I could not have predicted was that his rudder would become mine, although my instantaneous reaction to the first paragraph might have given me a hint: I don't know what this is, but this is true, I silently acknowledged, the words flashing across my brain as clearly and inexorably as the neon strip of news that once told people in Times Square what was happening in their world.

Like any child that feels he or she is beset on all sides by a lying, demanding, and manipulative world, I responded to a breath of fresh air— the authenticity of the Pilgrim's account of his experience—as if I were overdosing on oxygen. He could have been talking about making chopped liver and I would have felt the same. In the sixties, Henry Miller's super-energetic autobiography, *Sexus*, also had blown me up and away with its own kind of truth. But this writer's subject was religion, and in particular the Greek Orthodox Christian religion, and even more particularly, the life of silence and the Prayer of the Heart (a. k. a. the Jesus Prayer).

The monk's innocent and inspired invitation determined the course of my life. My eventual decision to exercise my free agency and switch teams caused a certain amount of confusion and a lot of suspicion for all of us: Jews, Greeks, and me. How could I be an Orthodox Christian when being a Greek Orthodox Christian means being Greek? And how could I not be a Jew when a Jew can never not be a Jew? To make it even more puzzling, I did not merely leave the Old Israel for the New but became a *fanatikos*—no translation needed. Whoever or whatever was driving my bus compelled me to take my new faith to the farthest reaches of my personal world: farther than most Greeks and so far away from the synagogue of my youth that I sometimes found myself at the point in outer space where the parallel lines of all faiths meet. The logic of fanaticism said that it was not possible to be an Orthodox Christian without becoming a monk. To those who knew me, this eager and abrupt departure from my former and decidedly uncelibate way of life was even more astonishing than my leap of faith. It wasn't as if it hadn't been brewing for thirty-three years, but what does the pot know about boiling water? I spent a major part of the next ten years protected from the ways of the world on Mount Athos, growing older in a place where ten years and growing older have no meaning. Stepping back through the looking glass, the shards often cut me, but here I am: your host.

In his autobiography, *Return to Greco*, Nikos Kazantzakis remarked that the only way he could repay a monk at St. Catherine's Monastery in Sinai for his hospitality was to make him doubt. In the same spirit, presenting an unorthodox view of Orthodox Christianity is the least I can do to repay this ancient, beautiful, and often compassionate and wise faith for the years I have enjoyed its hospitality. Therefore, in the pages that follow you will find history, mysticism, theology, philosophy, personal experience, a (very) little sex, and unabashedly blatant, uncensored, and unavoidable opinion.

Like my monk friend on Paros, I offer you a book. Unlike his offering, it is one for those who walk the golden mean by constantly straying from it, like bungee jumpers who fall away only to bounce back. It is odds-on to offend those members of the choir who already see their prayers rising to heaven like fragrant incense or who are secure in their possession of the One and Only Truth. It is a spiritual journey only as it reveals the humanity of monks. If what follows does seem a bit irreverent, well then, without a little irreverence nothing would ever change. And this book is about nothing if not change: the clash of irresistible forces, immovable objects, temporality, and eternity: the tensions without which there is no life.

The very serious Hermann Hesse wrote that laughter is where all the contradictions of life make sense, and it is in trying to control or avoid the inexorable rhythms of our own biology and a changing world that we are at both our most reflective and our most ludicrous. As the spread of modern technology forces us all to examine our spiritual aspirations and what it means to be human, a keen sense of humor becomes a necessity.

PART ONE

GETTING THERE

They change their clime, not their disposition,
who run beyond the sea.

Horace, *Epistles, I*

Dangling southeast from the plain of Thrace in northern Greece, from the underside of a tumid appendage called Chalkidiki (Khal-kee-dee-KEE), are three arthritic peninsulas that hang over the Aegean like exhausted teats from the skewed udder of a cow. The first two, Cassandra and Sithonia, are of no moment to our story. The third and easternmost one is where all the inaction is. For this is the Holy Mountain of Athos: Mount Athos, *Agion Oros*, the Garden of the Mother of God, the House of Unceasing Prayer, in which she who is ever pure is the only female allowed to dally, tour, or abide. This ban includes cats and chickens. The monks will tell you to disarm your rational mind; that the rats take flight at the utterance of a prayer, while the awkward availability of eggs is a daily miracle.

Looking at these wizened appendices on a map, a surgeon might reach for the scalpel. Hold on there, Abraham! Put up your knife and your judgment. For its physical beauty alone, Mount Athos deserves a second opinion. There are few places on earth, especially in that part claimed by the industrialized world, that teem with as much life in all its unedited magnificence and harshness, aspirations and constraints, as this unprepossessing cartographical squiggle, thirty-two miles long and six wide. More significant to this story, at the mere mention of the name of Athos, an Eastern Orthodox male will feverishly cross himself and pray that his Maker will allow him to set foot on the blessed soil at least once before he dies.

Agion Oros, by the grace of God and the Treaty of Lausanne (1923), is a self-governing Orthodox Christian monastic state under the loose protection and administration of Greece, which provides a resident civil governor, some customs officials, and a very few policemen. I confess I have not read the Treaty of Lausanne, which produced one of those periodic reorganizations of the eastern Mediterranean, but even if that document had transferred control of the peninsula to the Caliph of Mars, I don't believe it would have had more than a marginal effect on the lives of those who live there. When you enter Mount Athos you leave behind more than modern Greece. Athanasios, the founder of the Great Lavra – the first and still largest of the twenty major monasteries – means "not dead" or "eternal," and indeed this is a land that time forgot.

It also is a land that has forgotten time. Some monks wear watches, but here it is the sun and the seasons, and the eternal lives of the saints – events commemorated with bells, chimes, the rhythmic striking of mallet on *symandron*, and a succession of feasts, fasts, and funerals – that mark the passage of days, months, and years. In peacetime, the politics that concern *Agiorites* is who is alleged to have betrayed Orthodoxy and who has not. There are monks that have not spoken to other monks for thirty years because they disagree over the direction provided by their spiritual overlord, the Patriarch of Constantinople a.k.a. Istanbul, whose perpetual impotence is a persistent pin in the shirt – a reminder that for the past five hundred years the Turks have walled the patriarchs inside a tiny compound called the *Phanar* like a cask of Amontillado. Never mind the realities. In matters of faith, His All Holiness is the puissant absentee ruler of Mount Athos, which after all is all that matters to these men.

Well, not exactly all. One's ethnicity does not become completely irrelevant once one puts on the black. Nor does one immediately lose one's innate inclination to war. Athonites actively participated in the Greek struggle for independence, and during World War II some actively took up arms against the Nazis. During America's Bosnian adventure, the monks of the Serbian monastery, Hilandar, refused their hospitality to American monks. This little bit of rudeness reveals how high political passions ran because in both Greece and on the Holy Mountain hospitality isn't next to godliness. It *is* godliness.

Every journey begins with a crazy idea—some end there.

Reading about Mount Athos is one thing, but why would a *xenos* (foreigner) actually want to go there? A spiritual quest, a need for some peace and quiet, simple curiosity? A mistaken notion that Greece is everlastingly warm? A local Greek festival and a few too many *Opa!'s* and *ouzos*? Even in 1985, the year of my last journey there, the trip was not one you could book with your local travel agent. Just getting there is a lot of trouble. Mount Athos is not a sovereign state like the Vatican, but it is a self-governing territory. As such, travelers need written permission to enter. Even those who know how to work the maddening bureaucracy can encounter delay and even rejection.

Changed your mind? After all, why make all that effort to spend a few days with dirty, bearded men who would rather be left alone? Wouldn't you rather vacation on one of the islands, where you can sunbathe, swim, dance, and eat when and what you want? Where you will actually feel wanted? (Even if it is for your cash.) Where you will see beautiful Greek womens – every one like Aphrodite … with arms?… Mmm … ah! No? Well, I tried. Like hospitality, discouraging potential wannabes is a serious monastic tradition.

The process of getting to Mount Athos begins with getting the Greek government to intercede on your behalf. To start the ball rolling, the postulant must bear a letter of introduction to the Ministry for Northern Greece from the American ambassador in Athens or the consul in Thessalonica. The Ministry for Northern Greece, on the second floor of a gray building in Academy Street, controls the flow of visitors to the Holy Mountain. It is open on Wednesdays and Fridays from twelve to one, but sometimes it is not. This tiny window of opportunity periodically contracts when Greece's relations with other countries go south. Since Thessalonica seems to enjoy some kind of kind of immunity from diplomatic fallout, many people prefer to negotiate their passports there.

In either city an official issues a letter informing the *Epistasia*, the ruling body of Mount Athos, that Greece has approved the applicant as a very temporary immigrant, worthy of four days and three nights' stay on the Holy Mountain. A passport – the equivalent of food vouchers and a full hotel discount – will be issued by the monastic government in Karyes, the capital of Mount Athos.

Other than who you are, the Ministry for Northern Greece wants to know what you do for a living. This is a question that monks never ask at cocktail parties, but which the secular keepers of the key to the monastic kingdom have been asking since Jesus was a carpenter. Coincidently, at the time of my first visit to the Mountain, "carpenter" was how I described myself. I thought I was a shoo-in – even a little entitled. However, when a fellow pilgrim whispered to me that only foreigners who were professionals were getting in, I went through a brief dark night of the soul and unhesitatingly identified myself as a lawyer. Which I was but wasn't, having been granted an exit visa from law school but never taking the bar. There are quotas on visitors who are not Orthodox Christians, but unless you are an international terrorist, a woman, a non-Orthodox clergymen wearing his vestments, or the losing goalie on the A. C. Thessalonica soccer team, you are pretty much guaranteed entrance to Athos. Just don't carry a tool-box.

You don't have to be Greek to be Orthodox, but it helps.

The journey from Athens to Thessalonica to Mount Athos takes about fifteen hours, assuming no delays and good connections; which means it ordinarily takes about two days. You could fly, but pilgrimages are supposed to be long and uncomfortable, and the smoke on the flight would only require you to hold your breath for about forty minutes. While we wait for our train, gather round, and let me tell you a little about Greece and its church.

To even begin to understand Mount Athos it is necessary to understand that Greece is a Christian country, maybe the only one you will ever experience. What does it mean to be a Christian country? It is something that struck Lawrence Durrell, Henry Miller, and Philip Sherrard as immediately and palpably as if the *meltemi* had sent its searing, hot winds across the water from Africa. It means that when you step down onto the modest concrete of Athens airport, strewn with cigarette butts, plastic food containers, and the other detritus of the modern nomad, you walk over soil drenched not only with water broken at the birth of Western Civilization – Homer, Pericles, Phidias, Euripides, Plato, and Aphrodite – but also the blood, and tears, wine, and olive oil of the Eastern Orthodox Christian Church. To Greeks, being Orthodox is the same as being Greek. In Greece, the church, the government, and the way of life have been so knotted and gnarled by the winds of history that introducing change to any branch or root threatens the whole olive tree. The Orthodox Church is everywhere. Every Greek city has three hundred and sixty-five churches, but who's counting? Little chapels dot the agricultural countryside, the villages, and the commercial cities. Families build them, and families take care of them like family. If you build a chapel, it will keep the devil away from your relatives, your property, and assure your good fortune. Bearded priests in long blue robes – the equivalent of civvies as opposed to the ritual black –

are a presence in the streets, and you can spot at least a few black-robed monks and nuns at most communal events.

The presence of the Orthodox Church is far more than physical. Businesses close for feasts celebrating a major saint or some event in the life of Christ. Some municipalities still have laws forbidding the sale of dairy or meat products on Wednesdays and Fridays, the weekly fasting days – monastics also observe Mondays – when all animal foods are theocratically excluded from the national diet. One day, when I was in Athens, a Greek acquaintance of mine – who had been "away from the church" but had rediscovered his roots while going through a crisis – suddenly left my side and rushed into a shop to buy bread and a hunk of cheese for a homeless man. Clearly a *mitzvah*. The beneficiary of this largesse did not see it this way and stuffed the cheese into his pocket. "It's Friday," he admonished us from the full height of his moral advantage. "I'm fasting."

Along with signs making it a crime to smoke or spit on public transport, riders on municipal trains and buses are warned against blaspheming! Greeks celebrate the feast day of the saint they were named after as their birthday, and on that day, they open their houses to all and *give* gifts. The use of name days to record the passage of the years makes sense in a country where war and chaos often has made public records either unreliable or unavailable. In some villages where every child bears the name of the local saint, at meal times a cacophonous fugue of "Spiro!"s or "Ianni!"s or "Ekaterini!"s echoes through the narrows streets.

If you are not familiar with this church, it is not necessarily just because yours is a culture that is not very curious about others. In a touching effort to learn something about this oldest Christian church, my own mother took a course at the New School – on cults. Three years after my baptism had confirmed my having gone *geshmatt*, (i.e., apostatized) she innocently asked me, "Do *you people* celebrate Christmas?" Missions to the Third World aside, the modern Orthodox Church is a stranger to hard-core proselytism. For the most part, Greeks assume that everyone within easy reach who will become Orthodox already is, and the future is simply a matter of baptizing unknowing infants, while issuing an occasional green card to an aberration like me.

A monk is not a priest except sometimes.

Greece is a country in which clergy still have some clout, though ancient respect lives side-by-side with ancient suspicion. In fact, Greeks call *any* deep pocket that always seems to have room for more a "priest's pocket". Even though Orthodox whisper their transgressions to their priest in full view of the whole church, and not, like the Romans, through a grille, Greeks rarely go to their local priest for confession, fearful that as the *ouzo* flows in the neighborhood café those sacrosanct confidences might leak out of that very human human. Furthermore, priests are quasi-officials of the state, and the association of the church with the junta that ruled Greece during the nineteen-sixties greatly harmed its image. On the other hand, even suspect familiarity can be comforting. It may be that the everyday sight of these icons of stability, with their black to white beards and blue robes with ink stains that always seem to be seeping through their breast pocket is a needed reassurance that not everything is moving at warp speed. An airport security guard once apologetically ushered my bearded, black-robed self through a gate and onto a plane at the Athens airport even though my visa had long-since expired, simply because someone mistakenly informed him that I was a priest! More likely, the image of his grandma (*yiayia*) dressed for perpetual mourning, flashed before his eyes, and he didn't want to mess with *any*one in black, no matter what they actually were.

What is the difference between a priest and a monk? To the uninformed eye, they look similar – like geese and ducks – but a priest is not necessarily a monk, neither is a monk necessarily a priest, though both can be either. Mount Athos is a nation – a paper nation with no visible army or commercial paper – of monks, some of whom are priest-monks. A priest is a cleric to whom the sacrament of ordination gives the power to administer the other sacraments – baptism, confession, communion, and marriage. A man becomes a monk through the special sacrament of tonsure, which lies somewhere between ordination and marriage, since a monk is a committed bachelor whose token tonsure is a sign of his spiritual marriage to God. Unlike ordination, tonsure does not permit the recipient to administer the sacraments. At his initiation, the Orthodox monk is not required to expose his pate, as are monks in the West. In fact, all the Eastern monk loses is a strand of hair at the Biblical four "corners" of his head. Neither the monk nor anyone else may ever touch his hair again with a sharpened instrument. This includes his beard. A monk stroking his beard can mean many things: he is thinking some wise thought; he is thinking how he looks; he is thinking about dinner; or he is trying to remove something *from* dinner.

Since the church considers both fornication and adultery to be sins, a monk, who is married to God, must be celibate. Unless he is a monk, a priest who is out in the world must be married. *What?!* you exclaim. *Married priests?* Remember, you are in a land where people are so congenitally skeptical that they peel their fruit even after they wash it and retain the oil-stained sheet in which they catch their baby at baptism as proof that he or she has indeed been baptized; a few years later, they will collect a blood-stained sheet as evidence that a bride came to her marriage bed undefiled. Do you think people who so indulge the senses and are that suspicious would let an unmarried man, armed with spiritual allure, loose like a wolf among ewes? No, unmarried priests must be locked away together with other celibates who aren't priests.

If he does marry, a priest must make this decision prior to his ordination. His marriage to God being superior to his earthly union, he cannot follow it with the lesser sacrament, even though all sacraments are equal, independently interdependent, and on a spiritual par with each other. Is everything clear now? We are talking about two different levels of existence here, and even though what is bound or loosed above also is bound and loosed below, no amount of sophistry will force them to fit exactly over each other. So, baptism and communion are sacramental equals, but you can't receive communion unless you have been baptized. Until recently, the Roman Catholic Church, which historically has been more hierarchical, linear, and absurdly logical than its Eastern cousin, required communicants to make their confession prior to receiving the Eucharist, as if this purified them to receive the other sacrament that would purify them, while blocking bad thoughts in the interim. The Greek church did away with this affront to reason and the equality of mysteries years ago, perhaps inspired more by the leakiness of confession than a desire for theological consistency.

On the street, you can usually tell a priest by that strange hat he wears – the one with the brim on the top. That is, unless he is a priest-monk.

It's not so much knowing as not knowing.

Greek Orthodox theology is the New Testament pressed through the mesh of Greek culture and philosophy. The first thing the stranger needs to grasp is that it is antinomic. An antinomy is a contradiction in which both statements are absolutely true, all the time. It is the mind's attempt to bridge rational impossibilities, similar to what Herman Hesse did with a laugh. Antinomy literally means "what goes against the law". I do not mean the law of society, although Greeks do have difficulty dealing with authority, for instance, paying taxes. But while being on time for an appointment may be impossible, every Greek knows that God and men celebrate the same Eucharist at the same time on earth and in heaven. Impossible? No. Antinomical.

Orthodox theology begins with an antinomy – in fact, two of them: that Christ is Perfect Man and Perfect God, without admixture yet never separated; and the Holy Trinity consists of Three Beings, all independently fully God, yet dependent on the unfailing presence of the others. In other words, Christianity posits (how can we say this?) a "three equal" God, as in Donne's "Batter my heart, O Three-Person'd God," and not three equal Gods. Orthodox also believe that the bread and wine used in Holy Communion becomes the Body and Blood of Christ, without ever ceasing to be bread and wine. In other words, the host is *con*substantiated, not – as is the Roman belief – *tran*substantiated, in which the bread and wine cease to be such when they are changed into the divine elements. To the Orthodox – as to the Jews – God is simultaneously immanent and transcendent; in Holy Communion, the participant is able to experience both his or her own unceasing divinity and the constant humanity of God. Does this happen? (A good Jewish shrug.)

Orthodox Christianity, as I relentlessly insist without making any converts, is an Eastern religion. While their counterparts in the West stress the birth of God into the world as the divine act that guarantees salvation, Orthodox see Christmas only in the context of the Resurrection. Without this *re*birth, say the Orthodox, the Nativity would have been pointless. This sounds very close to the notion of karma. The antinomy is a product of Eastern philosophy, and an antidote to the either/or paradigm, the inability to rise above zero sum thinking that has been the bane of Western European thought and the author of almost every significant Christian heresy. For instance, Monothelites could not understand how one God could have two distinct though inseparable wills, while Monophysites had a problem with one God having two natures, also distinct but inseparable. Westerners who think of Christ as God or man, or God clothed in man, or even a God-man, also miss the point.

The second thing to know about Greek theology is that it is apophatic. The difference between apophatic and kataphatic is the same as that between a sculptor who chisels a statue from marble, and one who creates from clay. Literally, an apophasis means "after appearance", and kataphasis is "according to appearance". Being apophatic, the Orthodox Church tries to say only what God is not. It has abandoned this approach only when forced to do so by a perceived threat to its theological integrity. The Nicene Creed, the symbol of faith of the Orthodox Church, was a response to poorly reasoned, but compelling and fanatically held assertions of fact about the nature of Christ, the Trinity, and the God-bearer, Mary. The Creed begins with "I *believe* ..." not 'I *know.*' The *filioque*, the addition rejected by the Eastern Christian Church, is an attempt to define the exact nature of what no one can ever know: how the interior relationship of the three Persons of the Trinity actually works.

The art of the Orthodox Church, usually lumped under the misleading term, Byzantine, also is a meticulously studied response to the attempt to know by accumulation of facts. Byzantine art anticipated Renaissance perspective by going completely the other way. Thus, while the artists of Italy surrounded the viewer with the painting, artists further east wrote the larger images on the distance, thus separating the viewer from a sensual connection to the painting and the painting from this world.

All I ever needed to know about Greek, I learned from Zorba.

You can get around Mount Athos with surprisingly little Greek, and around the Orthodox Church with almost no Greek at all. How can this be? There are at least three reasons; no, four. First, communication in Greece is primarily through body language. Second, even most Greeks can't understand the Greek spoken in church. Third, Orthodoxy is a "way", requiring a road map more than a lexicon. And finally, at almost every monastery a monk who is only too willing to speak English will prevent you from practicing your Greek. Nevertheless, along with a glossary, you will find an appendix at the rear of this book that provides some useful language instruction under the heading "Hints for Speaking Well Greek".

The explanation for why you won't be the only one in church who doesn't understand the readings from the Gospel is that *koine* Greek, the tongue of the New Testament, was the lingua franca of the ancient world and disappeared with it. It does not have quite the same relation to modern Greek as Old English does to the language of Amy Tan, but you get the picture. We have enough trouble with the Elizabethan English of King James; just imagine if Chaucer had translated the Bible (for which, incidentally, he would have been burned). Most Orthodox hymns are baroque variations of Byzantine Greek, so convoluted and layered with meaning, aesthetics, and occasional cleverness that they clearly must have been written for God, because his people can't make head or tail of them. "Nobody understands the hymns," a chanter (*psaltis*) told me. "Not even the priests. The only thing you have to know is not to confuse a wedding and a funeral."

One of the most difficult tasks of the Greek Church in America has been to pry Greek-Americans away from ye olde incomprehensible language. The language that even their fathers couldn't understand is still part of that ethnic cliff top to which they cling with their nails – except for the one on the pinky, the length of which indicates that they won't do windows or floors. While it was the Catholic laity that forced their church to move away from the hocus pocus of Latin, the Greek faithful continue to challenge Paul's assertion that five words spoken with understanding are worth a thousand spoken in tongues. At the beginning of the 20th century, when a Hellene had the temerity to translate the New Testament into Modern Greek, the laity angrily rejected the innovation. Just forty years ago, when a Greek-American *psaltis* tried to introduce English into the liturgy, thugs set upon him as he exited the church!

While their motives were questionable, their understanding negligible, and their actions deplorable, and while it is difficult to inject the word, wisdom, into a sentence with such a damning and complicated predicate, this was their religion. So what if they didn't understand it – any of it. It was Greek. They professed a belief without borders, but belief is secondary to language, which, music excepted, is as close as you can get to the soul of a people. *This is our religion – the Greek Religion. If you can't accept it as we gave it to you, get your own*

In the first years after my baptism, I zealously demanded more English be used in the services. How dare they exclude me from understanding every *iota* of what was said in a church on American soil! When I finally got my wish, I often found the substance of what I heard embarrassing and far from uplifting; as for aesthetics, English fits Byzantine chant the way O. J.'s hand fit that glove. When forced by circumstance and necessity to engage in translation, as in most other things, Greeks stick with their own; furthermore, they believe that if they must make some allowance for English, it should, like children, be seen (for meaning, perhaps) but not heard. This condescension has spawned the quasi-language, Gringlish. Which is, after all, almost English. All that's been lost is sense, poetry, and beauty. King James must be rolling in his *taphos*.

Where's a McDonald's when you need one? Or an aspirin?

Ah. There's our train. The overnight express to Thessalonica. By now, the smoke you will experience en route shouldn't bother you. You have been breathing so much of it since your arrival that fresh air probably would make you sick. Smoke is synonymous with Greece: wood smoke, diesel smoke, coal smoke, cigarette smoke, smoke smoke … smoke drifting up from the refineries near Piraeus, from someone unsuccessfully trying to sell you the Parthenon, from tempers rubbed raw. If your lungs are seeking relief, don't stick your head out the window. Oncoming trains pass so close that when your body arrived in Thessalonica, your head would be in Athens.

Railroad carriages in Greece are unlike the democratic coaches of the United States, with row after row of seats facing forward until you reach the middle of the car, when they begin to face the other way. (A metaphor for life?) The second class coach you will experience on the Greek national railroad will be the kind favored by the rest of the civilized world. A series of compartments look onto a passageway that runs the length of the car along one side. Inside the compartments, two bench seats face each other, providing room for six to eight passengers. Individual doors and curtains provide a certain amount of privacy, ahem…. If you want real privacy, go first class. If uninterrupted sleep is a requirement, purchase a couchette.

You will need food and there is no dining car. Hurry. Buy a few *koulouria* before we board. *Koulouria* are little bagel-shaped breads covered with sesame seeds that street vendors sell throughout the day throughout Athens and Thessalonica. They have a crisp crust, and their crumb is only slightly heavier than air. *Koulouria* are at their best either early in the morning or during the evening rush hour, just after they are baked, because they go stale before they can even acquire a shelf life. My problem is that I usually eat them all before the train has left Athens. In case you get lucky and share a compartment with travel-savvy Greeks bearing enough food to feed the army at Troy, you could be feasting for eight hours on *moussaka, pastitsa,* chicken, *spanakopita, tyropita, baklava, risogala,* and *galatoboureko.* "*Fateh, fateh!*" "Eat, eat!" If fortune has truly smiled, there might be a bottle of *Demestica* and maybe even the aperitif called *ouzo.* If she has frowned, it will be the wine drink known as *retsina.*

Ouzo is the national beverage and it is made only in Greece. Its base is grape skins and comes in two kinds of bottles – one with a label and one that looks like all it needs is a rag stuffed into the neck to become a Molotov cocktail. One is homemade and the other has been store-prettified. No points for guessing which is the stronger. The anise added to *ouzo* gives it a licorice taste. *Ouzo* usually is sent out into the world rated at eighty proof (40% alcohol). When mixed with water, it turns cloudy. When mixed with your thought process, it turns that cloudy, too.

Retsina is the other alcoholic beverage that imprints itself on and sometimes in the brain of visitors to Greece in the shape of a horrendous hangover. Beware of Greeks bearing *retsina.* "The Greek taste for putting resin in the new wine makes it a struggle for anyone who is not used to it," writes the oinophile, Hugh Johnson, in his classic book, *Wine.* "*Retsina*, with its taste of turpentine, becomes a memory of Greece which is difficult ... to forget. No country expresses itself so uncompromisingly in its wine – but wine is hardly the word for it.... [The wine, however, is] distinctly better than the soggy hopelessness of the food ... in this gastronomic backwater."

There is more than one account of the origin of *retsina.* Irrefutable legend says that during the Turkish occupation, word spread throughout Crete that the hated foe was about to confiscate an entire vintage. Rather than give comfort to the enemy, the Greeks added pine resin to the new wine, thinking to make it undrinkable. But the Turks suddenly changed their collective minds and left the Cretans with *a lot* of undrinkable wine. They drank it. And they liked it! Or at least they pretended they did. There is another account that claims the vintners intentionally added the pine resin as a preservative. As if anyone could be so naïve as to believe that. It is true, however, that the Byzantines were drinking resinated wine in the 8th century.

If you are looking for something that will probably both give you a headache and eat its way through to your pancreas, do not refuse an offer of *raki* – Greek moonshine. *Raki* is paint thinner distilled from fruit and vegetable compost. It is difficult to escape at least a preliminary bout with this potent beverage. Upon your arrival at a monastery, the *archondaris* – the guest master – will almost invariably serve you a shot glass of *raki*, a tall glass of water, and a *loukoumi*—a gelatinous cube of sweetness generously coated with tooth-chilling confectioner's sugar. You may recognize *loukoumi* as "Turkish Delight," but you would be well advised not to try to impress your host with your discovery.

For Greeks, Turkey is no cause for thanksgiving.

The smile on the face of the Japanese man on the billboard across the subway tracks may assure you that you do not have to be Jewish to love Levy's rye bread, but if you are not Greek, you can never understand how and why they hate the Turks as much as they do. In Greece, as in many other parts of the world, persuading ancient enemies to patch things up and get on with life would require a national blood transfusion or an edict of a king or a prelate, and that age is long past. The Turks ruled Greece for close to four hundred years, governing mainly by benevolent neglect. While the Ottomans demanded little from their subject peoples except that they keep the peace and pay taxes, the *ram millet* were always aware of their inferior status. As if the Turks wanted to show they could do whatever they wanted whenever they wanted to do it, there were sporadic bloody persecutions and reprisals. Some Christians baited the Turks to martyr them, and others converted to Islam for the economic benefits, but, as happens in the wake of most conquests, most people did nothing. The Ottomans also conscripted Christian boys into their army to form the elite unit known as *Janissaries*. The invasion of Cyprus in 1974 gave birth to the rumor that the Turks put their Christian soldiers in the first wave of troops to hit the beach and didn't give them ammunition for their rifles. Whether this is true or not is irrelevant. It is what Greeks believe, what they want to believe, and, in truth, what they need to believe. Every day, for more than five centuries, the Orthodox Christian Patriarch of Constantinople has been forced to view the magnificent mosque – now a museum – once known as the Church of Hagia Sophia, "Holy Wisdom", from the windows of his beleaguered and insignificant *Phanar*.

Constantinople became Istanbul in 1930, exactly sixteen hundred years after Byzantium became Constantinople. "Istanbul", a popular song of the fifties, opined that why "Constantinople got the works" was "nobody's business but the Turks", but the songwriters, Jimmy Kennedy and Nat Simon, weren't Greek. The very name, Istanbul, is salt in an already gaping wound – a corruption of the Greek, *eis teen poleen,* meaning "in the city". The city on the Bosporus dominates Greek thought like the Acropolis dominates Athens. Constantinople is the Jerusalem of the Jews' now-realized "next year", the Moscow of the once-exiled white Russians, now also returned. Only Constantinople remains an unattained Promised Land. The Greeks came close once. When Greek armies drove the Turks out of Anatolia on the heels of the First World War, the English and the French – already busily carving out spheres of influence in the old Ottoman Empire – ordered them not to make any attempt on Constantinople. The City in Turkish hands sticks in the collective Greek throat like a fishbone, and they take pains to see that the wound does not heal. Every Tuesday is considered a bad day to begin any project because it was on Tuesday, May 29, 1453, that the Turks fulfilled an ancient prophecy by dragging their ships across land to the Golden Horn and capturing Constantinople. The Orthodox Church also dedicates every Tuesday to the beheaded forerunner of Christ, John the Baptist. Not a good day. The Greeks' refusal to let go was so prevalent that three years after the name change, the Turkish Post Office finally decided to no longer deliver any mail addressed to "Constantinople."

If, in the inconceivable future, Greeks ever get their wish, The City will come with a lot of unwanted Turks in it. While a repetition of the death swaps of the early 20th century would be unlikely, Greeks do not think highly of Turkish "barbarians" and would be hard-pressed to ascribe to them any quality not directly linked to lack of personal hygiene and congenital brutality. Greek Cypriots, too, would like to reclaim their lost territory, but also without their lost compatriots. "Oh, for the good old days," runs the familiar refrain. "We lived like brothers in Kyrenia – the

Turkeys and us. Like the precious oil running down Aaron's beard. We would give anything to get it back. But Kyrenia with Turks?... Mneh."

It is ironic that when the Turks finally did leave Mount Athos in 1913, at the end of the Balkan Wars, the last Turkish commander is supposed to have remarked "This is indeed a black day; but not for us. We did not disturb you in your desire for quiet. It is you who will have reason for regrets." Certainly, Mount Athos in the past hundred years or so, for all of its pride and – its monks would say – because of it, has not been without chaos. And it is true that the Turks most likely would have continued their policy of relative non-interference with The Mountain as a religious community. But what is freedom, anyway? And besides, who invented it?

Orthodox and Catholics: Christians separated by a common faith.

Constantinople is also the central player in the final splitting of the One, Holy, Catholic, and Apostolic church into its Orthodox and Roman Catholic confessions, the Orthodox being the ones who cross themselves with three fingers right to left and the Catholics, with four and left to right. The theological bases, the Pope and the *filioque*, are significant only in that they parallel the contrasting political ideals of Greece and Rome. Basically, the Orthodox Church functions like a loose union of independent city-states, while the Catholic Pope is the successor to the Roman emperor. There is no equivalent to the Pope in the Orthodox Church. With the exception of missionary churches, all Orthodox Christian churches are autocephalous – a good Greek word, literally meaning "one's own head".

In the early years of Christianity, there were four Patriarchates – Jerusalem, Antioch, Alexandria, and Rome. In the 4th century, the newly-enlightened Constantine made his capital city the fifth. The bishop of the Church at Rome was called the "first among equals" only out of respect for Peter's leadership of the apostles, which itself was due to a bad pun by Christ. "Thou art Peter," he said, "and upon this rock (*petros*) I will build my church." The Patriarchates continue, with Orthodox Moscow replacing Rome, but Alexandria, Antioch, Constantinople, and Jerusalem – names that were once names to be reckoned with – are now truly nominal. Perhaps as a sop to his ego and out of concern for his finances, the stranded Constantinopolitan prelate also bears the title of Ecumenical Patriarch, with suzerainty over all missions and churches in the Diaspora – the Americas, Australia, Asia, and most of Africa.

Every so often, a Great Synod of all the Orthodox Churches is called to discuss matters of dogma or Tradition. But not too often. The emperor, Constantine VI, convened the seventh and last one in '87 – that's 787 – to affirm the canonicity of the veneration of icons, and it very well might be the last one ever. The need for a convocation of churches to effect any change means that, in a real sense, the constitution of the Orthodox Church is set, with little chance of amendment. As in our federal system of secular government, however, the regulation of local traditions, including language, is the bailiwick of the national church. So while Orthodox boast that it is possible to walk into any Orthodox church anywhere on earth and know where you are in the Divine Liturgy, it is also possible that you will not feel exactly at home. Clearly, the Roman Church is in a better position to make changes if it wants to do so. Because of his position as the infallible Vicar of Christ, combining the secular and religious functions of the old Roman emperor (*pontifax maximus*), the Pope can convene an "ecumenical" council whenever he chooses, and he has chosen to do so fourteen times since the Great Divorce. "Greeks have no need for a Pope," a Greek mischievously told me, "because all of them believe that *they* are infallible."

The other theological bone of contention between the Roman and Orthodox Churches, the *filioque*, once again pits Greek and Roman world views against each other. In saying that the Holy Spirit proceeds from the Father *through* the Son, the Orthodox posit a triumvirate of ineffable equals; by saying that the Holy Spirit proceeds from the Father *and* the Son, the Catholic Church envisions a hierarchy of powers.

The questions of the primacy of the Pope and the insertion of the *filioque* into the Nicaean Creed were the main issues that prompted Cardinal Humbert of Silva – taking advantage of the death of Pope Leo IX in 1054 – to slap a bull of excommunication on the altar of Hagia Sofia; obeying an unspoken schoolyard protocol, the Ecumenical Patriarch reciprocated in kind. But this tit-for-tat had been going on for hundreds of years, through the Arian, Nestorian, Monophysite, and Monothelite heresies, with each side at different times espousing every one of these anathematized views while throwing excommunications at the other as if they were an inexhaustible quiver of darts. Miraculously, the church as a single entity had survived them all. Reunion was still a possibility until the spring of 1204, when a Frankish army, on its way to the Holy Land for the Fourth Crusade and in need of quick money to pay off its Venetian creditors for providing transport, parked itself in the Golden Horn. The Byzantine emperor had hardly been an innocent bystander, negotiating with the crusaders *and* the Seljuk Turks, and after the Constantinopolitans refused to pay for the blessed venture, the Franks overran the vulnerable sea wall. What was arguably the most enlightened city in the world – grisly executions and maimngs notwithstanding – opened its gates to the Dark Ages. The crusaders pillaged, looted, raped, and generally "sacked" the city sacred to their co-religionists for the three long and bloody days that victors in such matters traditionally devoted to profiteering. In his not-so-*Short History of Byzantium*, John Julian Norwich says that in terms of its effect on history, the sack of Constantinople was the worst single tragedy ever suffered by the Christian world. And the perpetrators were Christians!

The Franks didn't leave Constantinople for fifty-seven years, during which time they did absolutely nothing to improve the reputation of humankind. Their departure from The City was as ignominious as their entry had been treacherous. A Byzantine patrol out on reconnaissance simply walked through an unguarded gate. Compared to Western Christians, the Turks must have seemed like missionaries – a feeling that one of the Orthodox participants in the Council of Florence (1439) echoed when the Romans, as they had at the Council of Lyons (1274), tried to force the Byzantines into an acceptance of the Pope and the *filioque* in exchange for their help against the Ottomans. "Better the turban than the miter," he is alleged to have replied. Fourteen years later, he got his wish.

"Old men forget and all shall be forgot," wrote Shakespeare, in *Henry the Fifth*. Not so among those to whom forgiveness is practically a commandment. When a Roman cardinal recently requested permission to visit Athens, the Greek government agreed to receive him only as a political representative of the secular state known as the Vatican. After all, it's only been eight hundred years. Even longer since the last cordial meeting between the spiritual heads of the East and the West. Until Pope Paul VI's journey there in 1960, one thousand, three hundred and thirty-two years had elapsed since the last papal visit to the city on the Bosporus.

It is not for nothing, then, though little to do with doctrine, that while the Roman Church considers the Orthodox Church to be schismatic, that is, separated but redeemable, Orthodox Christians who care about such things regard Catholics as heretics and therefore irretrievably lost. To this day, although the Pope has said there is no salvation outside Catholicism, Orthodox Christians can receive Holy Communion in a Catholic church, but there is no quid pro quo. On the other hand, some Orthodox churches do allow African Copts, who are Monophysites and therefore anathematized heretics, to partake of the Eucharist. In their case, however, no Hatfield-McCoy history exists to make sure that the blood keeps dripping from an ancient wound.

But who with any experience of the variety of life cares if the churches are reunited? What would then happen to the little humility either of them have somehow retained? And who wants one, big clumsy, and inevitably super-corrupt church anyway? It's a cause with a lot of drummers and no real following. However, while it is not our goal to analyze this bitter separation, we do feel we have the right and perhaps, duty, to laugh at a situation in which both of these revered and ancient confessions, by maintaining and exploiting their mutual intransigence, contradict nearly every precept bequeathed by the one who gave them his name.

Charity begins at homelessness.

Christ was homeless. He was born in another man's barn and buried in another man's tomb. His father was a carpenter, and some surmise he followed in his steps, but in the three-year period covered by the Gospels, there is no mention of him holding down what we would call a job. Like Blanche DuBois in Tennessee Williams' *A Streetcar Named Desire*, he appears to have lived off "the kindness of strangers".

Greeks consider hospitality as fundamental to their identity as the Orthodox Church. In fact, *philoxenia*, the indiscriminate love of strangers, has been the defining aspiration of Greek life since before Homer, who used it as the pedestal for both *The Iliad* and *The Odyssey*. Hospitality does not merely command the host to treat all strangers with indiscriminate respect, but requires equal respect from those enjoying its benefits. Paris brought on the Trojan War by breaching Menelaus's hospitality, and Odysseus ended it by slaughtering his wife's suitors for their abuse of his. Zeus allowed terrible things to happen to good people because of Paris's breach of sacred

26

etiquette. Hector and Priam have many more of the qualities we consider admirable than do any of the Greeks, but that failed in the divine balance.

When I returned to the United States after my encounter with *The Way of a Pilgrim*, I immersed myself in a study of the Orthodox Church and learning basic *Demotiki* Greek. In December, 1975, believing I had learned enough about this exotic faith and myself to take the long leap into the baptismal font, I packed some warm clothes and a New Testament into a duffel bag and returned to Paros. My first visit, seven months before, had been preceded by all the planning it took to blindly point my finger at a map of Greece and abide by the result. What had I known about the real Greece anyway? My return that Christmas was another kind of no-brainer: Paros was where I had discovered an intimation of peace that I could not reconcile with my previous experience of the earth. On this island in the middle of the Aegean, the meanest jewel in the Kyklades chain draped around the sacred (pagan) island of Delos – this Paros that offered only an incomparable sunlight that mesmerized artists and renders its renowned marble translucent; this island that boasted thirty-seven monasteries (three live and thirty-four defunct) and the celebrated "Church of a Hundred Doors" – I was ready to offer myself up for baptism into the Eastern Orthodox Christian Church.

Thus it happened that on a gray Christmas Eve, I descended on the Holy Monastery of Longovarda. Christ entering Jerusalem on an ass? How about an ass entering Longovarda imagining he was Christ? Father G., my spiritual maître d', had spent much of the Second World War as an Anglican priest in Southeast London during the blitz. The parishes on either side of his had been totally destroyed. His was untouched. Whether he saw the destruction all around him as a punishment of the Church of England for its behavior and doctrine, I don't know, but he eventually embraced Orthodoxy as the "true church". As a result of his wartime experience, Father G. did not like surprises. A hello he wasn't ready for would immediately have him diving for the air raid shelter. Upon my arrival, he did not exactly spread palm fronds under my cloven hooves, but he received me with tempered enthusiasm and showed me to a guest room. I disregarded the less than fervid reception. In my position, Christ would have done no less.

After the liturgy the next morning, the day Jesus entered into the world as a babe, I responded to the refectory bell as if it were the starter's gun for a hundred-yard dash. In the company of my future brothers, I stood impatiently while we waited for the ancient abbot (*igoumenos*) to inch toward his place at the head of the table and bless the food. The monks' festive meal, on the day of Christ's birth, was spaghetti, fried potatoes, a herring-like fish, some crumbly cheese, and stale bread. And a carafe of acidic wine. And a cookie dusted in chalky confectioner's sugar. Head bowed in mock gratitude while one slightly open eye skeptically surveyed the spread, I began to reassess the impression – and the choice – I had made.

I could not stay at the monastery for my catechumenate without the blessing – the permission – of the bishop of the diocese, who resided on the neighboring island of Naxos. Since this was in the dark ages before videoconferencing, this necessitated a visit. While I awaited the episcopal summons, I rented a room – at fifty drachmas ($1.60) a night! – in Naousa, the isolated fishing village from which I had launched my life-bending adventure the previous spring. Then, it had been the monastery that unfailingly offered me free food. Now, it seemed as if every time I stepped into the street, some stranger dragged me into one of the two restaurants, forced me to sit at a long table strewn with culinary debris, and set a plate and a goblet in front of me! *"Fateh, fateh,"* they ordered. An ambivalent circular motion of the arm accompanied the words. It could have meant either, "Shovel it in" or "If you don't eat, I am going to flatten you with a bolo punch." And they provided entertainment! At practically every meal, a couple wearing laurel crowns dream-danced their way among the tables littered with the leavings of departed guests and a few passed out on the floor. What kind of place was this I had stumbled into? So what if every meal I ate twice a day for twelve days was lamb and fried potatoes and that by this time, I was a confirmed but not monastically certified vegetarian? Is this how people really lived here? Whatever happened to death, taxes, and being stuck with the bill? Was I being wrapped in the second coming of the Summer of Love?

What I did not know was that the Orthodox canons prohibit marriages during both Advent – the forty day fasting period before Christmas – and Great Lent, the more rigorous fast (*nisteia*) that precedes Easter (*Pascha*). That year, *Pascha* fell as early as it was possible according to the Eastern method of computing movable feasts; The *Triodion*, the three weeks of preparation for Lent, began just after Theophany – in the West, Epiphany – which falls on the thirteenth day after Christmas. The prohibition of celebrations during the fasts meant that if couples didn't tie the knot during the two weeks following Christmas, they couldn't until after Easter. Every meal to which I was invited was part of overlapping three-day wedding feasts celebrating who knows how many marriages!

But the hospitality didn't end with the onset of Lent, although now the meals were beans, rice, and *chorta* (wild greens). Whatever their motive – and there was a certain amount of prestige in having a guest and a repentant Israelite to boot – people in the town vied for the privilege of feeding me. I even began to expect it; and to think of it as my … well, right. The Yiddish for this is *"schnorring"*. But didn't Christ also *schnorr*? I suppose he did, my little lawyer, but hospitality is a two-way street, and he gave value in return. Who did you raise from the dead?

In contrast to the West, where everyone chooses what he or she will give up for Lent, in the Eastern precincts of Christianity everyone gives up the same thing: meat, dairy products, and fish. Weekday fare is *kserofagita* – literally, "dry food": beans, grains, legumes, vegetables, and fruit. While Greeks have managed to bend the rules to include vegetable oil, olive oil is out. On this part of the planet, you might as well order your heart to forego plasma. Has another people ever made such a sacrifice?

As is the case on many islands in the Aegean, the only oven (*fournos*) in the town of Naousa, on the island of Paros in the Kyklades, belonged to the baker. On weekend evenings during Lent, when the proscription against olive oil was lifted, the locals took their sealed clay pots of olive oil, chickpeas, olive oil, tomatoes, olive oil, garlic, olive oil, and basil, and olive oil to the bakery (also *fournos*). The next morning, they retrieved their pots. Back in their kitchens, they broke the seals, and an ambrosial fragrance heralded the entrance of *revethia* to the dinner table. For a taste of *revethia* I would have betrayed my own grandmother (who was an awful cook and wasn't very nice to me anyway).

I did not shop for my religion. My two sets of grandparents were secular Jews whose interest in religion ran from indifference to atheism. My mother knew a few Yiddish words; on Friday nights, she drove us to a Reform Temple, where my work-weary father found some relaxation criticizing the very distinguished-looking rabbi's remarkably undistinguished sermons. As I have mentioned, I had no apparent interest in religion at all while I was growing up; that applied double to Christianity as it was advertised in the United States and from my family, whose relatives and ancestors had only experienced its considerable down side. My first awareness that in Greece I was not in Kansas came when I was the recipient of this indiscriminate, heart and belly warming hospitality.

I can't say hospitality is unknown in the West, but I also wouldn't call it typical. Maybe we show it to friends; sometimes even to strangers. And without crossing the ocean, I have met some truly big hearts. But stop to talk with a homeless person, and you have labeled yourself "weird". In Greece at that time, to be homeless was a disgrace only in that it manifested the community's failure to provide. My Parian hosts might have been putting on a show for their neighbors, their priest, or their country; if they were, so what? There are mixed motives for everything, even for tending one's beard. But as a consequence of my initial experience on Paros, I have always equated hospitality with the Orthodox Church. I am sure that if I had been in Tibet and had a similar encounter with Buddhists that hadn't been born Jewish, I could have wound up wearing saffron instead of black. My point is this: Without this national exaltation of hospitality, there would be no story for me to tell, no real religion to write about, and you certainly would never be able to discover Mount Athos – with or without me. But don't get too comfortable. You get to be a guest at a monastery for three days. After that, it's work or leave.

Maintenance? You must be an unbeliever.

The overnight train to Thessalonica has other drawbacks besides the smoke. There are snoring neighbors and waking up aching all over and feeling dirty and like someone dumped a spoonful of ashes in your mouth. This is good for you. Saints have had similar experiences. Besides, taking the night train means getting an early start to Ouranopolis.

Thessalonica is the second-largest city in Greece and its population in 1985 was less than half of a million. The original settlers were Jews. Today, there are very few Jews. A long, curved esplanade separates the Aegean from high-rise, balconied apartments, restaurants, and clubs. Away from the two main streets, the city is a walker's delight, with many quiet squares, parks, and restaurants where you can walk through the kitchen to check what is cooking in olive oil today, and outdoor cafes. Once a crossroads of trade, Thessalonica is now a hub of university life. Students are everywhere and the nights are very young. The inevitable ruins are mainly medieval. The city claims the obligatory three hundred and sixty-five churches and one football stadium. Priests wish it were that easy to fill *their* seats. A few hours west of Thessalonica is Mount Olympus, aerie of Zeus and his eternally dysfunctional family. The mosaics of Pella, the capital of Alexander the Great's world-conquering Macedonia, lie thirty-five miles to the north. If you are going to Mount Athos, you go east.

Unlike American cities, there is no central bus station in Thessalonica. The terminal that serves Ouranopolis is about fifteen minutes by municipal bus from the train station. While walking will rearrange your twisted limbs and air out your enspittled and smoke-soaked clothing, you will almost certainly miss your connection, because the train arrives at about five thirty a.m. and the first bus to the far reaches of Chalkidiki leaves at six. The first bus is the only one that assures the traveler of arriving in time for the only boat making the coastal voyage to the Holy Mountain that day – weather permitting. Summer offers more options, since there are additional buses to handle the crowds. In any season, no scheduled bus departs with passengers on the curb. On Greek transport, overbooking is unknown. That number over the windshield indicating maximum capacity is purely decorative.

The expanded bus schedule is the only good reason for visiting Mount Athos in the summertime. By mid-July, the monks have had enough of the hordes of visitors, whether they be bona fide pilgrims, self-styled pilgrims, the curious, or nature-lovers. Two of the best times to visit the Holy Mountain are Christmas and Easter, since Greeks usually celebrate with their families. Measured against lamb roasting over an ash-pit, fish, spaghetti, and fried potatoes just don't cut it. A culinary tidbit: Greeks rarely eat goats; their milk makes them far too valuable. By the time goats are too old to do what no one pays them to do, their flesh has abandoned all claims to tenderness. Getting somebody's goat is considered a high level of hospitality, but old goat has all the flavor and texture of a young rubber band. It is so greasy that you may never get it to your mouth to make that discovery for yourself. Old goat is one meal that *retsina* complements beautifully.

The bus to Ouranopolis is a trusty, ancient Daimler-Benz – the DC-3 of the long-distance bus trade in countries below the economic Mendoza line. This is the only kind of vehicle that bus companies feel they can afford to lose should it slip off the seasonal ice or dust on mountain roads without rails and plunge a few hundred feet to final depreciation. Note the safety equipment, located in the narrow space between windscreen and sunroof. This consists of a wall-to-wall collage of icons, crosses, evil eyes, and the occasional chaste fifties-style pin-up with a smile like a small gondola, whose exaggerated curves are one of the benefits of drinking Coke. You will see a bus without wheels before one lacking a personalized icon screen.

Never talk to a Greek bus driver while his vehicle is in motion. You can be creeping up a mountain road with six inches and no guardrail between you and the exquisite valley a thousand feet below, and in his effort to please he will turn his toward you to reply. And never *never* hold up your hand to the driver's face to ask the fare with your fingers. A gesture with an open palm is a curse. The dreaded "evil eye" will immediately affix itself to the driver's soul, and he is far from his *yiayia*, who alone knows how to prepare the ancient cocktail that will plead his case with the devil. This is not another pathetic attempt at a joke. I was on a bus in Athens when another American did a full frontal digitalization of five drachmas, and it was two blocks before the driver could bring both bus and himself under control.

There are many models of monk, but they all come in black.

The bus arrives, the doors open, and we pile in. Your ticket will have a seat number, but there are no reserved seats. I slide over to a window and feel as if I am already on the Holy Mountain. Unlike the plane and the train, I am no longer with others who could be going anywhere. Carrying a company of strangers loosely bound by a common objective, the bus is the real transition between this world and the other: a three-hour journey that begins in the cultivated plains, winds through mountains hidden by morning mist, and then drops precipitously to the sparkling, white-capped, and empty sea. Across the aisle, a monks already sleeps. Another may appear to be, but a black, woolen prayer rope carries on with a life of its own; time-worn, it slips between time-worn fingers. Like cats, monks often seem to be sleeping; again, like cats, they do spend up to eighteen hours of the day involved in a world that has nothing to do with you. Up front, a monk stares straight ahead. He could be fixed on dinner, God, or the bend in the road where he expects to meet his maker. A national love of landscaping is not the reason why icon shelters, crosses, memorial lights, or flowers adorn almost every curve. A narrow curve is the place of choice to show off one's passing skills.

You will almost never see a monk reading a book. Or a newspaper. What could possibly be of current interest to them? Their only perspective on time is that they are getting older so what? And novels? Please. Besides, most abbots believe that unauthorized reading is as bad for the liver as speculative thinking. They hold writing in equally low regard: I continually forgot to confess to my abbot that I never stopped making notes about what I felt had been revealed to me and what I observed. Perhaps they were right – outside the monastic discipline, those thoughts have no meaning, and inside it they are unnecessary and distracting. Reading them years later, they are worse than code: intelligible, irrelevant, and embarrassing.

Some of the monks on the bus wear the only robes they have ever owned – an abridged and desiccated menu of every meal eaten over the past twenty years. Their shoes are scuffed and plugged, and soled with blown-out truck tires. These shabby monks are most likely the hermits and the *kalyve* and *kelli*-dwellers – the leaseholders of the quaint little ruins of stone and shale that dot the peninsula. They have to fend for themselves, have no insurance, go under, and are not survived. Like first-time home-buyers, every generation spawns a handful of hopefuls that fall in love with what they see at first sight and whisper to the wind, "If we just do this...."

Compare the habiliment of the loners with that of the *kenobites*, the ones who live in a cooperative community where the monks eat, work, and pray together – what we call a brotherhood. It is like comparing pa-and-pa businesses and corporations. The majority of monastic houses are *kenobitic*. Their representatives on the bus wear the best robes that having no money can buy, and black shoes polished to a sun-gleam. Several of them read, and they all have pension plans. No beacons blushing under a bush, they write books for the illumination of the world. Food, clothing, shelter, church, and a short-term sub-let on a cemetery plot – their monastery will take care of them from tonsure to grave.

Many of these brothers travel in consort with their abbot, around whom they fuss and hum as if over a queen bee. He responds in kind, playing the oriental potentate he is. The rule of the abbot of a monastery is absolute. His subjects can do nothing without his 'blessing'. He is the first to enter the church and the refectory. His monks bow their heads as he passes and kiss his hand before speaking to him. Although elected by the brotherhood, he makes a queen bee look like a president. In a monastery,

Caesar is the right hand of God. As each autocephalous (national) church is as supreme as the head of the Church of Rome, so every Athonite monastery, as long as it broaches no new dogma, is its own autocephalous church, acknowledging the spiritual, but not the administrative suzerainty, of the Patriarch of Constantinople.

Between the hermits and the *kenobites* are the *idiorrthymics*. These are the limited partnership monks: conservative, small-time capitalists who provide a balance to the socially progressive *kenobites*. *Idiorrhythmic* monks contract with their monasteries for room and board, in exchange for which they contribute some kind of work that helps the monastery sustain itself. Many do not inhabit cells, so much as suites. Unlike the *kenobites*, the *idiorrhythmics* do not give up their possessions – but, then, they have no pension plan. So far are they, in fact, from living the *kenobtic* ideal that sometimes their ruling council allows them to go into business for themselves and keep a good part of the profits from their 'obedience', that is, their monastic job. When, in the past, business included collecting the rents from real estate (*metochia*) in the world, and this lucrative grant was based on seniority, the difference in the circumstances of monks within the same monastery could be severe: some dressed in silks, while others, mainly the young, practically went naked.

The extent of the submission of *idiorrhythmic* monks to their abbot is not quite clear. They appear together only at services and in the refectory. Even attendance at those times of communal gathering is purely voluntary, and hence, very sporadic. Some eat in their rooms. *Idiorrhythmia* means "singular rhythm" – what we call walking to the beat of one's own drum. We are unlikely to encounter *idiorrhythmic* monks on the bus to Ouranopolis. I picture them taking taxis. I am not aware of their tipping habits.

Some of those not clad in black are bent on climbing the Mountain of Athos. In monastic parlance, people in the world are called *cosmoikoi*. There is a stigma in the word, as if the world is already halfway to hell. The majority of *xenoi*, however, are either Christian pilgrims or seekers after the most exotic religious practice west of the Indus River. The Orthodox will most likely be unshaven in homage to their hosts, a concession that adds to the uneasy feeling there is something "wrong" about the life one is temporarily forsaking. Some of the Greeks may have an old village chum or a relative on The Mountain. They chat with the monks, none of whom ever seem loath to talk. Nothing excites excess like deprivation.

Just because you aren't Orthodox doesn't mean you will go to hell.

The Orthodox Church believes in the Resurrection of Christ and the eventual resurrection of all humankind. However, it does not profess to know what the new creature will look like, except that it will have a body – though perhaps not one that we would recognize as such. Thus, until recently, cremation was illegal in Greece; there are still no crematoria. But neither are there boundaries excluding or including the "saved". If we think of salvation simply as "making whole", it ceases to be a buzzword of fanatics. Orthodox Christians believe that Orthodox have a pretty good shot at salvation. As for outsiders… (shrug)… who knows?

In keeping with its apophatic philosophy, the Orthodox Church has not examined the relationship of grace and works that constitute wholeness as definitively or extensively as churches in the West. It has respected the mystery, and the health of any religious pulse largely depends on admitting there is a lot it can't explain. As it creates no unnecessary dogma, there is space within what the Orthodox Church as a whole believes for people to wander in and out the way they do the physical church during long services. On the Sunday of Orthodoxy, the first Sunday of the Easter Fast, when the inventors of the fifty-nine recognized heresies are once more condemned to eternal perdition, I have often thought that if every person in church that day described what he or she truly believed, a hundred more heresies would be added to the list. But no one does ask. It's been a long time since the Orthodox Church had the secular power to launch a sustained Inquisition – not that at one point I personally wouldn't have given it the old college try. When it did, it did not deal out punishments with a light hand. Hundreds of thousands died in the strife that arose around the teachings of Arius in the 4th century. In the next century, the sainted anti-Semite, Cyril, Patriarch of Alexandria, used monks who had left the world for the Nitrean desert to cow opposition to his rigid views and instigated the murder of the noted philosopher, Hypatia. A contemporary called him a "monster, born and educated for the destruction of the church."

But doesn't the Orthodox Church have positions on issues like abortion, homosexuality, gay marriage, and evolution? It does, but I have never found a document raising them to the status of dogma. Why? Lack of power, decentralization, and an unwillingness to make statements when it doesn't have to, have forced this church to forsake judgment for mercy. To me, this apparent weakness is its strength. After the Ottoman yoke had been broken at the beginning of the 19th century, many of the Greek laity wanted those who had not just doubted but renounced their faith during the occupation to be punished, but the church wouldn't have it. As one of the Church Fathers put it, "You could throw away the entire New Testament as long as you kept the parable of the Prodigal Son." The English poet, Rupert Brooke (who is buried on the island of Skyros), wrote that there was more faith in doubt than in creeds – after all, even Christ on the cross had his doubts; but one prodigal son for whom the Orthodox Church did not kill the fatted calf was the doubter, Nikos Kazantzakis. For the views expressed in his novels – in particular, *The Last Temptation of Christ* – the church denied him burial in consecrated ground.

The writings of the Church Fathers are a storehouse of "right worship" (orthodoxy). Those seeking credibility in the Orthodox Christian world, must introduce their comments with "As the Fathers say...." – the equivalent of citing sources in a thesis. It is the key to receiving permission to add a little of your own. That said, I would be the last to admit that I have often taken liberties with this tradition. As the wisdom of ghettoed Eastern European Jews is so close to that of ragged monks living in the Egyptian Desert, I have often quoted anonymous Hasidic Jewish "Fathers" without raising an eyebrow among my Christian listeners. Both Hasidism and desert monasticism were at heart social movements, concerned more with living a faith than conforming to a rigid theology. Not surprisingly, the orthodox of both religions cited them for extremism and eventually excommunicated them. But it was hospitality, the hallmark of a living faith, not theology, that converted me.

Women are from Earth; men are from beyond Pluto.

One Hasidic tale that is accepted in any company concerns an angel that ridiculed a man waiting at the gates of heaven for letting his wife talk him into a sin. The Just Judge denied the man's application; but he also sent the angel to earth to experience marriage. Greek priests must marry and reveal themselves as subject to all the joys, sorrows, and infirmities of wedlock as any of their parishioners. If that's what it takes to be a priest, then why are women excluded from the priesthood? Don't women also experience all those things? The church gives the same reason for excluding women that prevailed in the Old Israel: in a world that did not understand menses and where touching blood made one ritually unclean, a woman priest would have been benched for at least a quarter of her life. Orthodox Christians may venerate Mary both as an obedient handmaid and as the Mother of God, but she could no more be a priest than if she had been a fornicator or adulteress. Although Number One in the panoply of saints, in icons she appears only as the *Theotokos*, or "She who bore God," and not, like other virginal saints, as a woman worthy of veneration on her own.

The sorry truth is that men, who base their identity almost wholly on money and power, are pathologically protective of their sand castle. Theologically, the church (building, congregation, and institution) is a woman, and priests are men who serve her. And yet, two thousand years into the Christian era, a priest still "churches" a forty-day old boy by carrying him around the altar, while if the baby is a girl, he stops at the Royal Gates. Until quite recently, if a priest divorced he could not marry again; now he can – so long as it was his wife who initiated the divorce! As if to show men how it feels, the formerly women-only Philoptochos ("lover of the poor") Society now admits men – yet it denies them the right to vote!

It could be said that the lot of women would be worse without a church, which at least teaches moral behavior and charity, but the bent, worn-out *yiayia* in black, her head covered as a token of submission to a masculine God, is not an attractive role model to young female Greeks. It can be little consolation to their daughters that not only do these same demeaned women fill the pews, but by virtue of their control of the household are the chief enablers of the traditions that oppress them. Why do they do this? My guess is as good as yours.

The word "religion" comes from *"religio"*, Latin for "to rebind". Religion engages the whole person. It is about relationships within oneself (including the divine), with others (including the divine), and with one's surroundings (including the divine). Not being a woman, I don't know for sure, but I think the nature and order of creation is self-evident to them by virtue of what takes place within their bodies. Their role as child-bearers means that history stretches behind, the future ahead, and both are in the present: the past is the unbroken chain of life, and there is little need to meditate on an afterlife when one knows (*gnorizo*) it first-hand in children.

And not only through their own children: I believe that women are more amenable to adopting the fruit of another womb because the impetus is a need to nurture, and not continue one's own line. Biology gives them a blessed fidelity to the business of living and to the Earth.

For women, therefore, theology is a luxury; for men it's a need. Men deposit their seed and are gone; the birth process is as unfathomable as the desire that draws them into it and as rife with personal insecurity as the rejection through which they must wade to participate. Why do men become addicted to useless games, keeping score and reveling in what looks like wasted time? As a man contemplates his role in creation – the mystery of it all and the odds against his succeeding – he perceives he really is as useless as the dog he kicks, and whether he succeeds in having a successor appears to be a matter of luck or grace. So when a man has a child, and especially a man-child, he is cigar-smoking ecstatic, especially if he is [relatively] sure it is his. By insisting on an apostolic succession within the priesthood, wherein every ordained minister can claim descent from one of the original apostles, men are only trying recreating their own credible chain of existence. Since, unlike women, they have no way of proving their connection with the present, men's knowledge of an afterlife also is theoretical.

The mind of a man is hopelessly analytical. It also is where he can safely entertain the illusion that he is safe and powerful. Only a man would ask how many angels could stand on the head of a pin – assuming angels have feet. A woman would point out that that is not what a pin is *for*.

Theology, the foredoomed attempt to understand the incomprehensible, inevitably sounds like the pseudo-logic of a madman, the more so because of the trance-like dispassion with which it is pursued, the intent of which is to dispel that very impression. But theology is madness – schizophrenic, even. How else could anyone burn God's creatures in the name of God? How else could I say that becoming a Christian made me more of a Jew, at the same time hating "the Jews" – as I once did – for their role in the death of Christ?

To most women with whom I have spoken, the fact that the residents of Mount Athos do not permit women even to enter is intolerable. I don't believe it's the particular beauty of the place that attracts them. There are many exotic places on this earth. I think it's more that they want to play the golf course of the club that won't have them as members just because they are women. This anger blinds them to the irony that if they were allowed on the Holy Mountain, what they would see and experience would not be Mount Athos but just one more beautiful place!

Intellectually, even morally, all right is on their side. Still, I think it shows a potentially tragic lack of psychological understanding and respect for the necessarily slow evolution of gender roles. We are talking about a place that in many ways has never left the 10th century, when political correctness approved of separation based on gender, and slavery was the fourth estate. In our own peculiar time, we are moving toward equality in all things, but in the case of Mount Athos, there is only one kind of equality that matters: man or woman, Greek or Jew, slave or free man, our souls are all equal before God. That has always been the case, so what is there to revise? It is no more open to change than Tradition, and Tradition is the Athonite chronicle. This is history that is still being lived, by people who are as devoted to their past as any ethnicity is to its particular heritage. By their presence, women would add an element that has no place in its long and continuous *tropos*. You cannot mix sugar and spice and everything nice with puppy dog's tails and expect either to pet or to eat the result.

Mommy, are we there yet?

The bus to Ouranopolis crosses a part of Greece that does not attract many tourists. A craggy topography dictated that this part of Thrace should be a region of little farms, and the two-lane road system, snaking around property and hills, ensures it will stay that way. Barring accidents, our transport stops just once, in Arneia, high among once-impassable mountains. The village consists of a small triangular *plaka*, the obligatory shade tree, and a few shops in which I never saw a customer. There is time to debark and stretch legs that have been in a vertical fetal position for hours. Breathe in that air! Certainly, it is a different ether from what you inhaled in Thessalonica, and most certainly different from the interesting vapors canned by the bus. There are two tables in front of the *kafeneion* across the square, and no chairs. A few passengers who are familiar with the village disappear into the back streets and return with dusty boxes of snacks and bottles of warm soda. Shivering in the chill air of early morning you may wonder what people do here for a living, forgetting that there are some places where what has always been done is still enough.

The bus descends out of the clouds and the dark waters of the Thracian Sea suddenly come into view. Instead of turning right, in the direction of Mount Athos, the driver goes north, enters the town of Stratoni, and negotiates the narrow palm-bordered streets of a residential neighborhood. Is the driver going home for lunch? He stops in front of a cinder-block house and drags two big cartons from the front of the bus onto the street. As if suddenly aware that his passengers are watching, he dashes to the door of the house to get the signed verification of his delivery.

On the road again, we run down the peninsula of Athos north of the border of the monastic state. Halfway to Ouranopolis is the place where Xerxes, the King of Kings of Persia, cut an isthmus to allow the passage of his ships from Asia Minor to Greece in the 5th century B.C. That's what absolute rulers do: they cut isthmuses; they tell people what their religion will be. But this despot didn't dig this ditch just for his amusement. Ten years earlier, Xerxes' father, Darius, had lost an enormous fleet – 250 ships, 20,000 men – unsuccessfully battling the violent weather off the southern tip of Athos. To the left of the road, on the north coast, is Ierissos, a town known as Acanthus until Roman times. There is no building in Ierissos older than 1932, the year in which a powerful earthquake leveled the town, buried it, dug it up again, and pounded it so flat that the highest point of the city was six inches above the ground. Most of the people in this area are descendants of the million and a half Greeks exchanged for a few Turks in 1922, the year that Mustapha Kemal Ataturk, first President of the Turkish Republic, cleaned his ethnic house. The Greek government confiscated much of the land it gave to the refugees from monastic owners.

Those who have established relations with one of the monasteries on the north side of The Mountain, or who already have their passports, de-bus and walk to the port to take passage down that coast in a *caique*, the ancient fishing boat that facilitates travel between the coastal monasteries. These graceful vessels, which once sported raked masts and red lateen sails and are now propelled by tubercular motors of indeterminate age, charge a pittance for carriage, kept low by lack of insurance. The monasteries on the north coast, more forbidding and less frequented than those on the other side, are almost all *idiorrhythmic*. Those on the south coast, which the shivering northerners scoffingly refer to as "the Riviera," practice the *kenobitic* way of life.

The weather on the north coast, which faces the Bosporus and the piercing winds coming out of Russia, can be vicious for many months of the year. It takes a certain kind of person – not necessarily a better one – to bear up to it, especially given the rarity and ineffectiveness of heating equipment. Nevertheless, the monks of that coast do seem to regard their more polite-living compatriots on the other side of the ridge as spineless candy-asses. For their part, the sweet-bottomed brethren in black from the south regard the individualistic northerners as latter-day barbarians.

Oh, Brother! In what Church art thou?

As if this *de facto* local schism weren't enough, the north coast boasts the monastery of Esphigmenou, which has been in a virtual state of secession from the Holy Mountain since 1964. In that year, the inmates of that establishment determined that the spiritual father of all Athos, the Patriarch of Constantinople, was at least a traitor to Orthodox Christianity and possibly a heretic, and they refused to commemorate him in their liturgies.

Refusing to commemorate a hierarch is tantamount to self-excommunication. The Nicaean Creed declares that the Orthodox Church is "apostolic". This means that every time an Orthodox priest serves the Divine Liturgy, the Orthodox mass, he must include through commemoration a hierarch who received his power to administer the sacraments through his direct descent from one of the twelve Apostles. In the Orthodox way of defeating normal human perspective, the clerical hierarchy is less a pyramid than a set of Russian dolls that fit inside each other. So, although there are more priests than bishops and more bishops than archbishops, wherever the priest is, so is the archbishop. In addition, the non-dualistic theology of the Orthodox Church affirms that the priest does not simply represent the bishop at the liturgy, but *is* the bishop in the same way that the bishop is not Christ's "vicar", but Christ, himself.

The corollary to the apostolic succession is that whoever commemorates a heretic is by association also a heretic. I believe the Esphigmenites had accused the Ecumenical Patriarch of entering into a dialogue with the Protestant and Catholic churches – a mortal sin known as "ecumenism". The only kind of inter-church dialogue acceptable to Orthodox zealots is unconditional surrender. The attempt to communicate with the Western confessions also may have confirmed a suspicion that His

All Holiness was leaning toward "modernism" – another unforgivable heresy to those mired in zealotry. Modernism is a crime that defies definition and can denote anything from adopting the Gregorian calendar to using upright toilets. It is a close-run thing as to which of these calcified stupidities is a greater affront to the spirit of Christianity. Religious crazies, no matter their confession, share one thing in common: unable to adjust to the present, all are anachronisms and proud of it. Some live in the irrecoverable past and others in the inconceivable future. But the behavior of the rebellious Athonites would have drawn no comment at all in 4th century Constantinople, when Christians fought each other in the streets over what faction they supported in the hippodrome and murdered each other over whether the precise word describing the relationship between the Father and the Son was *omoousion* ("the same essence") or *omoiousion* ("a like essence") – a matter of one *iota*.

Since they consider His All Holiness to be tinged with heresy, and refuse to commemorate him, the Esphigmenites have removed themselves from the fellowship of those monasteries that do. The rest of The Mountain has discovered it can live without them and the black, jolly roger-like flag stretched across their battlements that proclaims "[Our notion of] Orthodoxy or Death". As a non-Athonite monk whose monastery commemorates the Ecumenical Patriarch recently explained to me, "I do not know what *their* future will be; on the other hand, they are quite sure that I am going to hell."

The exact date of that sudden plunge is a matter of heated debate, since The Calendar is the single most prominent cause of the schisms that have plagued the Church of Greece in the past hundred years. Until 1923, all Orthodox churches abided by the Julian calendar, which the West had put aside in the 16th century in favor of the one recommended by Pope Gregory XIII. There is a difference of thirteen days between the two contenders. So what? you say. So what? I say. But anyone who has ever tried even unsuccessfully to read Stephen Hawking's *A Brief History of Time* must understand how even perceived differences in time can imperceptibly affect one's life. In this case, it was like slightly moving one of two concentric spheres off previously aligned coordinates, thereby creating an unbridgeable gap between two worlds.

Why the reluctance to make the leap? First, it was a matter of Tradition, and Tradition is, literally, what is "handed down" *without change*. Tradition is of greater importance to the church, which conceives of itself as the sole repository of absolute truth, than it is to the state, which cannot help but acknowledge that it neither operates alone in the world nor is that world unchanging. When the rivalry between the two was one of equals, it didn't make much difference, but when the balance tipped toward the state, then sticking with the old calendar became a cause. To calculate according to the ecclesiastical year emphasized the psychological divide and gave the religious arm a nuanced moral advantage when it possessed few others. Like "I was here first." Or "I am more Christian than you are." This is similar to the split created by the Jewish calendar, which already has its followers deep in the sixth millennium but has no bearing on their fiscal year.

Second, after the sack of Constantinople and the fall of The City, any agreement at all with the West was even more distasteful than it had been during the previous seven hundred years of separation. It was only when the Greeks won their independence in 1821 that the enlightened West suddenly came back into fashion. Even then, for more than a century, the Orthodox Church refused to go along with the state in the matter of the calendar.

In 1923, however, the Church of Greece, perhaps despairing of a return to Byzantium, or perhaps, after the enormous bloodshed in Anatolia the previous year, wanting to put any connection with Asiatic Greece in the past, decided to adopt the newer calendar. Outraged conservatives immediately declared the state church *anathema*, and nailed "Modernist" to its door. Since then the Greek Church has suffered a multitude of minor quakes, resulting in the birth of dozens of new sects – called "jurisdictions" – all claiming to be in The One and Only True line of descent from the Apostles. The governing bishops of these lanternless children of Diogenes each allege their historically non-apostolic canonicity by dispensation (*oikonomia*), like the Lost Tribes of Israel, returning to claim their inheritance but saying they lost the proof in a fire. The members of these new churches proudly call themselves *zylotes* – zealots. The church, i.e., where the vast majority of the people worship, uses another, less flattering word for them – *fanatikoi*. A *fanatikos* may smile at those he has left, and may even have cordial conversations with them. But make no mistake: like the Esphigmenites, he fully believes that when the two trains depart from the Station Styx, he is not the one on the express to the hot southern clime.

The real irony is that the calendar the zealots are (at least verbally) willing to die for is a pagan calendar. Rather that, I guess, than Rome. At least, Christian Rome. Esphigmenou aside, the Holy Mountain has remained outside this debate. While resolutely thirteen days behind the times, it has no problem remaining in communion – respecting the validity of each other's sacraments – with the new calendar Church of Greece. Like Jews, Athonites are no novices in the art of survival.

Easter (*Pascha*) is Easter for all Orthodox no matter what calendar they worship because it is a "moveable feast" dependent not on a date but on the lunar cycle. Easter usually occurs on a different date in the East and the West because Protestants and Catholics use a different formula in making their calculations from that employed by Orthodox. Both formulae are based on the new moon and the Vernal Equinox, but only the Orthodox one assures that Easter is always *after* Passover. Why is this important? How about because the Last Supper *is* the Jewish Passover? Rather than repent of this obvious absurdity, however, the Roman Church apparently can live with Easter egg on its face. Besides, how could the Pope be wrong? And Protestants? I guess there should have been ninety-six theses.

New wine must be put into new bottles – but keep the label.

Are Greeks Orthodox Christians who happen to be Greek, or are they Greeks who chance to be Orthodox? Whichever, and it probably differs from person to person, to be Greek is to be Orthodox is to be one of the "faithful". The latter admittedly is a very loose term. It has nothing to do with church attendance, which is as low as the fat content of some of our newer milks, or financial support – in Greece, the Orthodox Church is subsidized by the state – or belief in church doctrine, most of which is either unknown or as accurate as the last whisper in "Telegraph". Ninety-eight per cent of Greeks in Greece consider their faith fundamental to their identity, but only two per cent admit they attend church regularly. More than one Greek who has often seen me in church has innocently asked me when I had become Greek, when that should have been a tip-off that I was not. Going to church doesn't make a person religious any more than going to a garage makes him a car, but most Greeks see their religion simply as a part of the way things have always been – an heirloom that has been in the family past remembering, an ornament of everlasting Tradition. "Fast the way your *yiayia* fasted," is the popular catechism. Under the Turks, the church was a symbol that provoked a lot of ambivalence. In the villages, it represented resistance and continuity, but the virtual imprisonment of the Ecumenical Patriarch in the *Phanar* was a depressingly visible reminder to Greeks of their subservience. As might be expected, Orthodoxy is stronger in the country and on the islands than it is in urban centers, where an expanding bazaar of religions, cults, philosophies, and narcissisms compete for the faithfuls' attention.

To Greek-Americans, multi-racial, religiously pluralistic America is a very foreign land, and here it is more the Greekness of their church than the dogma that keeps them faithful. Many descendants of the original immigrants have discovered that to marry "outside" practically guarantees his or her disinheritance. If keeping the Olympic torch burning is their prime concern, it in part explains why church attendance in America is far higher than in the homeland, where there is no need to go to church to bear witness to one's ethnicity. When American Greeks do show up, however, it is often just before Holy Communion, so that their stay is no longer than absolutely necessary. Especially during the pro football season. This practice apparently does occasion some guilt. According to one of my Deep Throats, the reason Greeks head for the exit as soon as the priest brings the candle out of the altar on *Pascha* is that when they hear the verse, "Let God arise and let is enemies be scattered," they think it means them.

Modern Greece is experiencing what most "old" countries are going through. In times of insecurity, wherever people feel threatened by strangers or strange ideas, they retreat into the most defensible unit, their tribal culture, like a spider drawing in its legs. In the name of hope, in the fear of change, they carry their religion to the parapet like the doomed defenders of Constantinople parading the icon of the "Mother of God the Protectress" around the walls of their beleaguered city. But where people feel the ways of the past are embarrassing, irrelevant, or stifling, religion either disappears from their lives or charismatic sects spring up to snatch them away from the ancestral faith.

There is no First Amendment protecting freedom of worship in Greece, and who can worship what and where is complicated. For instance, while the constitution establishes Eastern Orthodoxy as the "prevailing religion", the state also pays the salaries of Muslim clerics! Judaism is the other recognized religion, but rabbis have to fend for themselves. Catholics, Greek Catholics (Uniates), and mainstream Protestants are saddled with legal disadvantages, the enforcement of which, however, seems arbitrary.

Although "Old Calendar" Orthodox churches are not persecuted, these renegades receive no state support. But they aren't the real problem. In fact, there is little to appeal to Greeks in any of the traditional Christian confessions. Start-up, low-rent, religions outwardly seem to be more in keeping with the times than stodgy old Orthodoxy, and its long-suffering Tradition. Because Evangelicals, Pentecostals, Mormons, and, in particular, Jehovah's Witnesses, have been too vigorous and successful in their efforts to make converts, the government has not only banned proselytism by these sects, but has even made their obtaining a permit for a house of worship dependent on the approval of the local Orthodox bishop.

Education in Orthodox Christianity is mandatory on all three levels of public school. During these classes, students of other faiths can either attend or just hang out. They are given no other options. Anti-Semitism is written into some of the textbooks. Attempts by Jewish organizations to have them expurgated have had mixed success.

Even when there is no visible threat or competition from strangers, the "evil eye" and *yiayia* (grandma) are ever ready to compete with the cross and the priest as they have done since before there was a cross and a priest. In the homes of the faithful, an ancient book of spells shares the shelf with the family Bible. In Thessalonica, on the feast day of the Beheading of John the Baptist, Christians jump through a ring of fire, just as their ancestors did when they strapped bronze greaves on their legs and sailed for Troy. Inhabitants of the island of Kalymnos celebrate *Pascha* with dynamite, though the origin of this quaint custom is obscure.

For all the rich history that has collected around Christianity over the past thousand years, it is important to remember that the faith of the Apostles has not so much triumphed over the Western world as it has come to an understanding with those beliefs that went before it. Paul the Apostle told the pagan Athenians that Christ was the "Unknown God" who they already worshipped. The handful of Jesuits who brought the Native Americans of Canada into the French Catholic fold in the 17th and 18th centuries succeeded for the same reason. On the other hand, working the old into the new is a lesson that Protestant churches never learned in the execution of their missionary zeal, a stubbornness that often resulted in the peevish, wholesale execution of local populations. Many potential Christians whose traditions contained large chunks of animism readily understood the benefits of eating one's savior, but it was not easy to sell an abstract deity and a barren cross. When you see a Christian baseball player go through a mystifying ritual every time he comes to the plate – spitting on his hands, tugging at his crotch, wiggling his shoes, and crossing himself – you are witnessing the survival of paganism and getting a glimpse into the history of religion.

Is our baseball player supplicating God for a hit, or trying to keep the devil away from his bat? (When you see him thanking God for getting a hit in his image, you are witnessing another and more troubling kind of confusion.) Monotheism is not a belief that comes easy to anyone brought up around the multiplicities of paganism, or, for that matter, with two sides to his or her brain. For all that Eastern and Western Christianity, Judaism, and Islam, have stressed the single Personhood of God, the concept that God is not a duality of good and evil is very difficult for *anyone* to accept. Eastern meditative philosophies favorably compare their no-God beliefs to the allegedly dualistic West, unwittingly creating their own dualism. But God and the devil are not opposites. The opposite of love is not hate, but indifference. In Orthodox Christianity, it is Michael the Archangel who wields the sword of the One and indivisible God against evil. How could God be evil, create evil, oppose evil, and embrace it? I don't know. Perhaps, as the American musical saint, Tom Waits, explains this most puzzling of all antinomies, "There ain't no devil – it's just God, when he's drunk."

"I can't think of a place that's more perfect for a person as perfect as [me]."

Some truly enlightened people are above superstition. For instance, me. Despite the proximity and temptation of the limpid, turquoise waters lapping the shores of Mount Athos, I never went swimming. I don't think I ever saw anyone else grasp the opportunity to get drunk on the wine dark sea, either. Whatever their reasons for abstaining, mine was not because I was sure I would be struck dead or, like Jonah, swallowed by a "great fish" as soon as I tested the temperature with my big toe. Oh no. The reason I did not go swimming was because I was certain that either my abbot would see my unmonastic-behavior-worthy-of-damnation in his crystal ball as soon as I dove in, or I would have to reveal my willful defection from dirt to him during my nightly confession.

My jousting with guilt was not confined to unauthorized swimming.

Although women no longer occupied my thoughts, my pinching shame over my inability to either prayerfully or willfully suppress nocturnal emissions often caused me to pass on the next morning's Holy Communion – as out-of-bounds to even inadvertent ejaculators as the Holy Mountain was to women. I imagined if I took communion after such an … accident, any of a number of bad things would happen: I would choke on the bread and wine, it would disappear or burst into flame while being conveyed to my mouth on the spoon, I would faint as I opened my lips, or I would be struck dumb when the priest asked me to state my name. (Seriously, I do have a law degree.)

On one occasion, desperate not to miss the daily manna without which I felt I could not get through the day, I finally found the cringing courage to ask my confessor for absolution. He was a priest of the dread Russian Church Outside of Russia, no less, which had the reputation of depriving people of communion for inhaling second-hand smoke. Father Hilarion listened with eyes closed and ear bent. Then he straightened up and smiled broadly.

"It happens to all of us," he said.

"Not Saint Anthony," I argued against myself.

Saint Anthony the Great, the first Christian monk, had somehow managed to become free from the need to "spill seed". The priest was unmoved.

"Take communion."

Who would have thought? The kingdom of heaven may be within, but it is equally true, as Anthony the Great [Withholder of Semen] himself said, "Hell is where I am." Incidentally, ROCOR is the only Orthodox sect that is in communion with Esphigmenou.

For the most part my weirdness was a product of fear; occasionally, it could produce something profitable. For instance, it once occurred to me that it would be a good idea to refrain from judging others because I had come to believe that behind closed doors all men became angels. In a place with doors for potentially thousands of monks, it had a very positive effect on my behavior. Of course, like anything that comes from the head and not the heart, it didn't last.

There are (some) heavenly bodies at heaven's gate.

It is less than thirty minutes from Ierissos to Ouranopolis, literally the "heavenly city", and the launching pad for those whose zeal – religious or otherwise – has brought them to Mount Athos. Less than half a century ago, the road between the two towns did not exist. Athonites and the Greek government had long ago agreed that no one would build a road from Xerxes' canal south to the Holy Mountain. If it was a written agreement, it has been lost, and toward the middle of the 20th century, local people took matters into their own hands and hacked the first crude road out of economic necessity. A few years later, with the approach of the one thousandth anniversary of Mount Athos, the government finished the road, enlarging and paving it, and wheeling the siege towers of modern technology up to the very walls of the Garden of the Mother of God.

Like Ierissos, Ouranopolis began its life as a camp for refugees from Asia Minor in the third decade of the 20th century. Its original name was Prosforion, meaning "holy offering", which is like calling Greenland Greenland. For thirty years, its only industry was despair. No one would have dreamed that this remote, low-lying and rock-sewn part of Greece, so little prized that it was handed over to destitute refugees with a "Good luck to you," would become a popular vacation spot. So popular has it become, that the pious have renamed it Pornopolis.

Just imagine: a parade of weary monks and pilgrims, having spent the past three hours in silent prayer and noxious smells, file off the bus and one by one and are forced to walk a gauntlet of tantalizing flesh. What a test! What exquisite torture! Do any of them imitate the bishop in ancient Antioch, who openly gawked at a naked harlot as she rode by while his fellow hierarchs huddled, heads together like it was fourth and goal to go on the one? "But she is beautiful!" he told them. What got him a collegial tongue-lashing, also earned a fond mention in the Life of Saint Pelagia (the Harlot). The bus arrives before it's time to put on the sunscreen, and the boat departs almost immediately for the Holy Mountain.

At the water's edge stands a massive stone tower (*pirgos*), built over the course of the 14th through 19th centuries. In the 1930s, it was occupied by an Englishman, Sidney Loch, and his legendary Australian wife, Joice. Even though the earthquake that leveled Ierissos passed right under it, the keep is as it appeared in photos from the late thirties. Although they were part of the worldwide Quaker relief effort, the Lochs had no discernible religion. They merely lived as if they did. Their experience of the Orthodox Church was, in many instances, an attempt to repair the ravages caused by ecclesial neglect and the fermentation of abstract theology in the dark waters of superstition and ignorance. Of course, they would never have put it that way.

Ms Loch modestly chronicled their service as doctors and advocates for the local population in *A Fringe of Blue*. Susanna de Vries has added a million or so details in *Blue Ribbons Bitter Bread*. When she died, in 1981, Ms Loch became the first and only non-Orthodox ever to receive a full Orthodox funeral. She is buried in Ouranopolis. My guess is that the Lochs, clearly no bluestockings, would have sided with the nudists against the prudists. They might have even skinny-dipped at night.

When the Friends sent the Lochs to the Middle East on a relief mission at the beginning of the Second World War, they left their tower in the care of an exiled Russian and her daughter. Marauding Communist partisans murdered both. Had they stayed, the Lochs would no doubt have shared the same fate.

So, what's the Russian?

Should you miss the boat or discover it's not running either because of its antiquated state or inclement weather, and the thought of spending another few hours in the fleshpot that surrounds you is tempting, intolerable, or both, it is possible to walk into the Holy Mountain. I did it once, in the company of two Athonite monks. We made our journey in the late fall, during a period of unpredictable weather when we might have been a week waiting for it to break. It was a walk that countless others had made; but probably not many who weren't seeking sanctuary from some bloody doctrinal war raging outside The Mountain or hunting game. Without this kind of motivation, it's an unnecessary slog. In our case, my companions were propelled by the kind of fear Cinderella had of her coach turning into a pumpkin: their abbot's blessing to travel expired at sunset the next day. My impatience came from another source: I didn't want to pay for a room.

The beginning was simple enough. Less than a kilometer south of Ouranopolis, we disturbed an official-looking gate that sported cobwebs dating back to the Greek Civil War. The evidence of disuse might merely have hinted at the existence of many other, unofficial entry points for those with less honorable reasons than ours – all right, theirs – to avoid customs or the *Epistasia*.

The map shows three monastic settlements between Ouranopolis and the first monastery on the Riviera – the Bulgarian Zografou, fifteen kilometers away as the double-headed eagle flies. Only one of these is inhabited. The Russian-occupied *kelli* with the mysterious name of Monoxilities, meaning "one dugout boat", seemed to be derelict until an elderly, derelict-looking monk showed up about a half hour after our arrival. He offered us a manger, and divided his meager meal of vegetables and orzo – a pellet-shaped pasta – into fourths. That evening, two young Greeks, a slightly older American, and an elderly Russian – strangers all – shared a cold dinner in silence and slept without fear. Forgotten was the fact that during the 19th century, the Russians tried to take over the entire Holy Mountain from others who shared their faith.

The desire of the Holy Emperor of All the Russias to acquire a seaport for his otherwise landlocked, Black Sea fleet prompted this aggressive adventure.

"We are only making our two little *skitis* a little bit bigger," I can imagine the Russians innocently pleading, "so as for us in Holy Russia to be able to have a place to send a small number of our devoted *poslushniks* (novices) who have recently got religion and wish to end their lives in prayer and contemplation."

Calling upon God to be their witness, they carefully sign themselves as if they were just learning the cross: forehead, belly, right shoulder, left shoulder. The tips of the thumb and the first two fingers of the right hand are joined, and the other two are pressed against the palm: together, they symbolize the Trinity and the two natures of Christ.

"The guns?" they continue, each holding his right hand over his heart as if he had trapped a butterfly there. "What guns? Oh, *those* guns. Well…. (Disarming though hearty chuckle.) They are for to kill rats and protect pious pilgrims from the many dangerous animals that roam on the Holy Mountain. (Cross cross cross.) And the pirates. (Cross cross cross.) And the Jews. (Cross cross cross cross cross.) Who wrote *The Protocols of the Elders of Zion*."

"Little Father," Czar Alexander II, threw thousands of "monks" into The Mountain. Calling Prophet Elijah and St. Andrew *skitis*, a term that

51

denotes a smaller dependency of one of the large monasteries, was intentionally duplicitous. They are as much *skitis* as the *QE2* is a *caique*. It is said that each *skiti* eventually teemed with five thousand seekers after the religious life. Including the mother house, Panteleimon, the "*Russikon*", there reputedly were fifteen thousand Russians in all. There is a chance that this figure is a slight exaggeration, and from the physical evidence, a quarter of that number is a more likely estimate, but the threat was real enough. Whatever the actual count, at the time Slavs significantly outnumbered Hellenes. The largest church in all of Mount Athos still belongs to Prophet Elijah, which now is under the aegis of the American-based Russian Orthodox Church Outside of Russia.

At one point, the Russians even landed troops on the Holy Mountain. But that was to quell an uprising of Russian monks! Made heady perhaps by their escape from the frozen tundra, these rebels had authored the heresy that "the name of God, being part of God, is in itself divine." They took over Panteleimon and usurped the abbacy. Funny, isn't it? That at the moment when a fresh wave of anti-Semitism was sweeping across Russia in the wake of the "discovery" of the allegedly seditious *Protocols*, Russian monks were proclaiming a quasi-Jewish doctrine – the unpronouncability of *Ha Shem*, the Name of God?

Lest this be a source of Hellenic gloating, let them remember that in the 14th century, the Bishop of Thessalonica also had occasion to call on the civil authority to expel Greek monks who believed they could see God through their navels. It's a good thing I wasn't there at the time, because I would have been included in the roundup, since at the nadir of my crusade for illumination I managed to pass up to thirteen hours a day in silent contentment, if not prayer, letting my mind and my heart go whither they would, at play in the poppy fields of the Lord.

In 1913, when the Greek flag flew over Mount Athos after an absence of four hundred and fifty years, the Romanovs' "hands across Athos" movement came to an abrupt halt. Ten years later, the Treaty of Lausanne confirmed the restoration of the ancient status quo guaranteed by the Treaty of Berlin that ended the Russo-Turkish War in 1878. The non-Greek monastic presence on Mount Athos was officially restricted to one major house each of Russian, Bulgarian, and Serbian persuasion, and the monastic state was placed under the protection of – but not assimilated by – Greece. Oddly enough, it was Greeks who soon had cause to fear being absorbed by Greece. Perhaps taking a page from Ataturk's transformation of Turkey into a secular state, the Hellenic government of General Panaglos tried to prohibit Greeks from becoming monks and residing on Mount Athos! It didn't succeed.

The neck of the peninsula is sparsely settled, and the forests have yet to show the effects of injudicious logging. Other than the Russian monk living out his days in terminal celibacy, the only other living creature we encountered on our trek was, of all things, an owl, sitting on top of a fence post and more startled to see us than we him. This was a formidable stump of a bird, snowy white, and with a menacing beak. We were obviously not so menacing. Besides, owls like fresh stuff, and every day we told ourselves we were walking carrion. More to the point, we probably smelled too rank to consider eating. With a wrinkle of his beak, he shut his eyes and allowed us to pass unmolested. At the abandoned *kelli* of the Holy Unmercenaries, the road bent sharply to the left, and disappeared upward toward the ridge that runs the length of The Mountain. Without hesitation, the monks left the track and continued along the shore. Perhaps they knew of a path, perhaps not. But they were from a monastery on the south coast, and this was the south coast, so I assumed they knew what they were doing. There were times when I had my doubts; especially when we had to push through water halfway up our thighs to get around headlands that we approached at the wrong time in the cycle of tides. My companions told me that their confidence stemmed from two sources: the blessing of their abbot, which did nothing for *my* confidence; and the presence of the overhead telephone line that eventually had to lead to a monastery, which did. Late on the second day, our rubber-sheathed breadcrumbs led us to the fortress-like *arsanas* (port) of Zografou. From there to my companions' monastery, Xenofondos, was a short walk along an established *monopati* (ancient footpath). I left them there and continued on to Panteleimon, where the kasha pot is always on and the borscht, unencumbered by vegetables, is a clear as Lake Baikal. Exhausted and hungry, to me it was the Ritz. I spent the night dreaming on a narrow, sprung cot among the faded glories and myths of Holy Russia.

Comrade, let us prey.

A *plion* is a largish seagoing vessel. A *plion* takes us from Ouranopolis to Dafni, the *arsanas* of Karyes, in about an hour and a quarter. On a mildly blustery day, it seems forever, with everybody on board huddling below the wildly pitching deck, ducking instinctively as the spray smashes against the glass, and getting violently sick. The shade of Darius's admiral, Mardonius, could doubtless tell why these boats do not run on really bad days.

Steaming resolutely along the rocky coast, the miles of gentle slopes and the spare shrubbery that give way to forests of conifers reveal little about the unique human life they support, but every minute takes us back dozens of years in a rush toward the first millennium. Scanning this invisible timeline marked by the occasional ruins of human habitation, ferocious animals aren't necessarily what comes to mind, but the animals that roam Mount Athos are not the domesticated kind.

Tales of encounters with the beasts of the Holy Mountain are as plentiful as miracles, accompanied by the rapid signing of crosses across the breast and upward looks to God as witness. Mount Athos is home to a large number of creatures we would categorize as unpleasant. Poisonous snakes, scorpions, wolves, wild boars, foxes … tourists. I worked in a garden once with a monk who calmly decapitated a pit adder with his spade without missing a beat. Returning from a service one morning, I found a scorpion on my pillow. A legend-become-fact tells of a thirty-foot boa constrictor, thick as a fallen tree, which rose from the road and attacked the logging truck that had run over it. The story is so vivid, and I have heard it and repeated it so often, that not only do I now half-believe it, but I actually think I might have been there when it happened.

That the following is true, however, I know for sure. While at the monastery of Konstamonitou, I was part of a small mule train making our way down to the *arsanas* to meet the morning boat from Ouranopolis, a descent of about forty minutes. We were riding single file and I was bringing up the rear, when the monk ahead of me shattered my prayer-like daydreams with a sharp command. Before he could utter another word, the lead monk dove off his mule as if he were diving into a drained pool. He hadn't reached the ground when a large, green, and fatally poisonous snake flew out of a tree, skimmed the empty saddle still hot from the monk's presence, and disappeared noisily into a bush! The monk picked himself up, slapped off some dust, put his *skufi* back on his head, and hoisted himself back up on his mule. Nobody even mentioned it. Had the snake been as smart as its Biblical reputation, it could have picked me off like one of the Sheriff of Nottingham's inept men-at-arms.

During the harsh and snowy winters, at least in those areas not protected by the civilizing radiance of the monasteries on the Riviera, monks travel in groups and carry large ironwood staves in case they should come across a hungry mother wolf and her cubs, or, more to the point, she them. It is a humbling thought how far down the food chain man slides without a weapon to protect him. In a not unusual display of xenophobia, Athonites say that the wolves come down from Bulgaria.

Rounding a headland, the bows of the *plion* point toward a square stone tower low on the shoreline. The fortress-like building is bristling with crenellations and looks like it means business. This is the *arsanas* of Zografou. Every monastery port has a similar keep. The builders no doubt hoped these forbidding stone towers would look just as forbidding to the pirates who used to drop in from time to time to collect the rent.

The Bulgarian monastery has a population of eight (including the abbot), about three hundred rooms, and very few visitors to take them up on their vouchers. Next to Zografou, on the other side of a creek, is the *arsanas* of the Monastery of Konstamonitou. Konstamonitou occupies a dank, depressing valley an hour's hard walk inland. There is no keep at this port – only a half-timber building. I suppose that when the corsairs came, the monks crossed over the stream and piled into their neighbors' fortification.

Continuing down the coast, the next port of call is the impressive Dochiareiou. This monastery climbs upward from the sea like one of the villages that charms visitors to the Greek islands. A stone wall thirty feet high surrounds the once-dying community, now suffering some sort of rebirth under a more youthful and modern regime. So close to Dochiareiou that you could imagine popping across for a cup of sugar, the low-lying compound with the long shoreline is Xenofondos. This monastery has been living a renaissance similar to Dochiareiou, but has been more successful, and now houses about forty enthusiastic young monks. The introduction of youngsters into older communities has not been without its internal problems. At Xenofondos there are a dozen or so bewildered, suspicious, and mostly elderly survivors from the hard times. Like older people everywhere, elderly monks have had difficulty adjusting to what they perceive to be radical changes. New regimes often demand more structure than what the holdover monks had been used to when their numbers were shrinking. Abbots exercise *oikonomia* in an attempt to accommodate them, but many have taken to *skitis* and *kellis*, where they can continue to live in the way of their generation.

The half hour's walk from Xenofondos to Panteleimon is ten minutes by boat. The monastery's green onion domes immediately tell you it is not Greek. Panteleimon is *not* a member of the Renaissance faction. A good part of Panteleimon, literally, the "all-merciful", was destroyed by fire in the 1970s, and these impressive, blackened shells have never been removed or rebuilt. The refectory is capable of accommodating eight hundred diners at a single seating. The monastery is so vast that the forty monks exported or deported from the Soviet Union must feel as if they actually have been sent to Siberia. On my two visits to the *Russikon* in the eighties, I think it was something more than paranoia that led me to feel that some of the inhabitants were KGB and there was a two-way mirror in my room – even though there was no mirror in any room, a mirror being a temptation to vanity. "Administrators" came and went, and not with a monastic mien. Under their floor-length robes, thick-soled black shoes squeaked across the wooden floors.

The history of the Russian Orthodox Church during the Soviet era did nothing to airbrush this impression. The hierarchs were openly subservient to the communist regime for seventy years. This collaboration resulted in the establishment in Yugoslavia in 1926 of a Russian Church in the Diaspora, which then split into *two* Churches in the Diaspora. The *pravoslavny* (believers) based their allegiance for the most part on the same issue of social status that brought about the Russian Revolution in the first place. The majority of the exiles were common people who were reluctant to totally abandon the church in Russia; they created the Metropolia. The land-owning "white" Russians, though a small minority, were the more vociferous critics of the stay-at-home Moscow Patriarchate; they formed the Holy Synod of the Russian Church Outside Russia. Of course, they did not have to negotiate the very real threat of total extermination, backed up by the murder of forty thousand Orthodox priests. Eventually, both emigré churches moved their headquarters to the United States, where ROCOR's platform of "no change whatever, whenever, and wherever" had great appeal to converts who saw themselves as Defenders of the Faith a safe eight thousand miles from Moscow and who were ready to die from the get-go for their adopted religion. Since America provided little opportunity for that, they consoled themselves with not eating meat during Lent, observing a rigorous fast before Holy Communion, and finding fault with others. I should know. I was once one of them.

While the Metropolia developed into the English-speaking Orthodox Church in America, the Church Outside Russia is still the Church for Russians Outside Russia, forget there is no reason for its being anywhere.

Isn't that Catherine the Great?

Leaving Panteleimon, the prow of the *plion* knifes into the bay, and about twenty minutes later, our vessel glides into Dafni. As it approaches the quay, a speck appears off to seaward. It is moving too fast for a vessel familiar with the pace of Athonite life. No, it is not a pirate ship. It is something far more threatening to The Mountain. It is a tour boat and if you are interested, the colors on deck soon will resolve themselves into bi- or mono-kinied passengers. Some wield binoculars while others soak up the Athonite sun, oblivious to the significance, and to some, the outrage of their presence. The Greeks, who have been responsible for a great deal of our attitude toward the law, are very skilled at circumventing it, and Mount Athos is not a signatory to any international convention on littoral rights. That the local law permits no women on Mount Athos does not mean that they cannot cruise or even heave-to *off* it.

Ironically, legend has it that the Theotokos, herself, created the ban known as the *avaton* as if she were a pagan deity jealously protecting her domain against human rivals. Nevertheless, on at least two occasions Orthodox kings allowed their queens to accompany them on visits and came away unscathed. Until the end of the 12th century, local Vlach women were a common sight in Karyes, having received permission to sell milk and eggs to the monks. However, the women weren't the only ones selling, and dairy products weren't the only goods on display: Vlach men were selling their wives and daughters to the monks, and I doubt they had a permit to do this. Exercising his leg from Constantinople, His All Holiness gave the Vlachs the terminal boot. Not that there is any evidence that the monks had anything against slavery on a humanitarian basis, or apparently, sex on any basis at all. But it did make them look even more parasitic and useless than their already unflattering popular image. Furthermore, ethics aside, slavery is an expensive institution to maintain when times are hard.

Seven hundred and fifty years after the expulsion of the Vlachs, women once again appeared on Mount Athos. After the Second World War Greeks crucified their own country with the blunt nails of civil war. Communist fought Nationalist. Neighbor betrayed neighbor, neighbor killed neighbor. Twice as many people died at the hands of their own countrymen as did fighting the Germans. Only ten per cent of the people fought on the Communist side, but they were the poorest and most desperate. The modern arms that the British had dropped into Greece during World War II found their way into the hands of both factions, somewhat equalizing the conflict. Accounts of Communist atrocities would make your stomach turn, although given a similar numerical inferiority there is no saying the Nationalists would have behaved any better. Considering who got to write the history of those times, they probable did *not* behave any better.

Communist partisans held whole towns and regions hostage by threats of death, retaliation, and grisly executions. Once an *Andarte*, always an *Andarte*. Anyone who defected might come home to find the members of his family dismembered with a knife in front of his own house. The *Andartes* entered Mount Athos to avoid capture or to raid the monasteries and taunt those for whom their atheistic religion had no use. With the *Andartes* came *Andartinas*, their women, who lounged around Karyes in their fatigues, smoking and drinking with their men, and (my overactive imagination would have me believe) offering themselves to monks. Like the Vlachs and the intrusive queens of yore, however, once the *Andartinas* were gone, it was as though they never happened. The tradition remains intact: no women have ever entered Mount Athos. Mary is 'ever-virgin', and so is her Garden.

At Dafni, our boat turns and backs its engines, a deckhand unbuckles the chain across the stern, and the human cargo pours out onto the concrete quay. A few police officers scrutinize the new arrivals for signs of femininity. They squint their eyes at young, thin men, and at debarkees who bear no signs of waging daily warfare with a beard. In the face of such a strict prohibition, how could one not at least attempt to subvert the *avaton*? That the attention of the customs officers is focused more on people leaving Mount Athos with its ancient treasures, so vast and so poorly catalogued that theft it not only tempting but rather easily accomplished, only increases the likelihood that the *avaton* is *virgo intactu* only in the minds of those who need to believe it is.

This may be the Riviera, but that town ain't nice.

The Dafni who gave her name to the dusty little port that serves Karyes is the mythological shepherdess who suffered transformation into a laurel tree rather than submit to the lustful god, Apollo – a theme which, after some tinkering, reappears in many of the *Lives of the [Christian] Saints*. Ovid describes the maiden as beautifully dressed and elegantly coiffed. If she had been able to foresee this future monument to her chastity, she might have succumbed to the sun god. Dafni is a café, two souvenir shops, Greek policemen searching for women, and, for an hour each day, a lot of coming and going. In this scraggy frontier port, we also can see monks who couldn't make it in the monasteries but couldn't leave Athos, either – the Aegean chapter of the "Harvard Underground". Some survive by making the rounds of the major monasteries. Few visitors are aware of their actual state because, at least until recently, Athonites felt as guilty about homelessness as other Greeks.

In Dafni, the visitor can choose between either proceeding inland to Karyes and getting his passport stamped, or bypassing authority, customs included, and stepping aboard the fragile-looking *caique* rocking gently on the other side of the quay and proceeding down the coast. By avoiding Karyes, you place yourself at the mercy of the first monastery you enter. Actually, this is not much of a risk. It is another delight peculiar to despots to sprinkle magnanimity like glitter. As long as the abbot approves and you don't leave his domain, you can stay there without a passport and for as long as you want. And provide free labor. Communist Albania used to offer roughly the same deal, except that "as long as you want" began with a mandatory two years of splitting rocks.

Like those who left the bus at Ierissos, most of the people who cross the quay and the gunwales of those ancient craft at Dafni have connections to a particular monastery. The design of the *caique* has not changed in the last two thousand years. It is the same boat whose decks filled with water during a storm on the Sea of Galilee, from which the faithless Peter screamed, "Master, master! Save us ere we perish!" If a storm should find a *caique* at sea today, those on board would still scream for help. As of old, no scupper holes pierce the gunwales to allow water to escape. There must be a reason for this, although I think it is simply an ancient example of a familiar attitude toward new technology when that advance will not greatly improve one's life: "It's always been done this way." Of course, the scupperless deck could be a simple reminder to sailors that they should not be at sea during a storm. The 20th century *caique* does have an engine. The throb of the motor should sound familiar. You guessed it – a Daimler-Benz. One engine fits everything.

From Dafni to Karyes is a trip.

Doors open and no driver in sight, a maroon bus, its battered nose pointing north, waits for those proceeding to Karyes. There are doors on the right side, front and rear. Maybe sixty seats of not too recent construction or upholstering. In a few spots, seats have been removed, but it would be a stretch to call it an attempt to provide wheelchair access. Around and above the driver's seat, the ubiquitous icon wall of religious trinketry and pictures – some Christian, many pagan – reassures passengers that a host of intercessors go before them to plead for their safe journey.

During tourist season, the overloaded vehicle resembles that can of peas bloated by botulism that you might see on the shelf of a village *katastima*. That eight-inch fan next to the icon of St. George slaying the banana slug is purely ornamental. Worse, the ancient, if reliable, Diamler-Benz engine is incapable of dragging its load up some of the very steep grades that decorate your route. From time to time, the driver will probably ask some of you to get off and walk, even if only a little way. The heat on Mount Athos during the summer is so intense that walking even a little way is a trial. The cold of winter presents its own problems, since the bus's tires are as bald as an eagle and have difficulty gripping the ice. So, while in the colder months there may be less people on the bus, the chances are that you will still have to get off and walk ... a little.

The ignition sparks life in at least three of the six cylinders. *Grigora grigora!* (Quickly! Quickly!) There is no grace period for stragglers. With a grinding of gears, the bus lurches forward. On the Dafni-Karyes express, a conductor collects fares. This truly is a safety device, since it allows the driver to concentrate on driving. The first quarter of a mile parallels the shoreline; then, the vehicle turns right and begins to ascend a ziggurat of switchbacks. Halfway to the top, we pause at Xeropotamou to let passengers off and perhaps board a monk bound for Karyes or the other side of The Mountain. Xeropotamou is one of a group of four progressive monasteries under the aegis of a charismatic superabbot who spends much of the year traveling around the Orthodox world making speeches, adherents, and enemies. He points out the tragic anomaly of the Orthodox Way in a world of faithlessness. Progressive, in this instance, has nothing to do with social policy, but means adherence to a way of life closer to the old monastic tradition as it was before anyone currently alive could testify that was the way it was.

One of the ways you can tell a progressively traditional monastery from a traditional, non-progressive monastery – aside from their respective cleanliness, order, and sense of purpose, and slovenliness, quiet chaos, and torpor – is the treatment of non-Orthodox visitors in the church and the refectory, which monks consider a "second church". Progressive monasteries do not allow the spiritually unwashed to eat with the monks or attend church services, and refuse them Holy Communion with politeness and an extensive lecture on the theological justification for their unfriendliness. They may provide a book in English that they believe rationally explains their position. Much of this literature unfortunately suffers from having been rendered into English by someone who is unaware that "render" has more than one meaning.

Like their progressive brethren, traditional monasteries let non-Orthodox visitors eat either before or after the monks and refuse them Holy Communion, but they don't tell them why. One is left to meditate on whether exclusion has any place in religion. Why Holy Communion, much less dinner, is not open to anyone of any or no religious persuasion who avows a need for spiritual nourishment. Or whether faith isn't an unfathomable, personal thing and why an omnipotent God needs defenders. Waxing *ad hominum*, you might ask why dirt and a scent of lingering urine impart a special sanctity to a monk. Then again, if you haven't by now been overwhelmed by your bias, you might ask why in our neck of the woods we say cleanliness is next to Godliness. Or whether there is any real virtue that is unerringly deducible from either. Which might lead to your wondering whether or not, along with a need to exalt oneself, there is a human compulsion to self-degradation – a love of intellectual order wed to an attraction to animal filth. Or you might just say, "What a beautiful place this is," and "How pious these people must be," and "How fortunate I am to be here."

The gears crunch as they struggle to find a match. The bus resumes its crawl up the rutted, dusty, rock-strewn road that is the main artery of the Athonite highway system. The rest of the network consists of the dirt road between Dafni and Simonopetra, the first monastery on the southern half of the Riviera, and the dirt road that descends from Karyes to Iveron, on the north coast. That is as far as the bus will go. That is as far as the bus can go. After that it is strictly a half-track track, slashed by overflowing streams running off the peninsula's extraordinary water supply, and choked by dense undergrowth produced by that same abundance.

There are a few other dirt roads carved out by the loggers who have contracted for much of Mount Athos. As these were constructed not to join monasteries but intentionally to avoid them, monks rarely use them. Isn't this what happens throughout nature when two species that are not immediately at odds with each other occupy the same territory?

Vehicular access being so restricted, the principal means of getting around the peninsula remain the *monopatis* – narrow goat-tracks that do not permit side-by-side travel. These paths are mostly up and sometimes down, which means you must be prepared to don and shed clothing like a magician. In the past, the Athonite Department of Public Works depended on constant usage to keep the undergrowth to the sides of the path, thus enabling monks to pass untroubled with room to swing their *comboskini*. Now, however, there are places where a machete would be a more suitable accessory. There may even come a time when no one at all will unthinkingly step on an adder or come around a bend and be face-to-face with a wild boar. For some whose gaze is fixed on a more distant future, the decrepit condition of the *monopatis* portends the "last times".

We're almost there.

Our bus crosses the great divide between north and south, the ridge that culminates in the snow-tipped peak of the Mountain of Athos, a true six thousand two hundred and forty feet on the not-far-off-the-vertical from the sea. There, the third in a chain of bonfires relayed the news of the fall of Troy to ancient Greece. As the drop from the ridge to Karyes is rather precipitous, it is customary for passengers to pray that the brakes are in at least as good condition as the engine.

The large complex on the left just before the last turn into the capital is the Russian *skiti* of St. Andrew's. No longer of any political moment, it is now home to five Greek monks devoted to preserving its treasures. As I have mentioned, the *skiti* is rather large. It is called a *skiti* for two reasons: one, it is a dependency of the Monastery of Vatopedi (i.e., it is on land belonging to that monastery and pays some kind of token rent); and two, no one has been allowed to add to the list of twenty major monasteries for the past six hundred years. Some of the halls of this pocket monastery bring to mind the Czar's summer palace in Petrograd. The grandeur is not all ostentation, however, because the Russian view of God is quite different from that of the Greeks. Russians appear to fear God more than they love him. Indeed, unless they are prostrating themselves, they stand in church until they drop, because there are no seats. Or, maybe, they love God in an unsentimental way that is unfamiliar to the West. The difference between Russian and Greek Orthodoxy is what distinguishes Zorba from Raskolnikov – to the Greeks, God is the Father of the Prodigal Son, while Russians view him as lethal and unforgiving of indiscretions no matter how hard he tries to convince them that he is indeed a God of mercy. God as enormous and unapproachable finds expression in the intimidating size of Russian churches as well as their monastic dwellings. I'm told that St. Peter's in Rome could fit inside the Church of St. Basil's in Moscow. Of course, it was a Russian who told me. On Mount Athos, both time and space have different dimensions.

Where is there?

There is no bus station in Karyes. The stone church directly opposite the dusty terminus, the *Protaton*, has been there almost as long as the monks. Don't let its garment of ordinariness deceive you. Believe me, inside that drab exterior is a blinding display of gold leaf, exquisite silverwork, and icons representing the heavenly patrons of the twenty ruling monasteries. You have to believe me because, unless your visit corresponds with a major feast day, the church is locked.

Originally, Karyes was also called Protaton, "head of the community". The name, Karyes, derives from the Greek word for hazelnut, and the trees that drop these nuts still surround the capital. The Church of the Protaton occupies a site that formerly hosted a temple to Apollo. Like the marines raising the Stars and Stripes over Iwo Jima, conquering Christians replaced the local temple with a church. This kind of religious trumping is commonplace. Wherever paganism had erected a shrine, Christianity – the new alpha male – felt obliged to build on top of it or destroy it. Throughout Greece, wherever you find a significant pagan complex, you will also find a church standing watch over it like a guard at a museum or a prison. Pagan metopes were pried out of temples and stone gods beheaded. The Plaka, the area below the Acropolis in Athens, is crawling with Christian places of worship. For a while, a church occupied a section of the ruined Parthenon. On Lycobetus, the only hill that rivals the height of the magnificent ancient compound dedicated to the pre-Christian *Parthenos*, Athena, stands a small token church, as if telling the world that Christianity has pissed here and therefore no gods shall be more exalted than God.

Karyes, in the geographical center of the peninsula, provides an unobstructed view of the sea to the north. But what you can see from the bus stop south is what there is to Karyes. Beyond the Church of the Protaton is a stone-paved square, some shops, some small wooden houses, the Athonite version of a greasy spoon, a suspect inn with two guestrooms, and not much else. Up through the 18th century, Karyes appears to have been a thriving market town, but the Turks' crackdown at the time of the Greek War of Independence reduced the monastic population of the Holy Mountain by two-thirds and put an end to its commerce.

The government of Mount Athos, resident at Karyes, operates under, but separate from, a civil governor who reports directly to the Greek Ministry of Foreign Affairs. It consists of three separate but interdependent bodies – a secular Trinity: the legislative body is a Holy *Synaxis* of all twenty of the ruling monasteries that convenes twice annually; the administrative body is a Holy Community of those same monasteries chaired by the representative of the Great Lavra; and the executive, the *Epistasia*, is composed of four representatives of four monastic groups of five monasteries each who take their seats on an annual rotation. It sounds more formidable than it is; ironically, because of its constitution. The constitution this government protects is the oldest continuous such document in existence, alleged to have been first put on paper in the 9th (?) century and guaranteed by the Byzantine Emperor. By the terms of this charter, Mount Athos not only is free of administrative interference from Constantinople/Istanbul, but each monastery is free of interference by any others, except in extreme cases. (Esphigmenou soon may help to define "extreme".) Monks are not under the jurisdiction of any secular court, though if a crime is committed, the Athonite government *may* turn the offender over to the state. Monks do not pay state taxes, nor are duties attached to goods going into or coming from the Holy Mountain. Understandably, these exemptions have caused a bit of grumbling among those who are impressed only by how parasitic monks and their whole monkdom seem to be.

The *Epistasia* is also the name of the administrative building where the body of the same name stamps its blessing on visitors' passports. As each member of the *Epistasia* is the guardian of one quadrant of this stamp, all four members must be present, at least in theory, to ratify any decision, including who visits The Mountain. The *Epistasia's* decisions in this regard are automatically binding on all the monasteries. Tourists coming from Ouranopolis usually arrive at Karyes between one and two in the afternoon. The *Epistasia* may or may not be open. The hours on the sign outside the building have as much to do with reality as the bus's legal capacity.

Once the government has stamped your passport and you have your game piece in hand, you are free to go *opou theleis*, "wherever you want" to go. Many visitors stay the night at Koutloumousi, the default house for the tired traveler that abuts the capital. The monks of Koutloumousi also are tired. Tired of tired travelers. They won't turn you away, but you might receive a rather different impression of monastic hospitality if you make your way to a monastery at a distance from Karyes. An hour or so will take you to Iveron, on the north coast. Three hours of walking will take you back to Zografou, home to those eight Bulgarian monks, where the abbot – a tall, kindly man – sits at the dinner table reading to his charges while they eat; it's fifty-fifty that they will not only kill the fatted vegi-calf on your arrival but ask you to join the brotherhood, with a decent shot at becoming abbot in a few years.

Well, good luck. *Kalos irthes* and *Kalo taxidi*. "Welcome" and "have a good trip." Oh. *O Theos voithi sas*. "May God help you."

Alone, Father Hierotheos, the late, *igoumenos* (abbot) and priest-monk of the Monastery of Longovarda, on Paros, might have discredited Gibbon's villainous description of the Eastern monk forever. A tireless worker for those inside and outside the monastery alike, he was – as so clearly pours forth from his eyes—a man of infinite compassion. No one was too lost, no task too menial, to receive his undivided attention. But those who make up monastic communities are a mixed lot, no better or worse than those in the world.

The rugged north (east) coast of Mount Athos, looking north from just south of the Monastery of Iverson, halfway down the peninsula.

Pilgrims, hikers, relatives, climbers, and the curious boarding the Athos bound boat at Ouranopolis. Note the incipient beard on the man in the foreground, a tradition for pilgrims.

This is Giovantsa, an *arsanas* (port) on the south coast of Mount Athos, now used by logging companies to help relieve the Holy Mountain of some of its excessive natural glory.

The Monastery of Dochiareiou on the south coast of Mount Athos. This busy-ness is typical of the modern monastic landscape where EU money is hard at work to who knows what end.

Saint Andrew, the enormous Russian *skiti* near Karyes—partly destroyed by fire in 1958. Now one monk who guards its wonder-working icon, "She who consoles the afflicted."

The Monastery of Simonopetra, the first establishment on the south coast south of Dafni. Since the advent of motor vehicles, the monastery's *arsanas* has been abandoned.

PART TWO

BEING THERE

And if I laugh at any mortal thing,
'Tis that I may not weep.

George Gordon, Lord Byron, *Don Juan, IV*

To become a monk is to discover that there is an edge at the end of the world, and you have fallen off it. As Martin Buber noted, in a Talmudic comment, you cannot worship God and Mammon *at the same altar*: you must destroy one way of perceiving before you can embark on another; otherwise, you are just replacing one idol with another. A monk takes vows to separate himself from worldly things; he owns nothing but his vows. Even his room is not his, but "ours". Tonsured monks give up all their possessions, sometimes to charity, sometimes to their monastery, and sometimes to the Orthodox Church. In theory, the vow of poverty is absolute. In reality, many monks still have families ready to support them.

A monk's aim in stripping the world from himself and he from the world is *theosis*, that is, entering again into God. In this quest, a sense of *metanoia*, of repentance, dominates his life even as his daily priority is prayer. *Metanoia – meta* (change) plus *noesis* (consciousness) – is described as "the change of the eye of the mind in the heart". It is not the eye, which can deceive, nor the mind, which is a barrel of monkeys, nor the heart, which would love to lose who we are in another. Like the celestial Trinity, each organ is absolutely sovereign, yet inseparably interdependent, although in this case, the sum is more than the parts.

Eternity is timeless and prayer is unconfined, but, on earth, a monk leads his life in conformity to a demanding and repetitive schedule in the monastery of his tonsure. Every day is slightly different according to whether it is a feast day or a fast and the particular saint being celebrated. Every day is also the same. He lives his life at the tangent of the circle of eternity and the line of history. He will tell you that his is a joyous life, but it is different kind of joy: he feels he has been given the key to eternity; but whether it opens the door for him will depend on God's mercy.

I realize that to talk about "a monk", or "the monk", is as misleading as talking about "the monastery". But, just as there are things that all monks do, all Athonite monasteries also have common features. One's always enters the compound through a double-gated square tower. The main church is always in the center of the compound and faces west so that those who enter are moving toward the rising sun. The refectory is either directly opposite the church door or at a right angle to it. The residential areas surround the church and are dotted with little chapels dedicated to favorite saints. But every monastery also has its own character. What determines that character of a monastery is the history, the abbot, the traditions, the part of the Greek world from which it draws most of its monks, its wealth, its reputation, and the direction in which the establishment is going, financially and spiritually. Food and accommodation also vary. In some monasteries, you will sleep on a poorly-sprung mattress in a large dormitory under a single bare light. Others may seem more like ski chalets, with well-appointed beds and individual reading lamps. Some serve meals that will have you staggering to those beds. At others, you might expect to see hungry birds pecking at the few grains in your dish as you exercise your jaws on a slightly green piece of week-old bread.

Konstamonitou is the most isolated monastery on Mount Athos. It is my adopted monastery – a compost of the infuriating and amusing, both modern and the anachronistic, purposeful and the aimless, the ethereal and the down-to-earth. Its reputation among Athonites is like Dodge City in the 1880s. A popular joke is that the other monasteries send their most cantankerous, dissatisfied brothers there to will learn what a bad monastery really is. Some of these exiles decide to stay. The monastery's frontier style of life probably suits them like it suited me. I could do anything I wanted there short of shooting craps in the refectory. Although, as in all monasteries, its monks pledged themselves to unwavering obedience, Konstamonitou was a corral full of congenitally ornery individuals who routinely avoided church for any number of vaguely legitimate or creative excuses. In this sense, it was the worst monastery I could have chosen.

The abbot of Konstamonitou is a young guy. He is also a "good guy". Not my observation, but that of a Greek monk who sat next to me on a trip from Karyes to Dafni. A careless comment, perhaps, but that oddball depiction convinced me to check out Konstamonitou as a possible long-term domicile. "Father A. was a very humble man … when he was a monk," my consultant added, with a mischievous expression on his face and a knowing look in his eye. Something happens to those ordained to a life of humble service, whether priest, abbot, or bishop. Possibly because the authority that attaches to the office does not depend on the personal character of the occupant. But while priests have superiors and abbots have an unspoken contract with their community, unless he commits some heinous crime, the man who sits on the episcopal throne has a literally God-given opportunity to act out to the end of his days. Even if he does infract some law or code, written or implied, the episcopal brotherhood is not unlike an old boys' network: there is always a vacant see to receive him, somewhere beyond the reach of rumor or fact.

Yeah, but he's got a great personality....

So what is the monastic day like? Rather than walk you through the typical day of the Perfect Monk of the Heavenly Monastery, let's lurch through twenty-four hours of my highly imperfect existence at Konstamonitou.

Just as the Jewish day begins at sunset, so it is for those who call themselves the New Israel. (Only at the *idiorrhythmic* Monastery of Iveron does the day begin at sunrise; why, I do not know.) The daily cycle of services therefore begins with Vespers (*esperinos*). The call to Vespers usually comes at around four o'clock in the afternoon, and signals the end of the working day. The hour varies with the seasons and not everyone makes it to Vespers all the time. Work takes precedence over formal prayer. When the *symandron* sounds with the urgent rhythm that allegedly accompanied the animals into the ark, monks do not just drop what they are doing to scuttle into the church, nor does anyone stand at the door counting them in pairs. The *symandron* is that long, flat piece of wood that the *ecclesiarch* – the churchwarden – strikes with a mallet. The story is that monks began to use "the wood" when the Turks forbade Christians to ring bells. (So many traditions seem to owe their origin to the need to show some kind of superiority by outsmarting an oppressor. When I was in Jerusalem, Muslims muezzins proved to be equally adaptive when the Israeli government temporarily forbade live performances, resorting to tape-recorded broadcasts to summon the faithful five times a day.)

At Vespers, it is often only the elderly monks who either hang out at the chanter's stand, tapping their fingers rhythmically, or sit slouched in the high-backed chairs (*stasida*) that line every available wall. Since Vespers is not a Eucharistic service, and I don't see why services that praise God repetitively and interminably and don't end with Holy Communion require my attendance, the need to meticulously fulfill my obedience – my daily duty to my brethren – suddenly becomes overwhelming, and I hasten to the refectory to prepare the tables for dinner. If it is a non-fasting day, in addition to the individual bowls or plates of food to be set at every place, there is cheese to cut and carafes of wine to fill, as well as putting out bread and the bowls of olives that must accompany every meal on pain of [my] death. To mess with a Greek's olives is like insulting his mother.

Vespers is over, and with the final *Amen*, the monks file out of the church and into the dining room. If the abbot has attended the service, the brotherhood will wait with bended necks for him to pass before them, and then follow him inside. We all stand while the abbot blesses the food. Only when he sits down do the rest of us spring into action. The priests and the *epitropoi* (administrators) – fully garbed with flowing headgear (*epikalimon*) and robes – spread their gowns and sit down gracefully on either side of the abbot. The other monks lift the long wooden benches away from the tables and try to keep the noise to a minimum. I sit at the low end of the lowest table with the other postulants and novices. We don't wear church regalia because we have none.

The *epitropos* is not an official position, but every monastery has at least one. These lieutenants keep the empire running smoothly while the emperor is off fighting his wars and the serfs are tilling the fields. My English monk-friend on the island of Paros, Father G., called them "personalities", and I have loved that term even as I have been suspicious of those it describes. Personality is no indication of character. "Personalities" create an unhealthy space that might not be there if they did not occupy it and wield a great deal of power. At meals and rituals they are positioned on either side of their lord, protecting him from communication like the now-ceremonial fans that once kept flies away from the host on the altar. Much of what the abbot hears from the brethren passes through the personalities, and it is through them that the brethren generally receive their instructions. The effect of the existence of *epitropoi* is to isolate the two essential signatories to the monastic compact from each other.

The monastic term for "refectory" is *trapeza*, with the accent on the first syllable. In the world, it means "table" or "bank". *Agia trapeza* means "holy table", and describes the altar in a church. After bowing to receive the abbot's weary blessing – a limp hand gesture, writing a cross – one of the monks retreats to a lectern and reads from the writings of a Church Father. The Greek he reads is at least a thousand years old, and few understand it. No big deal to me. The Prayer of the Heart, the Jesus Prayer, is what drove me and pulled me to where I am, so I busy myself with this mantra – "Lord Jesus Christ, Son of God, have mercy on me, a sinner" – when I am not mentally commenting on the atrocious eating habits of the monk across the table ("God, look at the way that disgusting pig eats…") or keeping an eye on the abbot to see if he is going to halt the proceedings before I have had time to eat all my food ("… and let me have time to stuff myself"). We eat in silence, save for muffled slurping. When the abbot finishes eating, he raises his hand to the reader to stop. At that moment, everyone also is finished. If the abbot finds the passage being read interesting, we sit immobile while I debate with my crabby conscience what effect eating another piece of stale bread might have on my participating in the Resurrection.

What does a monk eat? He eats very well, thank you, in the sense that what he eats and how much he eats have recently been declared to promote good health by those who prove with studies and facts what monks discovered by intuition. The basic monastic menu consists mostly of dry foods (*xerofagita*), such as beans and grains, and vegetables, fruits, and olives. In Greece, the olive is neither a fruit nor a vegetable, but a separate food group. The words for olive and mercy come from the same root – *eleas*. The national passion for the edible mercy and its derivatives approaches idolatry. An honest Greek menu would advertise a single dish: olive oil à la whatever-we-have-in-the-kitchen-today. Cheese and very fresh fish complete the monk's menu on days when the church calendar allows it. No meat is served. Ever.

The *typikon* (rule) permits wine on feast days, but not on fast days. Some monasteries even make their own plonk. These are not wines that gather bouquet as they age in dank cellars under the close supervision of a man in a white coat with a battery of thermometers weighing down his breast pocket. The measure of the vintage of Athonite wine is weeks, not years. Some monasteries toss wine that has passed its brief prime into a large wooden cask, the cobwebs across the lid creating a James Bond-like anti-theft system. Who would want to steal vinegar…? I'm glad you asked. Vinegar and sugar actually was the preferred beverage of one elderly monk who always sat across the table from me at Konstamonitou. In performing my obedience in the refectory, I noticed that whenever wine was permitted, the table in his vicinity not only was soaked with vinegar and sugar, but abounded with dead fruit flies. This suggested to me a very humane, even happy, way of putting an end to the plague of these little pests that were present at almost every meal at harvest time. Before closing up for the night, I placed a shallow dish of sugar and vinegar in the middle of a table. I felt a very little bit like Newton must have when the apple fell on his head or Archimedes as his body displaced the water in his bath. When I entered the refectory/lab the next morning, *Eureka!* – the tiny carcasses of more than fifty winged critters dotted the chipped enamel beach. Floating on the surface of the pond were a few dozen more who were similarly deceased by virtue of their vice.

"Hold on, you're movin' way too fast."

The *typikon* of all Orthodox monasteries prohibits animal products on one hundred eighty days of the year. That's every Monday, Wednesday, and Friday that isn't a major feast day, plus the four fasts: Great Lent (spring), the Apostles' Fast (early summer), the Fast before the Dormition of Mary (late summer), and Advent (late fall). Why the ritual abstinence? Prayer is nothing without the feeling that life itself is at stake, and bodily comforts sap this essential need. Nature never favors the soft. Throughout history, those who have focused on the inner life have generally agreed that comfort is anathema to the spirit. Food is essential to life; too much is soporific. Rich food eventually kills; the lion that eats too much becomes himself easy prey. The (wealthy) fat will succumb to the (spiritual) thin. The monk who prays even while he sleeps becomes the well-fed monk who sleeps while he prays. "Etcetera, etcetera, and so forth."

As the once-humble abbot of Konstamonitou remarked, "We sleep after we eat, because we are fit for nothing else." Eating is the gateway to the flesh, while fasting checks concupiscence and supports spiritual activity. An empty belly finds no solace in images of sexual pleasure. It wants to eat and it can't, so the mind helps it by escaping to where it is free of all bodily demands.

Okay, but why only half the year? Because just as silent prayer strives to diminish the effect of unavoidable thoughts without eliminating them, so the monk's goal is to subdue the passions, not remove them – "to live in the world, and not be of it". The Greek word, *apatheia*, means just that. While life without passions – the color and music of life – is unimaginable, so is a life submissive to appetites. But killing passions altogether would make a monk less human.

Success in controlling one's passions is often dependent not on will power but on the very grace being sought by the faster through prayer. As the right hand is not supposed to know what the left is doing as it gives alms, true fasters are not conscious they are not eating. It simply never occurs to them to eat. According to his chroniclers, the Ba'al Shem Tov, the founder of Hasidism, took seven loaves of bread with him when he went into to the mountains to pray and returned at the end of the week ignorant of the seven loaves still in his bag. Similarly, true prayers are unaware they are praying. The crippled Russian *strannik* of *The Way of a Pilgrim* yearns to know what it means to "pray without ceasing". Eventually, he *becomes* unceasing prayer. And yet, he is unaware that he has because the prayer is now as natural to him as breathing. He has been lifted out of the world while still walking in it.

Tradition with a small "t" requires Orthodox Christians to fast for one to three days before receiving Holy Communion. Forget that this is impossible, since the church prohibits fasting on Saturdays even though the Sabbath is now Sunday. Does fasting automatically prepare one for communion? Of course not. It is just as likely to prepare us to judge others who have not fasted and are not receiving communion. Fasting encourages one to concentrate mind and heart, but unless fasters are careful, they might be wielding a knife with the blade pointing inward. The truth is that fasting is easy for those who fast with their whole being, while for those who don't, what's the difference if they don't eat certain foods or less of them?

If I have given you the impression that I did not take adherence to monastic fasting seriously, for a long time I was in danger of making it my religion. I used to look forward to Lent, and especially the first week, more as a personal challenge than any great sacrifice. From sundown on the last Sunday before the Great Fast, until they participate Wednesday evening in a Eucharistic service known as the "Liturgy of the Pre-sanctified Gifts", monks – and at one time, laity, too – eat and drink nothing. Nada. Not even water. After the Eucharist, a simple meal, and then another absolute fast until the same liturgy on Friday. Tuesday for me was always the toughest day. By

Wednesday, I really didn't care if I ate or not. I once passed the first week at Mar Saba, an enormous, ancient, and barely inhabited monastery near the Dead Sea – as hot and dry a place for self-torture as you could ever desire. My room was on the fifth floor, maybe twenty feet from the cave/cell occupied in the 8th century by the renowned theologian, St. John of Damascus. What I remember of that experience is that by the third day, climbing the steps from the church to my room was taking me about half an hour. And that our meal on Wednesday was snails. Unless equally desperate, I probably will never eat snails again. They were delicious. Memorable. But enlightening? I loved beans and all that stuff the way others loved steak. A fast for me would have been being forced to eat cheesecake.

The monastic fast is quantitative as well as qualitative. Eating in moderation can be very beneficial to your health; abstaining from certain foods for a period of time can also contribute to the well-being of mind and body; weighing your oat flakes to see that you are only eating one teensy ounce of roughage does not. It is my totally uncorroborated yet firmly held belief that stress is the cause of every major disease to which we are susceptible that isn't caused by a bug – except those transmitted through sex. If you can't pass a scale without weighing yourself, or if you devote three-quarters of the time you spend at the market to squinting at the fine print to make sure that your prospective purchase does not contain even a smidgen of a canonically outlawed foodstuffs, are you not actually creating stress? While the body may be the temple of the soul, I have never heard that heaven is a reward for lowering one's cholesterol or taking two inches off one's waist.

Most important, short of refusing sugar if you are a diabetic, to turn away any kind of food offered in hospitality merely because it offends a rule of fasting, suggests that you just might not know what religion is about. The Hall of Famer, Sandy Koufax, who refused to pitch the first game of the 1965 World Series because it fell on Yom Kippur, once was invited to a barbecue at a teammate's house where the centerpiece was a roasted pig. When clued in, the flummoxed hostess managed to squeak a "What you would like to eat, Mr. Koufax?" The Dodger immortal – not an observant Jew but a very traditional one – is alleged to have nodded toward the spitted porker and said "I'll have some of that turkey."

"All things in moderation," advised the corpulent Doctor Johnson, the 18th century English man of letters not known for his moderation in anything. "Including moderation."

While believing that food's only purpose is to keep the body going until the soul shucks it off, monks can be very particular about the quality of that sustenance and extremely fastidious when it comes to where, what, and with what they eat. I don't recall ever seeing a dirty glass set out on a table at mealtime. And I was not exaggerating when I told you that a *trapezarius* that fails to put olives on the table at *any* meal puts his life in jeopardy. Many monks also seem to have special diets; more than what a normal amount of allergies or ulcers would prescribe. But a large number come from farms or villages, and, contrary to what one might think, people who grow up close to the land are probably less tolerant of a wide range of foods than city-dwellers like me, forced to forage in a wide variety of shops and restaurants. The bottom line is that monks, like anyone else, have foods they prefer and foods they won't eat without a direct order from the Ecumenical Patriarch. At Konstamonitou, I was cleaning up in the refectory when a monk, who had hurried back from an errand driven by his vision of the spaghetti with red sauce totally lost it when the only sauce left was white!

Whose life is it, anyway?

The short service that follows dinner is called *apodeipna* (literally, "after dinner"). A brief recitation of hymns and petitions focuses on the end of the day and the need for heavenly protection through the ensuing night. Alas, because there is no Eucharist to reward me for my attendance, it's another service I frequently skip. In the summer, while muffled voices ascend from the church like soap bubbles, I stand on one of the balconies, gossiping and smoking with the guys (just kidding, monks don't gossip) or take a walk in the purple hills outside the monastery. We must be back before dark, however, because that is when the huge gates of the monastery rumble shut to protect us against the ghosts of pirates past, and with only my purity to protect me I would not like to spend a night in the wild. The mules of Konstamonitou, safe within the walls, nightly attest to the presence of wolves in the neighborhood, catching the scent and bellowing like the geese that once saved Rome.

As the sun sets, I retire to *our* cell. The ideal monk has nothing; no place of his own to lay his head. I found Father G., my monk-friend on

Paros, to be scrupulous in this regard. When he told me that if I didn't like *The Way of a Pilgrim*, I should "put it back in *our* cell and find something else," I thought that either he had a roommate or I had inadvertently done or said something and been religiously shanghaied. But monks come from various backgrounds with various reasons for becoming monks, and not all of them are as painstaking about monastic traditions as Father G. Neither are those traditions inflexible. The worldly, powerful St. Jerome is said to have taken to the Egyptian desert with many of the luxuries that had garnished his life in Rome – Including a four-poster bed. When his monk mates complained of his exceptional treatment, his abbot replied, "Look at what he sacrificed to be here; what have you given up but your poverty?"

Father N., a grossly overweight Constantinopolitan, lived at Longovarda during my brief residence there. He had a wispy beard that didn't quite make it to his bulbous belly and a high-pitched voice. Father G. told me that the doctor who periodically visited the monastery, not wishing to offend His Portliness, referred to his obesity as a "dietological swelling". Father N. rarely attended church and took his meals in his cell. He was a perpetual novice, having determined he was not the kind of person who could forsake everything the world offered. Since he had given all his money to the monastery, it accommodated his singularities, and his cell was always covered with relatively current newspapers and the discarded wrappings of foodstuffs his sister sent him from the bazaars of Istan … Constantinople. Perhaps as a consequence of his boyhood in that brutally cold city, the elderly man was constantly shivering. He wore a sheepskin vest and fingerless gloves; the heat from his paraffin stove was as perpetual as his novitiate, and the accompanying smoke had turned the ceiling a greasy black. The food that had found a home on his robe could have fed the *trapeza* at the *Russikon*. I really liked Father N. The accident of his voice, pitched as if he had been a gelded guard in the sultan's seraglio, gave his every utterance the urgency of a 911 call. Belly aside, he was a dead-ringer for Alec Guinness's Fagin, and not without that unfortunate's charm.

Father N. was a kindly and generous person who, like Inspector Clouseau, suspected "everyone of everything and no one of nothing". It was in his Byzantine genes to be on guard constantly against treachery and conspiracies and to manufacture his own during lulls when none were available. He could discuss the schemes of world leaders as easily as the machinations of the "personalities" that ran the monastery. Father G.

disapproved of this brother's secular thoughts, his sensual conduct, and his gossip even as he hung on every word and quoted his suspicions to me as if they were gospel. I believe that the bond between these two *xenoi* (foreigners) was a mutual loathing of their abbot, who to the rest of Greece was a renowned *pneumatikos* (spiritual guide) and the man Father G. had sought out when he had determined that the Anglican Church was not a "true church".

In his youth, Father N. had run away to Paris, hoping to become an artist. He had lived in a small flat in Montmartre below the Church of the Sacre Coeur. At the age of thirty-seven, having decided his life was pointless, he determined to commit suicide. The path to the kitchen took him past his family's Bible, up to then a mere decoration. Desperate for a reason to live, he impulsively cracked the binding; the leaves settled at the first epistle of John, the great letter of love by the Apostle of Love. Father N. sold or gave away all he had and became as much of a monk as he knew himself capable of being.

I am quite certain that Orthodox Christianity's not permitting the burial of a suicide in consecrated ground had nothing to do with Father N.'s decision to live. In the present age, where the individual has been allowed to emerge from the mass, the right to privacy is expanding where it had never before even existed. My own view is that taking one's own life or the life of an unborn child is a terrible but personal choice. And that it seems harsh for a faith built on mercy to be more merciful toward a murderer – to whom it grants sanctuary – than to one who takes on herself the terrible burden of aborting the life within her, but the church's position cannot be easily dismissed as mere hypocrisy. For purely impersonal and practical reasons both church and state need to increase the human stock, and when the two were one and all there was, their unspoken logic was incontrovertible: no one could take a life but Caesar or God. As we move slowly away from that absolute, I wonder if its secular acceptance doesn't have as much to do with an innate consciousness of the consequences of overpopulation as with the evolution of morality.

On the other hand, our obsession with *prolonging* life when the flesh is wasted and the spirit wants to go makes no sense on any level. In this matter we might do well to visit an elephant's graveyard and contemplate the wisdom of these great beasts that have the intelligence to know when it is all right both to die and to let one die.

Home is where the prayer of the heart is.

The previous occupant of "our" cell in the monastery on Paros, the nephew of one of the *epitropoi*, had tried to jump to his death. As the window was only three feet from the ground, except for a few scrapes and a twisted knee, he emerged from the experience as unsound as ever. They removed him from the room, though not from the monastery, and upped his meds. They added bars to the window just in time for my arrival. As if it was the room that had caused him to leap. What nonsense. Well, after two months of the wintry wind that incessantly whined its way under the door, piling mounds of cold on the bare floorboards and spreading the frigid air with a trowel all around the room, I, too, was ready to jump. Except I no longer had the will even to do that.

Our cell at Konstamonitou is on the third floor facing the courtyard. The walls are whitewashed and cracked. There is a door latch, but its sole function is to keep out the winter wind and cold, an obedience it performs with considerable help from a small pot-bellied stove. I have about seven feet square in which to live my private life, but it is all I need. A thin straw mattress graces my narrow cot, and a board under the mattress lets me know how very thin it is. During the night, I often change my position as the board antagonizes the nerves in my hips. Under the bed rests a one-legged stool that makes sure I don't fall asleep when I sit down to pray. Low technology, but very effective. I – we – also have a rickety wooden lectern and an old bentwood chair. A paraffin lamp that gives off light the color of cheddar cheese keeps my nocturnal reading to a minimum. The few clothes I brought with me hang on nails on the back of the door. There is plenty of room to perform the prostrations I inflict on myself as part of my private devotions.

Round about midnight a knock on the door rouses me to perform my monastic "rule". This private exercise combines the reading of spiritual books and set prayers with making an assigned number of prostrations and running a woolen, knotted, prayer rope (*comboskini*) through one's fingers while reeling off the number of Jesus Prayers set for him by the abbot. It is as unprofitable to talk with another monk about his prayer rule as it is for people in the world to discuss their sex lives. Lack of insider knowledge encourages a comparable amount of boasting about one's prowess. If the number of monks who admit to five thousand prostrations a night is anywhere near accurate, the world is either quite safe from Satan or Mount

Athos should send a gymnastics team to the next Olympics. The abbot adapts the rule of each monk to what his perception of the individual's spiritual level In my case, my self-appraised aptitude is so high that to let another tamper with the bar is unthinkable.

A prostration is not exactly a pushup. We have learned that the word for prostration, *metanoia*, also means "repentance", "the change of the eye of the mind in the heart". I shall now demonstrate a proper *metanoia*: first, with knees bent and arms extended forward, I lean forward and drop to the floor; I am now in a position that resembles the yoga position known as the "cat cow"; next, I bend my neck until my forehead makes contact with the floor. My mind, ever seeking someplace to run, may even reflect on the observation that repentance mirrors the physical act of prostration: First, the knees buckle, literally taking one down a peg – I think it was Starbuck who when questioned about Ahab's humility replied, "I never yet saw him kneel." Then the body (within which is the heart) descends toward the floor, and finally the ever-thinking mind touches down. As it does so, I experience an ineffable harmony, a letting go, a relaxation of the ego that feels … I don't know…. "Right?" And surprisingly relaxing. I rise and repeat. And rise and repeat.

Of course, a *metanoia* can also be nothing more than a pushup. It takes time and repetition, it takes liking it, but not too much, for it to grow into a practice that claims a place in "the eye of the mind in the heart". In this, it is quite similar to the Psalter, the Book of Psalms. The *typikon* of every Orthodox monastery ensures that monks get to hear (or sleep through) all one hundred and fifty psalms every week during the cycle of services and to listen to the whole of the New Testament once a year. This, however, is not enough for me – the more so since the public reading is in Greek. Even though I cannot understand them, I am greatly offended by the way monks mumble and rush through the psalms as if a hot date awaits them in their cell. On my own, I read the Psalter and the New Testament once a week every week for ten years. That's at least five hundred and twenty times. Do I know the psalms by heart? (A blush.) Well, what can I say? "All thy waves and thy billows are gone over me." But I must tell you that my initial response to the Psalter was not quite as poetic. "What do these words have to do with me?" I carped, warding off one of the most beautiful, enduring experiences of my life. "It's unintelligible, archaic crap." But with no conscious effort, ninety per cent of that unintelligible, archaic crap gets stored in my heart. Throughout the day, one or another line sings to me; sometimes I effortlessly string them together and compose my own psalms.

My approach to the New Testament is somewhat different but with a similar result. It, too, begins with disdain: on first contact, compared with the lush, devious panorama of the Old Testament, the didactic simplicity of the Gospels has all the appeal of fast food. My reaction was not a singular one. I hear that a tribe in Uganda surprised their Christian missionaries by becoming Jewish because of a preference for the Old Testament tales. But it wasn't anything written that made me a Christian. It was the *person* of Christ; not what others wrote about him or what he was supposed to have said. I set out to devour scripture: if possible, to become it. I want to know (*gnorizo*) the New Testament so that I can speak, as Christ did, "with authority, and not as one of the scribes". I have no more interest in Biblical analysis than in unearthing the historical Jesus. Paul said that the wisdom of men is foolishness with God, and that strikes me as spot on. What is the point of deconstructing an ineffable experience unless it is to rationalize its power and thereby destroy it? In the name of what? Enlightenment? And these are supposedly religious people who commit this … this … crime? Surrendering the whole to the head?

After an obligatory trip to the *mairos*, I pray my way to the *kafeneion*, where I engage in my nightly attempt to reform young Father Bartholomew's faith to what I think it should be. It is so easy to poke logical holes in something so gossamer! It is even easier when that faith is in large part superstition and hand-me-down. These monastic bull sessions can last an hour or two. While I am torturing this poor, very helpful young man – perhaps partly in payment for speaking English when I am at least affecting a desire to learn Greek –, I remind myself that I am constantly saying the Prayer of the Heart, which tells me I am not. Sometimes, as we talk, I make (*plecko*) a *comboskini* out of black wool. It allows me to do something spiritually – and in some instances pecuniarily – profitable while I worse than waste another's time.

I was taught how to make prayer ropes during the eight days of my baptismal feast, when I wore white and was ruthlessly prohibited from doing any other kind of work. Although it is considered almost sacred knowledge, I am not alerting the Inquisition by telling you that the prayer rope knot is extremely complicated to set up and complete. My first one hundred knot rope took about twenty minutes per knot. Three knots per hour. A day and a half. And I was so proud of it!... It fell out of my pocket as I slid out of a car. *Sic transit gloria munde.*

Toward the end of my career, I could do seventy knots per hour – in the dark! Making prayer ropes paid in large part for whatever traveling I did during those years. Five dollars a pop isn't much; but multiply that by about half of the thirty-five hundred ropes I made, and that's a fair number of plane tickets. Of course, air travel was a lot cheaper in those days. I was amazed that so many people wanted them! And that I felt no compunction about commercializing my gift. But you can't hitch across the ocean, and hey, what's a poor boy to do? That what I collected so often exactly matched my immediate need convinced me that my enterprise was God's will.

In "the dark time, a couple of hours before dawn, when [in the world] the streets belong to the cops and the janitors with their mops," (Loesser, Frank, *Guys and Dolls*) the ecclesiarch makes his rounds, pounding on his *symandron*. It could be one o'clock; it could be three o'clock, depending on the season. His message is urgent: The water is rising! Hurry into the ark!

Doors creak open, latches click closed, and we make our separate ways to church. As I enter the *narthex* I make a prostration on the cold, marble floor and cross myself. In the cavernous nave, a solitary candle illumines the lectern of the monk mumbling the midnight office (*mesinichtikon*). In keeping with Konstamonitou's general lack of description, the main church is not a brilliant spokesbuilding for its kind. No murals hide the rough gray walls. The icons on the screen are second-rate: very much post-Byzantine and reflecting the Western humanism that impressed Greeks once they were free of their Ottoman past. As for the floor plan, if you've seen one Orthodox church, you've seen them all.

An *iconostasis*, the icon screen, separates the nave from the altar. At certain points in the service, things happen in the altar from which even the faithful are excluded, and a red curtain is drawn across the Royal Gates – the opening in the middle of the screen. Only ordained clergy may pass through this portal, also known as the Beautiful Gates. It is well known that a trespasser risks instant incineration should his toe cross the line that bridges the space like an invisible laser beam. Those who serve the liturgy in a non-ordained capacity use the north or south doors; these each bear an icon of one of the archangels – Gabriel or Michael – or a sainted deacon, thus indicating that these entrances are for helpers. Seen from the nave, the icon of Jesus is always to the right of the Royal Gates and Mary is always to the left of them. Except in the *kelli* of the *Axion Estin* ("worthy it is") icon of Mary, where, according to Athonite legend, the icons changed place of their own accord. John the Baptist is forever to the right of Christ, attending him whose sandals he said he was unworthy to unloose. The murals that sometimes decorate the walls on the sides and rear of the nave logically lead upward from earthly events and people to occupants and tableaux in heaven.

I venerate the icon of Christ; then I shuffle to the left and bow in front of the Royal Gates toward of the altar. Another shuffle to the sinister side has me venerating the silver-encased icon of Mary. I seek a vague kind of approval from an icon of Saint Nicholas that looks down at me from a pillar. Funny. I never feel I am fooling him.

In the middle of the floor is a mosaic eagle, and from this spot I bow to the choirs on either side of the nave and then to the rest of the brethren. I silently ask their forgiveness, and they silently tell me that it is God [in them] that forgives. It does not matter if anyone notices me or is there to hear the tree fall. My mere making the gesture inscribes it on the asset side of The Ledger. If the abbot is present, I walk to his throne, which is opposite the icon of Christ, and I hold out my cupped hands to receive his blessing. If he is absent, I do it anyway: his place will bless me.

That is the last that anyone will see of me until just before Holy Communion. My lack of proficiency in Greek acts as a shield against being asked to participate, freeing me to find the darkest and most obscure part of the church to pass the next three to six hours as I see fit – but always with my prayer rope in my hand. Since the services that precede the Divine Liturgy have no Eucharistic payoff, it is difficult for me to sit through them even with my whirling prayer counter. Consequently, I spend a good portion of the morning service (*orthros*) as I did Vespers, playing hooky in the refectory: cleaning up from the evening meal and making the place ready for "tea" or the meal that will immediately follow the Eucharist. If I am feeling particularly annoyed with my lot (or my brethren), I may sing "A Mighty Fortress is our God" or "Amazing Grace" or some other Protestant hymn. I don't care who hears me. I am one tough guy.

"I can't believe that you're in love with me."

The morning service is a seemingly endless procession of psalms and hymns that eventually gives way to one of eight looped readings from the Gospel: one for each of the eight musical "tones" that flavor the service. Eastern chant is antiphonic. A lone *psaltis* chants, and from the opposite side of the church another responds. While a choir of monks may congregate around the music stand, only one *psaltis* chants the melody at any one time; another "holds the *ison*", a bass note that keeps the hymn on course. Byzantine chant is like Byzantine art in that while it allows a wide range of individual expression, it also insists that the personal touch stay within certain forms. For people whose egos poison their voice with the sugar of self-flattery, this can be a struggle. I have heard a chanter refer to the ultra-personal work of a rival as "Turkish love songs". You can't get any lower than that. I am told and I believe that the most heated disagreements in churches in the world are between the priest and his choirmaster over who is the real leader of the service. Is it music or the spoken or chanted word that is the prime mover in ritual? In the Orthodox Church, this town is big enough for both, but partisans can make sure that it isn't. Like the apostles of science and religion.

Outside, the gray of the false dawn draws the buildings without shadow. With timing born of centuries of repetition and a little luck, the the first blessing of the Divine Liturgy resounds through the church as the first chord of the sun vaults the surrounding rooftops and pours through the window behind the altar. "For the peace of the world, let us pray to the Lord," chants the deacon, standing in front of the Royal Gates, or in his absence, the priest, from within. This is our group mission statement. This is religious theater at its best: the enactment/reenactment of the life of Christ, from his birth in the manger to the years of his ministry, and on to his passion, death, and resurrection. From litanies of supplication, the service proceeds logically and organically to the revelation of the written Word, when a monk reads the daily epistle from the *Apostolos* and the priest reads from the *Evangelion*. This ends the Liturgy of the Catechumens, open to all.

At this point, if there are any non-baptized in the nave, they are ushered outside, and the doors are shut as firmly as the monastery gates at sunset. The curtain is drawn across the Royal Gates, instantly creating a "Holy of Holies", accessible only to the ordained and the prayers of Believers. Commences forthwith the Liturgy of the Faithful: the enactment of the mystery of consubstantiation. To the Orthodox, this isn't about memorials or symbolism. This *is*. The *epiclesis*, in which the assembled faithful invoke the Holy Spirit to consubstantiate the bread and wine, *is* the Crucifixion, and hard on its heels, in Holy Communion, we will experience the Resurrection. This death and reappearance of Christ happens every day as if it never happened before. It is one of many places in Orthodox worship where linear history meets eternity and dumbfounds logic.

The *epiclesis* is the holiest moment of the service. On Sunday and on major feast days – that is, the fourteen feasts of Christ – when the risen Lord is ineffably present, the monks remain standing. On all other days, they fall to their knees and prostrate themselves as the priest raises the Gifts toward Heaven. The *epiclesis* is also the holiest moment of the Orthodox Christian year and of the past two thousand years. The priest doesn't just ask that the Holy Spirit enter the bread and wine in the mystery on the Cross; he asks that the hearts of everyone present be changed to allow them to receive the consubstantiated elements: for the spirit to heal or ignore their flaws, patch up their leaks, and make them fit vessels – something they cannot do themselves. If the mystical fit is not there, the prince will take his slipper and move on. The interdependence of the individual and the community is abundantly clear: no one is "saved" unless all are.

And yet now the mystery deepens: nowhere is the line between God and man more clearly drawn than in the Eucharist, just as it is there that they never are closer. God gives himself, and man receives him. Man gives himself as best he can and God receives him. At every Divine Liturgy, the priest offers Holy Communion to whoever wants it. The chance to be in God for a little while – a taste of *theosis*. And yet it takes a cattle prod to get most Greeks to accept his offer! Monks and *cosmoikoi* alike. What is it? Laziness? Fear? Pride? Most excuses seem to originate in a pious self-assessment of one's own unworthiness: "I am not worthy of Christ;" "I have not fasted;" "I had a nocturnal emission and am unclean." Puh-leez. This is the church version of "My cat ate my homework." Who *could* be "worthy" of God? Who needs whom more? "Worthiness" has nothing to do with Holy Communion. It's anathema to its spirit. The sacrament is a gift. If anything, judging oneself – and thence with very little effort one's neighbor – might very well make one "*un*worthy". If there is such a thing as "worthiness", it is only one more grace for which to pray.

On Mount Athos, the monks of the *kenobitic* houses need a very convincing excuse *not* to receive the Gifts. As the curtain is pulled away from the Royal Gates, monks emerge from every cranny and form a line in front of the cup. All may be equal before God, but they approach in a jealously guarded order of seniority. Orthodox use real bread in the Eucharist and mix both elements in the chalice. Shutting their eyes and opening their mouths wide in a horrendous display of dental neglect and miasma, all receive Christ from the same chalice and spoon. Aesthetics aside, in these days of highly communicable and deadly diseases, this to me is an extreme act of faith. Maybe not so much for monks, quarantined as they are, but the ritual is the same in churches in the world. It can be very educational to watch the faces of those who approach the cup as they host the battle between the spiritual reward promised and the bacterial punishment they fear.

I believe I have at least hinted at how much I have been looking forward to this moment. Beneath all the inflexibility and superstition that cover it like misguided paint, Orthodox Christianity is intellectually rich and sensually satisfying, available to anyone who wants to take the time to learn about it. And yet I couldn't care less about the inner workings or even the existence of the Holy Trinity. Even less about whether Mary had a little lamb or was a virgin when she gave birth to the Christ child. Or if she remained one the rest of her days. All that matters to me is that some time ago I received a shattering revelation: Through the person of Christ, I know that I am both human and divine, and that is all I can know. This is humbling and exhilarating. In the person of Christ, I found what I could not find in Judaism: a Friend of Friends: someone like me: someone who was willing to die for me; someone who, like me, could not save himself from himself. Not an unpronounceable Name or a notional *Shechinah*. Not abstract transcendence and supersubjective immanence, but a man. This is why I became a Christian. Without the person of Christ in the bread and wine, I truly believe that I can do nothing.

Studying did not produce this knowledge; therefore, I cannot honor it with my mind. Only through the Prayer of the Heart and Holy Communion do I stand on Jacob's ladder between Earth and Heaven with a view of all that is around me, above, and below, feeling reports coming in from all the provinces and the ages and reporting to them in return. Orthodoxy is a "sacramental" church. The Greek word for sacrament is *mysterion*, and Orthodoxy revels in its mysteries. Every Eucharist celebrated on any day around the world happens at exactly the same celestial time. Forget the so-called "realities". When I receive the Body and Blood of Christ, I am in the company of all who are at present alive on earth and all who have ever lived and will live. This is as real as it gets. It is not just something no one can take from me; it is something I can never and have never been able to take away from myself. And believe me, I have tried.

It is easy to say that one sees God in everything, but everyone has only one revelation that takes on the quality of a *mysterion*, even as one is entitled to only one baptism. I can renounce Christianity, but my revelation, my glimpse into the workings of time and place, will always be Christian. I can no more wipe this away than Lady Macbeth could get rid of her damn spot. Holy Communion is so precious and real to me that I am not surprised that the church commands that if a drop or a morsel touches the floor, that piece of the floor must be hacked out and burned. Communion and mystical prayer are what make every day that I am in the monastery worthwhile. That and having one brand new thought. New, at least, to me.

After receiving Holy Communion, I slowly retreat. Since I am in the presence of a king, I never turn my back to the cup. I feel my way toward a table on which rests a basket of small bread cubes called *antidoron*, literally, "instead of the gifts". *Antidoron* is cut from what remains of the *prosphora* (bread) after the priest has removed the Host, which he places in the communion chalice. *Antidoron* is not consecrated, but it is blessed. It has two functions: in the case of those who have communicated, it helps to ensure that no consecrated bread remains in the communicant's mouth; those who have not been to the chalice receive it as a token from priest's hand at the end of the service, a kind of consolation prize. *Antidoron* also tastes good – especially if you haven't eaten anything else for about twelve hours.

If it is a feast day, there may be a short *artoklassia* service, in which the priest celebrates the biblical multiplication of the loaves by blessing five sweetened loaves of bread. These will be cut up and distributed to the monks in the refectory. Or, on almost any day, there may be a memorial service for the departed, in which the priest blesses a mound of *koliva*, a concoction of boiled wheat, raisins, almonds, powdered sugar, and parsley. This is then spooned into the cupped hands of a line of monks – either as they exit the church or in the *trapeze* – who shovel it into their mouths and lick their fingers clean, not for the taste, but out of respect for the blessing. Greeks love their dead, who are present in every Divine Liturgy in the candles the living light; for many, the memorial day of their departed is the most sacred day of the year, *Pascha* included. The genuine solace and hope they find in this is nothing to pooh-pooh. It provides a vertical dimension crucial to understanding one's place in the world. Unfortunately, it can also approach ancestor worship.

Although services in the world usually end with a sermon, some priests make their pitch after reading from the Gospel, when they are assured of still having an audience. On Mount Athos, either tradition or common sense dictates that a wise abbot gives no sermon after a foodless seven hours of church. (On a major feast day, this can be eighteen hours.) Perhaps he has run out of things to say. After all, Athonites celebrate the Divine Liturgy almost every day of the year. Instead of talking to a potentially hostile and certainly hungry crowd, the abbot leads a procession of black-clothed bellies into the *trapeza*. On fasting days, the morning "tea" is a hearty mini-meal of bread, tahini, jam, leftovers, and – will wonders never cease? – olives. On non-fasting days, it's a real meal.

Following *trapeza*, it's time for a little kip, and then off to work to keep the house functioning and in repair, all in the service of the liturgical cycle without which there would be no reason for the buildings even being there. While every monastery has its own hallowed *typikon*, they all contain the elements described above. The Athonite *typikon* is an amalgam of the Rule of St. Theodore, first abbot of the huge monastery of Studion, in Constantinople, and the Western Rule of St. Benedict, formulated before the Great Schism. The monastic *typikon* is an attempt to defeat time by submitting to it while not being bound by it. The mysteries of noetic prayer and Holy Communion temporarily release a monk from temporality, and he enters another existence; at the same time, he is a creature living in time, experiencing most of what existence has to offer. Except sex.

"Monks' madness" isn't just for monks.

I am an expert on celibacy but not the history of celibacy. From what I have gathered, for a long time religious abstinence seems to have been a local matter, with different churches and dioceses having different rules. There is, however, the possibility that it was all a mistake, and, as the monastic researcher working in the Vatican library discovered to his infinite anguish while perusing the original texts, the word actually was "celebrate".

Indeed, that anything female is prohibited from entering or abiding in the Holy Mountain may appear to be one of those absurdities that hang around the extremes of any closed system; but it is only apparently ironic that without the ecstatic pleasure men and women find in sex and the natural tension between them, it's a good bet there would be no Mount Athos and no monasticism. But there is, so what went wrong?

In pagan societies, sex and gods were practically identical. Gods had sex with humans whenever they felt like it, marriage be damned, and produced little tykes called demigods. Most of the offspring, like Herakles and Dionysius, lived very confused lives as semi-immortals. Monotheism could not tolerate this kind of ambiguity or behavior. Because it is a tautology that a god that created through sex isn't essentially superior to the beings he creates, there had to be an absolute separation. Having sex had to be made a sign of the beast, however relatively bestial that creature was.

Fornication is not forbidden by the Ten Commandments. The Old Testament condemned adultery because potentially it was disruptive of a fragile social order; otherwise, it seems just to have let nature take its course. Marriage wasn't necessarily one-on-one, and from my reading, I don't recall any discrimination against bastards. As for love, did Jacob "love" Rachel? Or, like David re Bathsheba – and many a future man – was it pure desire? I may be wrong, but while there is lot of satisfying of carnal appetites in the Old Testament, I don't get the feeling that many men and women loved much about their partners that wasn't physical.

When men *knew* women, it was in the sense of knowledge as power, not understanding. To have sex with someone was not to empower them in any way but to take away their power. Discount the Song of Songs, and heterosexual sex in the Old Israel pretty much began and ended with begat, an act closer to an expression of violence than of love. It wasn't only women that discovered this to their detriment: Samson, Sisera, and Holofernes paid heavily for following their desires long before the satiated Balzac lamented "There goes a novel." David's lament that he thinks Jonathan loved him in a way that was better than a woman's love may be commenting on homoerotic sex, male-to-male understanding, or both. One thing that was definitely forbidden was masturbation, and not because it could make you go blind – a sexual act had to at least have the potential for making babies.

In the New Testament, sex is for making babies, and that within wedlock. Anything else takes one's focus off heaven. Sex is not an expression of love but a … necessity. A duty. An … inescapable sin, a consequence of Adam's disobedience. As the creator of Christianity, Paul struggled mightily with sexual issues in many of his epistles; sometimes, he says things that to us are outrageous, at other times, he makes sense. At one point, perhaps frustrated by trying to catch lightning in a bottle, he says, "… [I]t is better to marry than to burn." Clearly, not a ringing endorsement of marriage; but a warning against random fornication coming out of his own experience. He never denies the power of sensual urges; his own warfare has had, in his eyes, its triumphs and its despair. He complains about having been given "a thorn in the flesh" that he can't dislodge. For a man of his charisma, it's not hard to guess what was pricking him.

Paul could not allow sex to be a source of pleasure. For the "Faithful", pleasure comes only from doing the will of God. So when sex pulls in one direction, and God pulls in another, "how is one to live in the world without becoming of it?" To find pleasure in sex must be a sin, and since some degree of pleasure is inevitable, sex is confirmed as an innate sin. What can be done about this? If men and women must reproduce, they must sin, voluntarily or involuntarily. The more conservative Orthodox congregations still separate the sexes in church – like kids from bad homes being reprogrammed by a couple of hours in school. No doubt this is as successful a deterrent as ye olde bundling board.

In the modern world, with effective means of birth control available, and ways of creating a child without two people even being present, sex has become … what? Third world countries continue to mindlessly churn out and kill their young, but what is sex to us? A vehicle for pleasure only? With a glorified egocentricity demanding immediate gratification, pregnancy is only an option. Where people continue to have sex way beyond the age at which a hundred years ago they would have been dead, it's not even that.

So what is this thing called sex beyond its baby-making function? Other than fun? Is it an expression of love? Something that makes us believe we're in love? Is it as useless as the appendix? Some say that for men, sex is an attempt to crawl back into the womb, the way that the search for or worship of God is an attempt to return to the boundless bliss of nothingness. Like prayer, our need for God and our need for sex elude us even when we think we have explained both to our own satisfaction – a complacency that is inherently short-lived. Both sex and the worship of God are passions sewn into our being. Fear of authority or disease has never stopped people from having sex; no amount of persecution has stopped people from seeking a divine explanation for their existence or an intercessor for their woes. When one or the other of these passions controls one's life, the results are as disastrous as for any other kind of fanaticism. To experience all God is or that sex can offer demands *apatheia*, a word that sounds like "apathy" but is concerned rather with living a balanced life.

Sex and God appeal to different parts of our nature, but they have this powerful and indispensable quality in common: they mediate between our aloneness and the aloneness of others: they are efforts at rebinding (i.e., religion), to make use of if we will. We know (*ksero*) a lot more than the ancients, but cerebral knowledge of God or sex has little to do with the experience of either: Both remain mysteries, impervious to kataphatic or apophatic analysis; in the deepest sense, incommunicable. I've read enough attempts to transmit both to say this with some authority. Some writers come closer than others. I've tried, myself, but I always can tell by the dead spot in my reader's eye or voice that some little, very big thing is missing. Both sex and God are "I" experiences: personal and ineffable. We can think we are sharing, but we really don't; not in our groans, not in our words, not even in our silence. When we go to church, we think we share God, but we don't. It is a gathering place in which, while all may pray to him as a group, each meets him individually. And yet there is such a need to try! To find a way out of ourselves (*ekstasia*) and into the mystery of life; to overcome our fear of a lonely, meaningless death by communicating our emotional experience to others. Occasionally, rarely, in both worlds, we get a glimpse; we know (*gnorizo*) that something like a spark of lightning has bridged the gap between us, even as God's finger almost touches Adam's. But do we ever know (*gnorizo*) what either God or sex is for the other? It is said that one will know God only in death, and don't we call orgasms, "little deaths"?

When a man becomes a monk or a woman becomes a nun, he or she is sacrificing a part of their humanity in the reasonable expectation that it will make their life at least more manageable and allow them to focus on their profession. Like pruning leaves to make flowers grow. They know that if the opportunity for sex arises it will probably happen, so they avoid it. With modern values, it's hard to see the point. But these days, we don't stand around on street corners, either, debating theology – as they did in

Constantinople of old. We don't consider the need to find answers to such things a matter of life or death (perhaps because death does not seem so immediate); yet we constantly make choices that to a celibate would seem even sillier at best and at worst, soul-destroying. For instance, hop-scotching through relationships; abusing relationships, substances, and talents; squandering money on expensive toys and comforts; playing cat-and-mouse with authority; at the end of which all we can sing is "I did it my way."

There is no way of knowing for sure, but my feeling is that a majority of monastics have either renounced all sex or are just are not interested in it. After a few years of abstinence, away from visible reminders of what you might be missing, it is even difficult to remember what sex was. Like any habit, if you stop using it, it stops using you. The whole system shuts down, and it takes what feels like a miracle to restart it. Indeed, my journey back into sexuality was much more difficult than the trip out, which was occasioned not simply by an overwhelming preference for God over a depth of human companionship that eluded me, but the sheer physical and emotional exhaustion that was a consequence of the life I had been living. From what I hear, however, my painful return to sexuality has not been the experience of other many longtime celibates. I would be putting the lie to what I have just said if I could speak for them, but the image of a monk being released from his celibacy like a popped cork on a bottle of champagne is so attractive that, even if it were completely apocryphal, people who have never left the world would still probably call a desire to bed everyone in sight "monks' madness".

I do not think I would be guilty of hyperbole if I guessed that, oh, ninety per cent of the current population of the world to whom life on earth is hell would have no trouble understanding why a person would choose to live outside of his or her body and the many painful shackles of the flesh. Or why, sex aside, a good part of that other ten percent wouldn't prefer the company of their own sex. Think of it: no one to understand and no need to be understood. Women could eat all they wanted and men could break wind without worrying who they might or might not impress. Good riddance to sex, marriage, and kids!

I will now tell you something I have told very few others: at one point in my search for otherworldiness, I actually managed to erase all gender distinctions. I could look at a beautiful woman and feel nothing. Talk with her and not hear the musicality of her voice. Have the same reaction to

Sophia Loren as to Babe Ruth. How could I do such a thing? I've asked myself that exact question many times while hitting my head against a wall and have only this to offer: as you must skin a moose before you can make moose soup, to think and act as I did, you must have no sex drive. Like a moose, it may cross your path, but at this point, assuming you have a gun, killing it is actually quite easy: just point and shoot. Skinning it and getting it into the pot may be more difficult, but once it is there, leave the rest to time. I blamed sex for my former way of life. I could not even think of my sexual adventures without a feeling of revulsion reminiscent of Alex's "treatment" in *A Clockwork Orange*. If you have no copulatory urge, it's easy to strip others of their bodies and imagine them to be only souls. Thinking you have become enlightened, you have become very, very stupid. Moose soup, at least, is probably nourishing.

Blame it on Willie Sutton.

But what about that *other* kind of sex? You know. "Erotic brotherly love?" After all, when it wasn't rumors of monks raping their way through the countryside like the hairy Jewish satyrs of Eastern Europe, assumptions about homosexuality used to be the yellow police tape by which the world identified a presumably weird way of life. I mean, what "real" man wears a dress? And do they wear anything under it? Equating monasticism with homosexuality has allowed people to dismiss the cloistered life without ever considering it might be a choice for your average Joe or Jo. My own mother, whom you will meet, thought that because I was unmarried and lived in San Francisco, I had to be gay. It didn't matter that I lived in Berkeley. Wasn't Berkeley *close* to San Francisco?

One of those newspaper fillers that entertain us when a story fails to fill a column assures me that seven per cent of all monks are gay, but I have no idea how anyone could have compiled that statistic. I find it difficult to imagine a census-taker paddling up some river in northern Thailand or raising himself in a wicker basket to one of the monastic aeries of Meteora in Greece and asking monks to complete his survey. Perhaps what they are really saying is that seven per cent of each monk is gay. An arm here, a leg there – maybe the occasional nose. That would be reasonable.

Well, if some monks have no interest in sex, and homosexuality is not rife, are there monks who do have "a bit on the side"? I don't know. Most likely there are and always have been. Few would question the assertion that spiritual power is an awesome aphrodisiac. Combine it with prohibited conduct, and the temptation becomes well-nigh irresistible to both potential participants. In the world, Orthodox sometimes move erring clerics around to new locales like musical smallpox. Monks, however, live too far from the kitchen to feel the worst of the heat. And while most peoples aren't as fussy about Americans when it comes to bodily smells.… Well, who knows? Almost no one bathed in the 10th century. Nevertheless, I imagine that most of the sex that monks engage in passes through the world as jokes.

In the absence of visible temptations, do monks take things into their own hands? I have never heard any comment on the practice of masturbation among monks that is not merely an extrapolation on H. L. Mencken's, "How can I believe you are telling the truth, when I know, in your place, I would lie?" Perhaps the "seven per cent gay" people have done some as yet unpublished work in this critical area, but the only survey of which I have any knowledge involved interviews with five hundred Jesuits. Four hundred and ninety-eight replied, yes, they did masturbate. The other two had no arms.

By the way, most monks wear work clothes under their "dresses".

"Who are those guys?"

The life of an Eastern Christian monk demands celibacy; it does not require silence. It isn't possible to be a little celibate, but it is possible to be relatively silent. There are *hesychasts*, monks who do practice absolute silence in the pursuit of mystical *theosis* through the Jesus Prayer, but that is their personal and often unauthorized choice.

There are no silent orders in Orthodox monasticism equivalent to those in the Catholic world. There are no orders in Orthodox monasticism at all: no houses given to teaching, caring for the poor, the sick, etc. There are no friars among the Orthodox except for a few monks who have taken it upon themselves to wander, and a few others who believe that God sent them into the world to preach. Some might even call Orthodox monasticism *dis*orderly, and the Orthodox monks' garb does nothing to dispel this image. "Clothes that on another would have looked like rags discarded in the street, on him looked stolen," Conrad says of a marginal seaman in *The Nigger of the Narcissus*. And certainly, compared for instance to well-kempt Dominicans, Orthodox monastics do look as if they are homeless. But isn't that how they should look? Since they own nothing, if they did look sleek and prosperous, it would be like a man on a diet ordering a chocolate egg cream with skimmed milk.

There are no orders in the monastic tradition of the Eastern church, but there are echelons. These stages reflect the degree of a man's acceptance into the community and a decision to take vows that increasingly limit his mobility and expand his restraints. Anyone can become a monk. Nobody asks an applicant for his I.Q. or his rap sheet. The postulant at the monastery gates is a guest for three days and then he becomes a novice. The novice who makes it through the first wave of temptations urging him to leave becomes a *rasophor* monk by tonsure. The *rasophor* wears the *rason* (tunic) of a monk, but he is under no obligation to remain in the monastery if things do not work out. The abbot tonsures the persevering *rasophor* into the ranks of the *microschema*, the "small habit" monks. The *microschema* monk takes vows of poverty, chastity, and obedience, and swears to make the monastery of his tonsure his home for life. The *megaloschema*, the monk of "great habit", is the Eagle Scout of monasticism. There are very few of these: the daily prayer rule and general asceticism is reputedly so demanding that a Greek monk usually attains this rank at the same time he hears his last rites. In Russia, this practice is without exception.

What criteria determine one's ascent from rung to rung on the monastic ladder of accomplishment? There are only two: persistence and acclimatization to the way of life. In other words, obedience and patience. Disappointing as it may be to those searching for some visible sign of holiness, the demands made on an Eastern Orthodox monk to demonstrate his spiritual acuity go no further than this. Just as no one demotes Orthodox saints for not having any recent miracles to their credit, no one cashiers a monk for failing to meet a monthly quota of good deeds or too many absences from church. Once a monk, always a monk and nothing but a monk. Like some government jobs, short of resignation, you have to work really hard to get yourself tossed.

Soldiers depend upon those around them, and monks fight their battles alone; yet both are warned against making personal friends. Temporal ties may end at any time, and neither species of combatant can afford the emotional expense of separation. The only lasting relationship a monk develops is with his Creator. If he loves others, it is through him. My last girlfriend prior to my jumping into the monk pool walked away shaking her head (I hope, sadly) when I told her that this Christ-mediated love was the only kind I could offer her. My proposal was either incomprehensible or unacceptable, and it didn't matter which. When I remember that conversation, I cringe and want to hit my head against the wall again; but at the time, it made perfect sense to me because I was already thinking like a *monakhos*, and a monk is focused on one thing and one thing only.

Committing to a single relationship does not negate the fact that the monastery is the monk's family, for the aim of monasticism is not to focus on the monk but on God in him. Honoring the immanent God in his brother frees the monk to serve his brethren, and in so doing to be "in" the transcendent God. In a working monastery, there are jealousies, misunderstandings, and rebellions; there is anger, loyalty, and blood-love among *sympatriotes* (countrymen): everything you have in a family in the world except the conflicts caused by sex and sometimes consequent progeny. The monastery is the monk's battleground in his effort to live with others in a God-pleasing way. It is also his wilderness, the place that will try his spirit. Only prayer connects a monk with the world, even as it releases him from it.

The committed monk who takes his vows seriously will stay in the monastery of his tonsure for the rest of his life, and his bones will rest there until the Resurrection. His abbot determines his way of life, and the monk's obedience to his abbot is as absolute as if the abbot were God. In fact, his submission to his abbot is another partial atonement for Adam's disobedience. Once he has put himself in his abbot's hands, his job is only to do. Whether this is its own reward or a foot in the door of Heaven is immaterial. Obedience is the pawn ticket that guarantees the integrity of his soul.

Only on rare occasions does the monk leave his monastery even temporarily. For instance, the abbot may send him on an errand in or outside the Holy Mountain, or sickness may send him to a hospital in the world. On even rarer occasions may a monk transfer his residence to another monastery and his obedience to another abbot. Discontent with one's place is hardly unique to monasticism, but a monk's vows forbid him to act on that malaise. No one respects a wandering monk because they doubt his integrity and his commitment, which may be the only things for which they may respect him at all. Dissatisfaction with one's place initiates an internal struggle the way angry thoughts long to become angry words. If he does not confess those thoughts to his spiritual elder whenever they arise, they will stay with him, and one day when he relaxes his vigilance they will push him out of his monastery as surely as failing to dump one's personal baggage periodically will eventually break one's back.

"*Oy vay!*" was the lamentation of my Israeli friends in 1977, on the first of my two visits to Jerusalem. "We finally get you to come, and you're a Christian!" Like, it wasn't *my* fault. Besides, Jerusalem disappointed me, too. I expected all the inhabitants of the "Place of Peace" to be levitating, flapping their wings, smiling beatifically, and giving precise directions and correct change. What a shock! This city, holy to three major faiths, is one of the earthiest places on Earth, and those who live there are surprisingly concerned with eking out the same mundane existence as people with a much less prestigious address.

Gibbon drew his less than flattering description of the first Egyptian monks from ignorance and prejudice, but the image of angelic monks hovering above the Holy Mountain is equally erroneous. How we regard monks is a pretty accurate reflection of where we imagine ourselves to be relative to our own faith. Some of us need monks to be crazy, others need them to be saints; literature and history provide us with both. Monks disappoint us when we discover they are only men. Unfortunately, by advocating an unabashedly moral view of the world, the religious, in the words of Jerry Seinfeld, hang "quite a matzoh ball" on the end of their nose: "Man (or Woman) of the Cloth." Advertising one's superiority is a peril of any trade, but especially this one.

There's nothing unusual about this reaction. We're human: we feel justified in being suspicious of people who fight for the rights of cats and are uncharitable toward humans. Sometimes we *are* justified. But because people in the morality business appear to have set themselves above common, bumbling, more or less opportunistic and relativistic humanity, when they fail to live up to their avowals, we seize the opportunity and react as if we'd caught them speeding in a construction zone and were morally entitled to double their fine.

If anything, sex aside, monks live closer to their basic needs than people in the world. When you see monks come in from a day in the fields or putting new tiles on a roof, you realize that many of these angels are pretty tough characters who do very hard manual work for little apparent reward. A glance at the architecture of every one of the ruling monasteries of Mount Athos, with their thick stone walls and towers with overhanging machicolations, will tell you that they have not relied solely on God for their protection. The history of the inhabitants of the Holy Mountain is similar to that of any of the other peoples whose fate has been to live at that crossroads of the world that floats on and circles the eastern Mediterranean; who suffered frequent pillage and destruction at the hands of Muslim pirates and fellow Christians and learned what it takes to survive.

The mind is a terrible thing to use.

In Jerusalem, I shared digs at the Russian Excavations with a Serbian Orthodox novice who had been a journalist in Sibenic, a seaside city in Croatia, before briefly settling into a Russian monastery in Upper New York State, where the abbot quickly found him nonconforming and expendable. The impetus (boot to the butt) behind my own move to Jerusalem was similar, even if the toe on my *tuchus* was Greek. The Russian Excavations is the name given to an archaeological effort begun in the 19th century by the czars. With their extinction, it passed into the neglect of the American-based ROCOR. As the monastic presence at this site, our job consisted primarily of sitting in the kitchen with an aged, yellow wall blocking our view of the alleged spot on which Pilate allegedly washed his hands while we drank tepid, black tea, watched the flies devour the rotting fruit that Russians consider a delicacy, and picked at leftovers from the table of the abbot, whose rumored hedonism and venality made him more base than ascetic.

We also ran errands. One day, the Serb returned from the Monastery of Abraham's Oak at Mamre, near the flash-point West Bank city of Hebron, with a gash on his forehead and a smile on his lips. A mob of angry Palestinians had mistaken his beard and black robe for the trappings of an Orthodox Jew and stoned him as he got off the bus. Sitting with him in the dingy kitchen, emptying the ever-ready samovar and flicking cockroaches off excavated bread, I revealed I had been born among the Israelites. His response to this disclosure, which a number of Orthodox Faithful have taken as a sign of the truth of their belief, was akin to that of my mother's Greek dentist when he learned that I had embraced the faith of his fathers.

"What?" the Hellenic *ogdhondyiatros* had exclaimed, while savaging her gums with his pick. "He went to the best law school in America, and he chooses a religion for peasants and idiots!?"

"How could you do such a thing!?" the Serb exclaimed with equal vehemence, angry spittle catching on the barbs of his graying moustache. "Judaism is far superior to Christianity! And do you know why [you idiot]? Because it has no theology!"

Now, this may come as a shock to graduates of the Jewish Theological Seminary, but his point was that, theologically, Judaism is as simple as monotheism gets, and how can you get any simpler than monotheism? How much less can you say than the *Sh'ma*? That "God is One."

The Serb, however, was bent on stripping monotheism of any remaining flesh, and having identified a form of nothingness ("Oh, the horror! The horror!"), he tumbled into the vacuum of his own creation. That night, he tried to discover whether there was indeed a Heaven. In his bedroom, separated from mine by a thin wall through which both of us easily could have heard the sounds of the sex neither of us were having, the distraught monastic drained a bottle of *slivovica* (plum brandy), smashed it on the floor, and then rolled over and over on the shards. Perhaps what he experienced as he writhed on the grimy linoleum in his dank bedroom among tank traps of broken glass was the ultimate isolation in the anteroom of death to which his rational mind had brought him before his time and for which he needed expiation. The alcohol also minimized the possibility of infection inside the straitjacket in which they shipped him back to the United States.

A sad story, but in the western precincts of the secular world are we any less deluded? Don't we set our mind hopeless tasks without accepting their hopelessness? For instance, we take pride in a belief that in this life we can effect significant changes in our essential nature with a little hard work, a variety of drugs, or soft wishes. We insist on characters in novels changing or we have no interest in them. But this quixotic notion would appall any theologian as well as any scientist with the possible exception of Dr. Frankenstein and maybe the Wizard of Oz.

As a species, we have no choice but to keep ahead of anything that threatens us whether organic or of our own creation, but merciless Nature and a merciful God are in complete agreement on the inability of the average human to effect a meaningful transformation within him or herself. "Which of you," says Christ, "by taking thought can add one cubit to his [inner or outer] stature?" Or lose an ounce of weight beyond the dictates of his or her body. Our software may change, but the hardware remains the same. Saul, the Jewish fanatic, became Paul, the Christian fanatic. We can do with our talent what we will – even modify our behavior to some extent – but that does not change what or who we are. When we think we are changing, we are mimicking computers in the same way that they mimic us, simply exiting one file and opening up another one from the same folder. Even if we think we have deleted and destroyed them, they are lurking somewhere in our hard drive, waiting for our diligent inner hacker to decide on the moment to retrieve them.

Since we think they are gone, their reappearance can surprise and discomfit us. And it happens all the time, to all of us. Did my immersing myself in the Psalter or devouring the New Testament change me? Did the Jesus Prayer or Holy Communion effect something lasting in me? I don't think so. I was older, yes. Time no doubt had some effect, mellowed me somewhat and gave me a little unavoidable wisdom, but that would have happened anywhere. On leaving the world of monasticism, I was appalled to discover how little my experience had altered who I was. Others thought I had changed, but they have only seen the trailer to the movie.

The realization of our impotence is the *sine qua non* of religious wisdom. Christ, himself, replied to those who remarked on the inconsistency of his perfectly human behavior, particularly his anger, by saying that even physicians cannot heal themselves. Which does not mean that we are wasting our time trying to "better" ourselves, even if we can't say what "bettering" is. The desire to "better" ourselves is in our nature. It's something we can't help doing: the stuff of pilgrimage, sometimes rewarding, sometimes not, and sometimes its own reward. After all, do we ever stop trying to change the world we live in, no matter how frustrating that is and how futile that appears to be?

Who knows? We just might play an active part in evolution: inadvertently, we might pass on a valuable way of seeing things to someone who would then begin life that little bit "better". And how does one accomplish even this little miracle? In just that way. Seraphim of Sarov, Russia's best-loved saint, said, "Acquire the Spirit of Peace and a thousand souls will be saved around you." Others will learn by watching you; not by who you think you are or what you think you are teaching. The way babies learn.

I read somewhere that Thomas Merton, the celebrated Trappist (now *that's* an oxymoron), replied to Mark Van Doren's question about how monks deal with change by saying that a monk does not change; he becomes more who he is. A monk becomes more fully realized as he realizes his place both among his fellows and in Creation. Who we are to ourselves may be a matter of thought or imagination and be subject to rude awakenings, but the healthy monk finds himself in prayer, and prayer is not a matter of thought or imagination. The purpose of saying the words of the Jesus Prayer is apophatic: to eliminate the words one by one until only the unnamable source is left. The last word to disappear is the name "Jesus." After that, we are communicating beyond words.

When a monk picks up a prayer rope, he has no expectations; no inflated opinion of his worth; no knowledge other than that he breathes and in that breath is life; no belief that he can ever control the thoughts that jump around in his had. The only desire he has is the desire to have the desire to pray. The Fathers tell us that God takes account only of the quantity of our prayers – our perseverance, our steadfastness – because we can no more affect the quality of our prayers than change who we are. Most likely the prayer rope is just something physical that relaxes or releases the grip the mind has on the soul. The abbot of Bourazerei, the *skiti* where I spent my first winter on Mount Athos, was a disciple of a renowned Athonite *hesychast*, the Elder, Joseph. Every monk in his care practiced a common prayer rule that consisted of praying the Prayer of the Heart in his cell for about four hours nightly before going to church. He was expected to stand on his feet, away from a wall, and say upward of fifty thousand Jesus Prayers. That's right – five-o thousand. If the purpose of the prayer rope is to release the mind, why were the monks at Bourazerei responsible for *fifty thousand* Jesus prayers a night? Wouldn't they lose count? Exactly.

Who put the orange juice in my orange juice?

The brass ring on the Greek Orthodox Christian merry-go-round is *theosis* – the return of the unchanged soul into God. For spiritual guidance on this journey there are a very few monks whom others acknowledge to be living *pneumatikoi.* As in most mentoring relationships, how successful these holy fathers are partly depends on the listener's receptivity, his or her willingness to commit him or herself into the elder's hands, and the guru's integrity. I use both genders because spiritual elders have a following among women, too. Sometimes *pneumatikoi* extend their talents to external events, and sometimes they peek into the future, though there is no evidence that as a group they are any more successful at the latter than your average television weatherman. Does this sound familiar to followers of other faiths?

During the course of my wanderings in the Orthodox world, I met many of these revered guides. Some had the gaunt appearance of the astheniac, as if the effort of moving back and forth between the spiritual and terrestrial worlds or supporting a sinful world on their shoulders left them physically exhausted. Others were corpulent with an inclination to recline, as if worn out by their toil in the realm of the spirit as a farmer in his wheat field, forever removing the rocks that sit on his seeds and nick the blades of his plow. Fat or thin, the pupils of their eyes were uniformly pale, their flesh often transparent, and their hands suspiciously soft: for the most part, they were also addicted to heat. It is as if they had sacrificed the protection of their bodies for a more ethereal kind and laid themselves naked, like molting crabs, shivering in the slightest current while awaiting the awesome breath of the spirit. When most of them blessed me, it felt like it was the last one they would ever give.

Lest I give the impression of having joined forces with Edward Gibbon, let me say that many of these men are probably quite humble and simple people, with a healthy fear of overstepping themselves and their talents. The most famous of Athonite *pneumatikoi*, Father P., whose hospitality I abused for about ten minutes one day as we sat on the bank of a dry creek, munching (his) cherries, was a wiry little man, physically fit and verbally direct. I may hate authority, but I also fear it; while I may not have been impressed by what I heard from the lips of some of these holy men, I was unfailingly respectful. Besides, when I sought them out, I was convinced I was truly seeking some sort of direction. But was I seeking guidance on how to approach the bewildering maze of options in any moment? Or was I searching for someone to tell me in detail what my particular life would or should be as if it had already been written? In my case, did it matter? My conviction to the contrary, I think my asking for spiritual advice was more like W. C. Fields' phoning doctors to ask what they charged for a visit just so he could spend a few joyous moments haggling over the price before hanging up on them.

Still, I am suspicious of spiritual specialists. To me, most of them have seemed like the kind of auto mechanic who can sell you an engine when all you need is a fuel pump because the only thing you know about your car is that it's not running. It's not all their fault, however. Beware of projection. If what you look for in a "man of the spirit" is for him to wrap himself around you, you will feel him cover you with light as with a garment as surely as you can convince yourself that your lust for a courtesan is love. Similarly, if you thirst for the spirit, you will find it, and what you find will probably deceive you: in the order of things it is the spirit that finds *you*. What, then, do I think makes someone a true man of the spirit? The most human people I have met have been the most spiritual, and vice-versa. I'm sure you've met at least one: someone who is tuned into every individual dial on the human radio and pays attention to every piece of personal news as if it was a front page story; who makes you feel as if you matter without exalting you. A renowned Jewish *tzaddik*, a comfort to his people in the Russian Pale, humbly described his own gift in this way: "What I do is very easy. I hear people answering their own questions just by the way that they ask them."

While Russians have surrounded Saint Seraphim with the light of transfiguration, I don't think he, himself, would have a problem with defining any person of spirit – parent, friend, teacher, child, stranger – as one who in no way imposes his or her beliefs on anyone but by example reveals what it means to be perfectly human; as someone who uses his or her free will to be compassionate to all. Someone like Joice Loch. As I have said, it wasn't what Christ said or did that made me a Christian; it was his person.

Modern saints keep their heads.

The priest at Stavrovouni, in Cyprus, where I spent the most incessantly cold winter of my life, was another such an individual. When I set out from Boston for Jerusalem in January, 1978, four months after my baptism, I had no intention of visiting Cyprus. In fact, I knew less about the island than Mao Tse Tung, who asked his guest, the Cypriot President-Archbishop Makarios, if his six hundred thousand people countrymen all lived in one block of flats. I went to Cyprus because when I was in Athens, a Greek ship owner told me that I would have better luck finding a vessel bound for Haifa if I went first to Cyprus – not surprisingly, in one of his ships. Thinking my new faith required me to trust everyone, I believed him. A passage of thirty-eight hours took us first to Crete, then to Rhodes, and finally to the port of Limassol, on the south coast of Aphrodite's isle. In Limassol, I wandered the docks like the tormented prophet, Jonah, looking for a ship; but there were no ships. In fact, for the next six weeks, fierce winter winds prevented any sea-going craft from putting into or leaving the unprotected port, trapping me there like Odysseus. I didn't have the comforting arms of Circe as consolation, but then, I didn't want them. I could have taken a plane, but then I couldn't have called myself a pilgrim, and I took immense pride in that humble name. Besides, Cyprus to Tel Aviv by air was, based on mileage, the most expensive flight in the world. I did, however, have normal physical needs, such as a roof over my head and food,

Thus it was that late on a moonless February night, two soldiers in a jeep of the Cyprus National Guard deposited me and my duffel bag atop the highest mountain in the eastern Troodos range, in front of Stavrovouni, the oldest monastery in the Christian world, and then drove back down the six miles of narrow dirt road and hairpin turns to the military compound at its base. This is not a simple sentence, and it was not a simple act of hospitality. It was two years after the Turkish invasion of the island and the English commandant of the camp didn't want strangers of any kind hanging around. His unceremonious dumping me at the door had no effect on my genuine gratitude for the lift. Anyone who has ever hitchhiked knows that there is nothing like seeing any house in front of you when your mind has begun to entertain the goblins of a night out in the cold.

The monastery was dark and silent. My genuine gratitude went out like a match. The door was ajar but not open. My imagination did its usual dirty work, but I was more desperate for shelter. Inside, a broad wooden staircase on the right led to the second floor. I felt my way slowly up the treads. As I did so, I heard footsteps cross a creaking wooden floor and saw the light of a lantern approaching the stairs from above. As my eyes came level with the top step, I saw in the lamplight the face of a well-padded monk with a narrow white beard, high cheekbones of good cheer, and kindly eyes that advertised the serenity within. He lowered his light to the floor and wrapped his arms around me as if he had found the original prodigal son.

When I met him, Father A. was in his mid-fifties and had spent seventeen years as priest and lone custodian of the isolated monastery, caring for a couple of disturbed men, his elderly parents, and a few monastic refugees from the north. He cleaned and cooked, and served a full cycle of services daily. He also served coffee to strangers and put them up overnight. Like the liturgy he performed so faithfully, it was not necessary for me to understand what Father A. said. Neither was it necessary for me to feel that I was making myself understood. Beyond the normal Greek-English barrier was the one imposed by Cypriot Greek, a dialect I have often been told is understood only by Cretans. No matter. The warmth of caring radiated from him, and the little "Ehh" he uttered when I finished speaking always felt like the most deeply considered advice. He cared for everyone equally regardless of personality or agenda. He wanted me to become a monk, but he never pushed it. Whenever I left, he blessed me, and when I returned, months or years later, he would smile and ask me, *"Menete edhoh, Ioannis?"* "Are you staying now?"

This chunky, apple-cheeked priest of Stavrovouni was what the Jewish *hasid* must have had in mind when asked by another what wisdom he had heard on a visit to a famous *Maggid* (teacher) in a faraway town.

"Heard?" he replied. "You think I walked all that way to hear something? I went there to see how he laces up his shoes!"

Father A. was also the confessor for many, many *cosmoikoi*. On the Greek-speaking part of the island, home to about four hundred and fifty thousand Orthodox Christians, there were only four priests whom their bishop had blessed to hear confession. If you are thinking it's not rocket science, you're right. It's much harder. It's got no formulas or standardized parts. That's why there were only four.

Prior to my last visit to Stavrovouni, the abbot of the three monastic houses of which that aerie was the crown jewel had been killed when the tractor he was driving tipped over into a ditch and crushed him. The search for a successor did not point toward the obvious choice, my friend the priest. Why not? Hand-in-hand with the wisdom shown in selecting Father A. as a confessor went the primeval human foolishness – not peculiar to Greeks or Cypriots – of social classism. The priest's people were peasants. How could a peasant, no matter how gifted, assume the abbacy of the oldest Christian monastery in the world?

It took the fearlessness of youth to break the social code. Eleven educated young men from Limassol put a hammerlock on the decision-maker in this arena, the Bishop of Larnaca, spiritual lord of eastern Cyprus. "We will all become monks at Stavrovouni," they offered, "but only if you make Father A. the abbot." The bishop capitulated. Along with a rejuvenated monastery and a commendation from the Department of Tourism, he acquired a reputation for truly progressive thinking.

Will there be baseball in heaven?

It is clubhouse lore more than patristic wisdom that men go to seminary to learn about their religion and lose their faith. After leaving the monastic life, I attended a Russian Orthodox cemet … seminary in Pennsylvania for a year. Seminarians at the two more prestigious Orthodox priest schools in America somewhat uncharitably called St. Tikhon's, "a reform school for Slavic delinquents". I went there because an ill-tempered Russian priest got tired of my complaining about the world and told me the world had a far better case against me. My reactive assessment of him as a pietistic clod might have been correct, but no *pneumatikos* could have served me better.

If I couldn't make it as a monk, thought I, the priesthood represented an acceptable compromise. There is great comfort in logic, if only for a while. It's what kept me in law school. "If one couldn't be interested in Constitutional law," I had argued with myself, "what could one possibly be interested in?" I have never practiced law. I did not choose St. Tikhon's because of its Konstamonitouian reputation. I went there because it was the least academic and most liturgically oriented of the three kosher seminaries: the place I could receive Holy Communion daily and most easily practice the Jesus Prayer. I quacked and waddled, but I still thought of myself as a Greek monk.

Whatever my intentions had been on entering that institution, it proved to be a kind of pressure chamber that prevented spiritual bends as I moved between one world and another. I was no more a priest than I was a monk or a lawyer. Priests must believe what they preach to others. They cannot quietly go to bed with their private heresies the way monks and laymen can. At seminary I continued to receive Holy Communion as if I were in a "progressive" Athonite monastery and not among Russians who awaited the second coming of Nicholas the Second and took the same jaundiced view of the Eucharist that Elizabethans took of baths. I spent half of my "bright college year" substituting the entire works of George Eliot for the syllabus and the other half walking and schmoozing with Father V. Borichevsky. We were often late for church, and when I finally did take my place among the baritones in the choir and he departed for the altar, I would open a copy of *The Mill on the Floss* inside my hymnal. Of course, I took the precaution of covering it with brown paper on the front of which I had inked a great purple cross; on the spine, I drew another, more delicate cross and the hand-printed appellation, "Themillon T. Hefloss." Had anyone asked, he was one of the more obscure Church Fathers.

Father V.'s gifts were as different from those of Father A. as his ability to be a source of illumination to others was similar. Father V. was a priest and the Dean of Faculty. He had nine children and a difficult marriage. As far as I knew, he never made more than seventy-five hundred dollars a year. Second-hand books were the walls of his farmhouse, but his purchases had not kept up with the structural needs of his dilapidated barn. As gravity lowered the leaning walls toward an inevitable merging with the horizontal, the priest mused on whether he or the barn would fall down first. He talked about baseball, the weather, and the animals in the fields with the wonder and exuberance of a ten-year old, and he shared his excitement with everyone.

Father V. created peace wherever he went solely by his presence, realigning the confused particles of troubled and angry souls like a magnet. In the year after I left the seminary, I visited him with my Jewish girlfriend – the first woman I'd been with in a mere dozen years. (I later discovered, to my horror, it was thirteen!) Driving toward his house, something made me ask her a crazy question: "Would you like Father V. to hear your confession?" Who ever heard of such a thing? A Jew? Confessing to a Russian Orthodox Christian priest? "Ask and it shall be...." She said she would.

Father V.'s house was furnished in the elaborate chaos common to many Russian households. Nothing was thrown out – ever. On every visit it felt as if everything had been pushed a little to make room for something else or just to find breathing space. His wife always made an affectionate show of barely tolerating new additions to the mess. After we had hunted for the plates of food that she swore were there, the four of us sat where we could and chatted for a while about nothing in particular. Finally, the moment of truth – or how much of it I was prepared to reveal – arrived. The priest asked me if I wanted to make my confession; I nodded and we went upstairs. What I told him never seemed to matter. As he sheltered my bowed head with his stole and said a few introductory words, I felt he knew me so deeply that I had already confessed in detail.

On the way downstairs I asked him about the possibility of his hearing my companion's confession. He laughed. "Fifty years as a priest," he said, "and I have never heard a Jew's confession! Well, why not?" Though he was an ordained cleric in an ethnic church notorious for its anti-Semitism, the two of them went upstairs. The priest and the woman I was living with in sin were together for over an hour. When they descended it was clear they were the best of friends. As we drove away I awkwardly asked "how it had been for her". As if they were the ones having sex. She said that he was indeed a wonderful man but that the hour she spent confessing had been unnecessary.

"While we were sitting around the living room after lunch, talking about this and that," she informed me, her voice tinged with awe, "he answered all the questions I had!" She added that, with the kindest and wisest of smiles, he had thanked her: "… for making John [a.k.a. Richard] human."

Father V. fell before his barn. He died of cancer. His doctor reported that he took nothing to ease his pain, and that in his final moments he looked as at peace "as if he had been watching television". I was astonished to hear that the last name on his lips was mine. Not his wife, not his friends, not his colleagues, but someone who needed him.

Saints wouldn't be saints and we humans wouldn't be a little lower than angels without imperfections. What would it be like to be perfect (assuming that was possible)? How could you relate to anyone or they to you? What if your life were a succession of perfect little circles – as I often thought my was – and not a spiral? Perfection is death. When I can remember to, I pity perfectly beautiful women. How lonely they must be! When I said that the Fathers A. and V. were examples of what it meant to be perfectly human I was including their many and glaring faults. For example, Father A. was quick tempered and had difficulty delegating work. Shame on him for spending seventeen years caring without any help for all who came to him! Father V. ... (hah) well, Father V. never exercised! That's how bad *he* was!

I will now confess what I never confessed to any of my confessors: I continually looked for faults in others like a pig hunting for truffles. Especially in those I admired or, like Father V., I loved. Every flaw I found made them more like me; it also lessened the pressure for me to be more like them.

What is this fengshui stuff?

While you are standing in the middle of Karyes, consult your internal compass and point your feet in the least promising direction. Turn right at the end of the stone wall and climb the rocky steps that lead north – up, up, and away. The municipal path ends at the highway to Dafni. Pause to catch your breath and let the blood resettle in your thighs. Look both ways and cross to the dirt road that runs between two low stone walls through a long archway of overhanging trees. This little bit of New England skirts the gardens behind St. Andrew and connects with the dirt road that runs through the 'burbs, a sparsely settled area of *kellia* and the smaller stone cottages known as *kalyves*.

About a half mile along this path, you will come upon an anomaly: a cut stone thoroughfare. Not tarmac, not concrete, but large blocks of tawny stone. The tolerance of the joints suggests the Appian Way. Was it a chain-gang or a labor of love that created this yellow brick road in the wilderness? Who knows? Perhaps Romans did build the highway and just left it when the peninsula no longer fit in with their strategic needs in the neighborhood. The road leads to Vatopedi, a huge monastery on the north coast that from the sea bears an alarming resemblance to California's San Quentin State Prison, but at its upper end it simply ends. Perhaps the builders were monks, and the road was one of those monastic tasks where the purpose disappears with the doing. Remember, in the world of the monk, obedience and love are synonymous.

Whose labor built the monasteries? Who knows? Who built the Roman Colosseum or the pyramids of Egypt? Chartres Cathedrale? All tombs of the unknown laborer. Who designed them? For thousands of years, most of what men created was anonymous so that all praise went either to their sovereign, to their gods, or to God. The residents of Mount Athos may live in the Garden of the Mother of God and dwell on the indwelling of the Holy Spirit, but it is their buildings that set their peninsula apart from the world. They frequently point to the story of the construction of Simonopetra, the most spectacularly situated of the Athonite monasteries, as proof that faith is rewarded and the Faithful protected. Simonopetra is a massive, three storey compound built on an almost vertical cliff. Because it rests atop an enormous concrete pedestal scarffed into the steep slope, if viewed from the sea it looks ten storeys tall. An ancient, two-tiered aqueduct connects it with the hills behind like an umbilical cord.

As with all the major houses, a patriarch of Constantinople established Simonopetra by charter. Some of the monasteries also are *stavropegic*, meaning that the builders incorporated a piece of the True Cross into the foundation. This piece of wood is not the rarity it might seem. After Helen, mother of Constantine, reputedly discovered the True Cross in Jerusalem in 327, she is alleged to have had it sawn into nineteen pieces for not very safe keeping, since all but four were lost. That still left a lot of wood. Tradition alleges that twelve thousand pieces of varying sizes are scattered throughout the Christian world. Even I have a splinter.

Simonopetra took decades to complete and involved hauling material up from a hostile sea, seven hundred feet below. It is a staple of Athonite history that the builders balked when they saw the perilous site, but a glass of wine slipping from a workman's hand and tumbling hundreds of feet to the shore without the loss of a drop persuaded them the work was blessed. This miracle was embellished so we now know not a single life was lost in the construction. Substantial as the structure is, Simonopetra looks as shaky as that London Bridge of song. The patching of many cycles of style and fortune may give it that quality. Perhaps because of the compound's precarious perch, the mind's eye of the Californian already sees it sliding uninsured into the sea. But then the founders built this monastery, like all the others, with the expectation that it would last no longer than their lifetime. For all anyone knew, many expected, and some no doubt hoped, that might also be the end of the world.

Every monastery on the Holy Mountain claims that some miraculous event accompanied its foundation. The occupants of one even swear to the wandering of an icon across the water from Constantinople a good five hundred years before the arrival of Athanasios, the first Athonite.

There are dozens of stories about how an icon's interposition saved monks and monasteries from pirates or Turks or Catalans, sometimes creating a fog that hid the buildings or threw the invaders into confusion so that they slaughtered each other.

Miracles are to Mount Athos as we regard legends. Not an expression of fact so much as a vision of a different, timeless world. If you don't believe in miracles other than those you encounter every day, you'll be shaking your head all day at such massive credulity. The careless attitude toward time makes the chronological histories of Athonite monasteries difficult to follow – more like a box full of anecdotes than a book. Monks attribute everything that happens to the activity of the divine in their common lives, whether for the good or for the bad; if it is for the good, it is a sign of God's mercy; if for the bad, it is because it is deserved – proof of his just judgment.

The miracle attending the founding of Konstamonitou is that it was ever built. It is the worst sited monastery on the Holy Mountain, and it has the worst weather. Located at the southern end of a valley, it receives no cooling sea breezes from the West during the long and humid summer, while howling north winds bring down snow in the winter. Which is all it deserves since its godparents were folly and fraternal bickering. Two brothers received a grant to build the house in the latter part of the 10th century; but when urgent business took one of them elsewhere, he left everything in his brother's hands. You know the story of the man marooned on an island who built two churches: the one he went to and the one he didn't? On the trusting brother's return from the world, he took one look at what his sibling had wrought and left in an unfraternal but understandable snit to build his own monastery on a nearby slope. There are other tales about Konstamonitou's foundation, including the one shared by other monasteries, to whit, that it was built by Constantine the Great. If true, it must have been his shade, since the emperor saint died about six hundred years before the first monk set foot on Mount Athos. Perhaps in answer to the displeased brother's unspoken prayers, fire and the Catalans destroyed Konstamonitou twice in the first three centuries of its existence. But it rose again, while the breakaway house merely passed into disuse.

Nobody visits Konstamonitou without a strong motivation to do so. It is a nondescript squat little square. It does not even get a point of a lone star in Baedeker's guide to places to stay on the Grand Monastic Tour. But there are those of us who love it. Despite its rocky beginnings and cruel swipes from a world history to which Mount Athos in large part has been peripheral, Konstamonitou has maintained its place among the ruling monasteries, no matter that place is twentieth and last in the pecking order at Karyes. While the peninsula abounds in abandoned minor residential projects, and a few large establishments perished along the way, all of the monasteries that still function, if not flourish, can trace their pedigree to within hailing distance of Athanasios' founding of the Great Lavra.

Fire, wars, and earthquakes have ensured that Fraunce's Tavern, near the Battery in New York, is probably older than eighty per cent of buildings on the Holy Mountain, but most monasteries can still boast sections or towers that have seen nearly a millennium. Contrast the ephemeral permanence of Athos with the permanent transience of modern Athens, where iron rods project skyward from hastily erected cement huts in tearful anticipation of a structural resolution never to be realized – and until then, untaxed. Like the monks it shelters, The Mountain's very persistence might be its greatest miracle.

Your Grace, it's for you – I think it's a Jew.

While methods and materials of construction have undergone considerable change since Mount Athos parted company with the world, they affect only comfort, a temptation with which the monk is familiar, and which he fights with simple food, cold water, and a hard bed. Electricity and the internal combustion engine are another story. Electricity changes the shape of the day and the nature of communication, while the automobile is arguably the dominant invention of the last century, uprooting people and whole towns from traditional ways of doing and being. The automobile, and the ease of electronically transmitting voices and images, has not only fostered the notion that one place is as good as the next, but that there is some virtue – and no great difficulty – in discovering this for oneself. Both electricity and the internal combustion engine are capable of transforming any society, including a monastic one.

There is electricity on Mount Athos, but as yet it is contained. A few monasteries – and even some small *kellia* – own gas-powered generators that provide light and have the capacity to operate machine tools. While all the monasteries have telephone sets, the only electrical connection between Mount Athos and the world is the one, lonely telephone line that guides monks through the wilderness to centers of civilization. The development of the Athonite telephone network, however, is not far behind the experience of the rest of rural Greece, where expansion into the islands and rural areas has depended on the return of the native. A Greek makes his fortune overseas, returns to the *patris* and forks over a large sum of money to run a line from the town out to his property. Then everyone on the route siphons electricity from his service for a relatively minimal hook-up fee.

On Mount Athos, it is unlikely that the cost of running a telephone line the length of the peninsula was a great financial burden. Either it was a group effort, or it was paid for by the Great Lavra, the original and largest of the Greek establishments. Great Lavra is also the second wealthiest monastery (after Vatopedi) and the one closest to the southern tip. Some think it was a waste of money because the actual use of the telephone is conditioned by the fact that Greece, like most Mediterranean societies, is a street culture. Greek monks shout their message into the receiver as if it were merely some silly convention required by progress. On the other hand, Father G. on Paros knew how a telephone worked and hated it for the potential to destroy pure silence that he saw in everything modern and to escape which he had fled the memory of the V-rockets, the Anglican Church, and England.

The telephone has greatly facilitated the circulation of the fleas of rumor that bite everyone on the Holy Mountain. Now, instead of waiting perhaps days or weeks for a piece of juicily distorted news, the latest morsel of *fliaria* (nonsense) is only a dial tone away.

It has also created clairvoyants. I had a taste of this even before I became Orthodox, when I was on Paros, enjoying the amazing hospitality of the Naousans. After two weeks in freebie paradise, the Bishop of Naxos and Paros summoned me to appear at his court to receive his blessing to reside at Longovarda while I prepared to become a Christian. Father G., who accompanied me, made the journey to the island of Naxos slightly longer by refusing to acknowledge the modern asphalt road and zigzagging his way through fields all the way to Parokia, the capital and main port of Paros.

Why I was in such a hurry to get to Parokia, where we took passage on the *S. S. Kyklades*, I do not know. The *Kyklades* was known to locals and tourists alike as the "Sick Sick Cyclades" for its unendearing ability to yaw sadistically in even the calmest sea. And the sea was not calm, my friends. It was winter, and I was violently ill before we turned the headland and staggered east toward Naxos. Short, choppy seas and a screaming north wind had us heeling over to the point where in the eye of my mind our bottom was exposed to the merciless pounding of the waves. I can't say this with certainty, because the eyes that were in my face were fixed masochistically on the horizon, watching it rise and fall and rise and fall. Our noble vessel, having established its ability to roll, now angled her way up a crest and pitched forward and down into the following trough. This activity brought on the yaw – that most nauseating of motions, which only an elephant has been able to replicate on land. I increased my discomfort by stubbornly refusing to offer the contents of my stomach to Poseidon.

It took about a life and a half to crawl across the narrow strait. When we staggered ashore on Naxos, dinner was out of the question. My interior refectory was a shambles. I spent the night stabilizing my wracked equilibrium under a threadbare woolen blanket in a heatless hotel, shivering like a can of paint in a mixing machine even as I tried to warm my chest with fleshless knees. I glared at my snoring companion on his cot, as soundly asleep on his back as Snoopy on the roof of his doghouse. Maybe there is something to not walking on asphalt roads.

The following day, on legs that wouldn't stand up and a stomach that could keep nothing down, I stood before the spiritual lord of two islands, three live and thirty-four defunct monasteries, and waited. Head bowed for fear of throwing up, I heard my friend presumably plead my case while I tried to keep my mind off my condition by contemplating an ancient mosaic of a peacock set in the marble floor.

When Father G. had finished what I imagined was a glowing description of my humble self, His Grace chewed on a few words and a bit of his alabaster beard; then he slowly rose from his throne, the miter resting on his white hair looking too heavy for his head. Capturing a Hebrew is no small coup for an island prelate. As loudly as Paul shouting from Mars hill, the hierarch quoted scripture for all two of us to hear.

"'I saw you while you were still under the fig tree!'" he bellowed.

On another day, I might have appreciated being told that I had walked out of the Bible, but on this one, my problem was walking out of the room. I believe a more correct description of how he knew of my presence on Paros would be: "I heard about you on the telephone from the butcher in

Naousa whose brother is a monk at Longovarda." *Dhen eimai dho kai vlachas.* (Literally, "I am not a shepherd.") I'm from Brooklyn. We sell bridges – we don't buy them.

His Grace, however, must have thought that I did, because he wasn't finished. He squinted into the future.

"Your name will be John," the lord of such decisions accurately foretold.

I had no beef with that. John the Baptist, last of the prophets and first of the apostles, was one of my favorite Biblical characters. Maybe the bishop had taken his cue from my emaciated and pallid visage. But no, nothing so mundane as that.

"As the Baptist was the forerunner of Christ," he continued, vigorously shaking his staff to both God and his absent flock, "so you shall be a forerunner to your people!"

They still are waiting.

I don't know if His Grace also foresaw that it would be some time before I became John. Exactly three months after my interview, on the feast day of the Annunciation, an unerring intelligence (not mine) drove me from Longovarda like a failed Adam leaving Paradise. Nil Sorski, a Russian hermit of the 15th century who met the Prayer of the Heart on Mount Athos, says that so long as a person retains a shred of belief that anyone or anything can help him, he will remain in the spiritual pit. This includes one's own effort, luck, and the Lone Ranger. Even faith in God. In the end, it took a fall off a bike on the Brooklyn Bridge that cracked my head open and overwhelmed my resistance.

As I lay watching an expanding pool of my own blood, not having had a thought about God in months, I heard myself silently say *It doesn't matter if I live or die because I know Christ is with me.* This startling news produced an incredible feeling of peace: a stillness outside time or place. Someone else might have spent a few days with a headache and forgotten about it. Me? No. Way. My life was no longer my own. I went looking for the first baptismal font that would take me.

It took a bit longer than that. At the first church I went to, I was given two pages of mimeographed notes and told to return in the evening. Did I return to Paros? Well ... I couldn't. By scribbling my farewell note to the bishop on a scrap of brown paper retrieved from the floor of the main post office in Athens, I had burned that bridge. Once I had envisioned being baptized in the deep, ancient font that adorned the Church of a Thousand Doors in Parokia; my actual baptism took place in a green oil drum in the living room of a monastery near Boston that was not exactly mainstream Orthodox.

Am I my brother's brother?

Although I have been an abject failure in carrying forward the work of John the Baptist, I have had an equal lack of success in trying to use my "conversion" (ugh!) to demythologize the church's ancient portrait of the Jew as Christ-killer, since the sweet Greek Orthodox woman who smiles at me and says, "Judaism is a good religion, too," cannot see any conflict between this and the Gospel account of who killed Christ that is priests raise to a pogrom pitch during Holy Week. Perhaps she is a natural antinomist. The undeniable fact that Jesus was a Jew makes anti-Semitism a tragic paradox. And yet, as I have already confessed, in the years of my fanaticism, I was as uncharitable to my people as anyone who had never met a Jew, much less was and always will be one!

The relationship between Jews and Christians is as weird as it is natural. It is weird, because for a hundred fifty years after the death of Christ, all were considered Jews. It is natural, because their very reason for being depended on radically different answers as to whether or not the Messiah had indeed come in the person of Jesus.

For a long time, the overwhelmingly more numerous Jews probably regarded Christianity more like a pesky gnat than a serious rival. The existence of a trading network of Jewish colonies throughout the Roman world had made Jews very valuable to the empire, and they enjoyed what we would today call a most-favored nation status. But when Simeon Bar Kochba led the second great Jewish revolt that the Romans crushed in 135, all that changed.

In the wake of their defeat, all Jews were banned from inhabiting Jerusalem and the rest of Judea as well. While the Jewish Christians were swept out with the rest, not even they wanted to be associated with a people who had made such dangerous pests of themselves. Although it was too late to maintain a foothold in the Holy Land, the Christians made a clean break. The former Chief rabbi, Eleazar, to whom the bloody fourteen-year war must have seemed like the end of the world, undoubtedly had made their decision easier by declaring Bar Kochba to be the true Messiah. Rome appreciated brave men, but not foolish acts, and crucified both the alleged Messiah and his prophet – the same punishment that they had conferred on Christ and, in fact, awarded to all criminals who were not Roman citizens. (Paul, a citizen, was beheaded.) Eventually, the ability to organize and communicate, which had appealed to the Romans when the Jews were in their good graces, brought commercial privileges to Christians; not surprisingly, the new sect gained many converts from among fellow Jews.

Christians now began to establish little differences from Jewish practices that would help to maintain separation – just as Paul had advised when he argued with Peter about the need for Christians to be circumcised. Passover became *Pascha*, *Sh'vouth* became Pentecost, Chanukah became Christmas. The Jewish Sabbath was Saturday? Christians rested on Sunday – although they still believed that God completed his work on Saturday. Jews fasted on Monday and Thursday – the two weekdays on which portions of the Torah were read? Christians would fast on Wednesday and Friday – the appointed days of the betrayal and the crucifixion of Christ. Jews can't eat pork or shellfish? (Remember, this was before Chinese restaurants.) To the Christian, nothing is *traif*. The Star of David has six points? The Christian star has eight. Little things – stuff that, "precept by precept, line by line," creates a deep and unbridgeable abyss, so that the shared vision is lost, leaving only the fact of alienation.

But the Jews had forfeited more than their privileged position. They were now stateless, reduced to the status of gypsies and persecuted as such. As was predicted in the Book of Genesis when Cain slew his brother, the Jews would henceforth wander the earth. The ancient psychologist clearly knew what he was talking about when he forecast that everyone would raise their hand against them, but no one would wipe them out. Their suffering on earth would end only with the coming of the Messiah. When the Christians came to power in the 4th century, the Messiah became the Son of God, and pitiless logic led them to add the unabsolvable crime of deicide to the Jews' burden. This gave a moral advantage to those who might otherwise have felt some pity or offered succor to their fallen brothers. So what if this charge ironically made heretics of its advocates, since according to the Council of Chalcedon, in 451, it was the perfect man, Jesus, and not perfect God, who died on the cross?

Get your kicks on route *exsinde-exsi*.

If you set out to design an invention to bring out the worst in people, it would look very much like the automobile. But then, as with most inventions, the collateral damage wasn't part of the design. The automobile is capable of doing to humility and repose on the Holy Mountain what the telephone did for silence. The phone destroys privacy while appearing to enhance it; the car destroys freedom while appearing to expand it, turning everyone into a Marco Polo and an alpha male, creating a new and exciting world with only one person in it (and the occasional passenger). Whether the weapon is a Lamborghini or a Yugo makes no difference: every driver finds some reason to think and act as if they own the road. To use or not to use is no longer a choice. But for the moment, that applies only to the world.

Alas, my opinions, as usual, do not speak for everyone – not even those to whom silence, however relative, has been essential. Do younger monks not see the internal combustion engine as a spiritual concession to modern times? Why should they? They've never known anything else. And how many older monks do you think would turn down a ride? Old age is very humbling. For many, the new age cannot come too soon, but not every monk regards the automobile as either predestined or a second coming. Father G., staunch enemy of the asphalt road, had to be drugged and bound with cords before he would ride in a motor vehicle of any sort, and at the mere perceived threat, some older Athonites have scattered to *kellis* like sheep fleeing before wolves. Motor vehicles, whether on rails or roads and whatever illusions they carry with them, ultimately mean people. When the road to Ouranopolis opened in 1963, Mount Athos aged a thousand years.

Are motor vehicles necessary in a place where time is a backbencher? No. But need has as little bearing on the inverted psychology of newness as the consideration of consequences. A major industry, advertising, bets its existence on this truth: Build it, and they will find a use for it. Or at least a dream. Access to the half-tracks owned by Great Lavra, Iveron, and Simonopetra does not come with your passport, but motor vehicles are not new to you, and they are not why you're here. You have experienced the headaches, and came here to escape such things. To many monks it is still a thrill. When you see one bouncing along happily in the back of a jeep, you are seeing an innocent experiencing the uncommon joys of speed and physical power. Check in with him after a day or two in rush hour traffic, say, on Route I-80 East, out of San Francisco, and he might have a different view. So far, there has been no cry for public transport.

Besides introducing the notion of possibility to what has been forever, the appearance of motor vehicles on Mount Athos has had an immediate effect on wolves. Once was a time when the gray beasts could rely on an occasional meal of careless mule up and down The Mountain. As a fever like that which afflicted Toad in *The Wind in the Willows* swept through the sacred peninsula in anticipation of the motor car, however, the monasteries gave all of their mules to Konstamonitou, the most isolated of the major houses, and one of only two that did not have either a motor vehicle friendly dirt road connecting it with the sea or was directly on the sea itself. The thirty monks of Konstamonitou are very zealous in their care of the wonderful but obstinate creatures, but now and then, one of their charges gets the urge to assert its independence and ignore the closing of the gates at sunset, and the agony attending its mistake can be heard for miles. It makes a wonderful parable for abbots to tell to monks with the urge to go walkabout.

The eclipse of the mule is a shame because that beast is the apotheosis of animal technology on the Holy Mountain. A donkey is not a mule. A donkey has two ears and four legs and a tendency to be stubborn, but there the similarity ends. Mules are superior to donkeys in traversing dangerous trails because a mule will always place its hind hooves exactly where its fore hooves have been. There is no guesswork in it. Watch your cat as it traverses the dinner table without disturbing a fork. The donkey does not offer this feature in any model. Perhaps that – along with its blinking, infuriating obstinacy – is why Greeks believe that the donkey is a gift of the devil.

In the years of my close association with the lunatic fringe, I once boarded a mule for a night trip to an *agripnia* (all-night vigil) celebrating the annual feast day of a *fanatikos kelli* in Kavsokalivia ("burned houses"), a semi-eremitic community in the rugged foothills southwest of the Mountain of Athos. Stealing though the moonless night to worship in secret, I felt like I was an early Christian avoiding the persecuting Romans – the vast majority of the Orthodox Church. We descended eight hundred feet on a trail I saw only on our ascent the following morning. All that slipping and sliding and rocks I'd heard rolling off the path but never landing? The entire length of the ribbon-like trail ran a foot from the edge of a precipice from which one could have dropped a plumb line to the sea.

Had I not made it, I would have been spared an experience that made me wonder what any of us were doing at this remote site, isolated by our own choosing not only from human contact but from those of our own kind whom we had judged as being a little too familiar with the ways of the world. There must have been two hundred *zylotes* at the *kelli* that night. They ate, drank, and sang songs from dusk until dawn. Occasionally, some entered the church to take their place in the choir as the service moved inexorably from the Ninth Hour to Vespers to the Midnight Office to Matins and through the Divine Liturgy. And there I was, thinking this was indeed a strange way to prepare for Holy Communion, and wasn't that the reason we all were there, God damn it!? Apparently not. The chalice came out and went back in, *intactu*. I could have forced my way in, but, frankly, I was scared. What if they were offended by my over-familiarity with the cup? They might have stripped me of my *fanatikos* button!

Hi ho, hi ho, it's off the cliff we go.

Wild animals and treacherous trails aren't the only natural dangers on Mount Athos. In the dense forests and look-alike valleys, one can get lost and never found, and the sea has swept many a monk off a rocky path, never to be seen again. The weather can also make radical changes in the topography, and there is nothing to warn the traveler on foot but word of mouth.

The Romanian *skiti* of Timion Prodromos is on the tip of the peninsula, an hour's walk from Great Lavra. Having tired of Greeks, I once spent a couple of weeks at the *skiti*, doing what the Romanian monks did – which was the same as what Greek monks do – and eating Romanian food, featuring *mamaliga* (polenta). On my departure, I decided I wanted to visit (the always "dread") Karoulia, the remote and rocky place between the sky and the sea to which a certain breed of monk banish themselves when they can no longer live among or anywhere near others. A mile out from Timion Prodromos, a fork indicated that there was a high road to the right, and a low road to the left. I wasn't in a climbing mood. Not long after beginning my descent, I came to a halt where a rockslide had cut the trail. An unbroken slope of pulverized black stone fell a good three hundred feet to the sea, waves gnawing at its feet. From where I stood, I could see that there was a footpath worn into the slide by numerous passages across it. When I call it a footpath, I am being literal. It was about a foot wide. In length, it was about an eighth of a mile. Something over two hundred yards. I can only imagine the patience and unassuming bravery that went into making that little ledge. Not the donkey-like obstinacy and stupidity that I was about to exhibit. *Okay,* I said, *I can do this,* and I tightened my belt.

About twenty steps onto the slide, the path disappeared. I knew it was there, because I had seen it when I was at a distance from it.... Hadn't I? Or had it been the always-blamable devil? What ev. Now, all I could even *feel* of the path was the postcard on which I was standing. Go back? That meant climbing. Besides, I *never* go *back*. Besides besides, I was carrying my prayer rope. Where was my alleged faith!?

I imagine nothing tempts the mercy of God like an unnecessary test, as if there weren't enough trials in the course of a day to bring one to the point of despair. I reached mine faster than an engine with a busted thermostat. Topographically, I was blind. I could shout, but it would be half a clap. I could cry, but the thirsty shale would have sucked up my tears. Who would find my crushed and mangled body? Would it be the mule-starved wolves? Or the razor-beaked birds that dined on those afflicted with hubris? The only thing going faster than my prayer rope was my heart. I prayed to everybody, including my high school tennis coach, who taught me how to cheat. I made impossible vows, the performance of which depended on a guarantee of my safety.

An eighth of a mile isn't all that long, unless you measure your progress by the inch. When I was about ten feet shy of my goal, and safety beckoned like Salome dropping her veils, I was tempted to make a run for it. I looked down to my left and didn't. Most accidents happen within half a mile of home. My lips mumbling a mile a minute, I shuffled onward. Minutes later, my foot crossed the line that divided black, treacherous gravel from dusty terra firma. When my other foot pulled up alongside its fellow I felt as if I had landed on Plymouth Rock. As I took my first unlabored breath of the past half hour, my vows disappeared faster than the Pilgrims' promises to the Indians.

As sure as death and taxes…. Okay, monks don't pay taxes.

If the elder generation is changing the shape of the age pyramid throughout the world, this is old hat in Athos. While medical treatment is far from sophisticated and not always available, a monastery itself is a kind of spiritual and a physical hospital, in the ancient Asclepian tradition that respected the dialogue between body and soul: when having a psychosomatic illness meant that you were the opposite of insane. It is a workplace that is also a retirement community. Every monastery has an infirmary, the principal function of which appears to be less curative than the maintenance of mental and emotional stability. This dedicated room is kept as warm as resources will allow. The heat mingles with the unwashed bodies of those who reside there to produce a miasma from which one would think germs would leave of their own accord. A serious illness sometimes warrants a trip to Thessalonica, but monks subject most sicknesses to either prayer or denial or to treatment with lemon juice, the bruited healing properties of which occupy a dimension far beyond Vitamin C. and make it a serious rival of the olive. In the case of rheumatoid arthritis, it is applied in the form of soaked poultices. Joint inflammation is not uncommon in a damp place where heat out of season is not merely an alien concept, but frowned on by Tradition.

"The season" is from November 21st to March 25th. Monks light the first fires on the Feast of the Entrance of Mary into the Temple, and on the Feast of the Annunciation, they bank the last embers, shut down the flues, and sweep away the ashes. As many a bone-chilled visitor to Greece can attest, what religious call "the season" does not always correspond to winter, the season. Beginning in late October, the winds come out of Russia, force their way through the Bosporus, and ravage the Aegean, bringing four or five months of relentless, unmarketable cold, with an occasional day in the seventies that has you looking up and about in the cloudless sky for who turned on the switch.

There are times when Athonites recognize local remedies as inadequate and an affliction forces them to resort to the advances available at pharmacies in the outside world. When I left Konstamonitou, Father B., the young monk who worried about my soul as much as I worried about his inability to smile, promised to carve a postcard-sized icon of John the Baptist on a block of rosewood and send it to me in New York. Weeks passed, and no icon. I wrote to him, inquiring as to the progress he was making on my gift. His response was plaintive. For the past three weeks, he wrote, he had been suffering from *diskiliohtees,* a beautiful word that my dictionary translated as "constipation". A direct consequence of this affliction was that he could not sit down for any length of time and therefore had been unable to complete "our" project.

The pitiful plight of my one-time housemate immediately aroused in me a selfless compassion. With my next letter, I enclosed three boxes of Ex-Lax, along with the facetious command to get back to work. Whether his recovery was due to the treatment, or to being conditioned to obedience, I do not know, but the magnificent icon arrived shortly after, carved by the steady hand of a workman clearly comfortable with his seat. In the ancient tradition that all shall pass and be forgot, no signature or initials allowed anyone who did not know him to praise the artist for a job well done.

When all else fails, it is usually only a short, swift trip to the monastery graveyard. While I do not wish to dwell on a subject that makes outsiders queasy even as it gives insiders hope, the Athonite way of death deserves some discussion, if only for the sharp contrast with that which surrounds *our* shuffling off this mortal coil. No long line of limousines wending their way to the cemetery escorted by motorcycles, no polished hardwood casket to keep the worms from their work, no sunken bronze plate to fool visitors into thinking they are not in a repository of the dead, no eulogy or obituary.

No, in Mount Athos, after a short church service, the deceased, whoever he is and no matter how many decades he has spent in the monastery, is carried on a rough plank to the graveyard and dumped into an open pit like the soul-deprived carcass he now is. Old wine in the vinegar vat. Sometimes, the plank is lowered on top of him to give the corpse a little protection from the falling clods of earth before he is covered over with dirt. A monk sticks a jury-rigged wooden cross into the disturbed ground. And that is that. Like a junked car: wrecked or obsolete, what does is matter how it got there? And who can pass an automobile graveyard without getting a creepy sense of one's own mortality?

The crude cross, blank where a name might be, more closely resembles the marker stuck into the soil of a potted plant – the one that gives you information about the care of your purchase – than a memorial. Well, why should it be anything more? Cemeteries on Mount Athos do not take up much space, because after three years, the whitened bones of the dead are unearthed. The skull is tagged with an I.D., the skeleton is thrown on a heap, and the whole package is placed in a *leipsanon* – a bone storeroom – in the company of everyone who has ever died there, to await the general Resurrection. On that day, they will all find their way back together into whatever as-yet-unknown physical configuration is consistent with that event. Some seem to think they know when that day will be; many have thought they knew. The piles of bones remain. In the *leipsanon* at Mar Saba, in Israel, there is a collection of over sixteen hundred skulls that owe their place to a single event – a visit to the monastery by Persians in 617. Incidentally, Mar Saba does not have an official cemetery; instead, the bodies are thrown into a sewer in front of the church and pulled out after two years, by which time rats have picked the bones clean. When a monk is dead, he is gone, brother. As I have mentioned, friendships are not encouraged.

For the bones of those already adjudged saints, however, and which can therefore intercede with God, there is a different fate. Hands, thigh-bones, pieces of skull – if bearing the mark of a Turkish axe, so much the better – are stored in beautifully crafted boxes in the church and brought out by a priest for the delectation of (Orthodox) visitors the way the guest master proffers squares of *loukoumi*.

The mainstream Orthodox Church is very down to earth concerning the limits of human knowledge and has little to say about the afterlife except that it exists. About the future afterlife, they are even more reticent. The canons consider the Book of Revelation to be so dangerously speculative that they do not allow it to be read in church. It is not surprising, therefore, that Greeks love it…. Okay, so does the soul need the body to effect its return? This is a point of passionate theological dispute. Perhaps why the skull – the last known address of the soul – receives such heady treatment. But what happens to souls before Judgment Day? Is there a pre-Heaven Heaven? Where did Enoch and Elijah go – the only humans besides the incarnate Christ that the Bible says did not die? Is "falling asleep," as Mary is alleged to have done, a metaphor for the limit of our knowledge as well as the strength of our hopes? It is no accident that the Dormition (Assumption) of Mary, celebrated on August 15th, is the last major feast in the yearly liturgical cycle that begins on the first day of September, just as the first feast is Mary's birth.

An I for an I, but not my tooth!

Along with lemons, herbs are very popular among the healing profession on Mount Athos. The hot, enamel mugs of tea that greet monks every morning after four or five or more hours in a stone cold church contain a profuse infusion of an adventurous bouquet of variegated leaves collectively called "mountain tea". Considering the harsh climate and lack of heat on The Mountain, most monks are remarkably healthy, although hypochondria is one of the more acceptable comforts. Especially when there is no one to make a diagnosis, ailments can offer an unlimited source of complaints and camaraderie. A doctor comes around every few months, but that still gives monks plenty of time to develop a meaningful relationship with some real or imagined illness.

However he might protest about the ephemeral quality of his physical state, the monastic diet and the relative freedom from the stress occasioned by the fight for physical survival and procreation and not chasing women and all the intermediate goals that are stepping stones to that ultimate end are conducive to the long, healthy life that many monks seem to see as such an affliction. In the ten years I spent in that world, living much of the time in threadbare clothing in stone buildings without heat, I was not sick a single day! Not one. Even my brain-numbing headaches took the decade off. There is also considerable physical exercise, whether from the monastic labors concerned with maintenance and sustenance, or the effort required to get practically anywhere on the peninsula, or making *metanoias*, the spiritual push-ups done in one's cell at night. I slept between four and six hours a day (including the morning nap) and don't recall ever feeling tired. If many monks appear to be overweight, I imagine it is mostly due to the general immobility of age or the need to provide oneself with copious amounts of internal heat during the winter in the absence of external sources.

The care of one's teeth is not a subject often dealt with in monastic guidebooks; as a result, I paid dearly for my pious disregard of oral maintenance. It is hard to imagine an aching tooth, but if there were any dental hypochondriacs, a visit to the dentist (*ogdhondyiatros*) that resides in Karyes would provide a reality check. His office does not know electricity in any form. The whirring of his primitive drill comes from vigorously pumping a foot-pedal. No certificate of graduation from – or even attendance at – a professional school adorns the wall of his modest office, and where he received his training, and in what, is a mystery that is not a sacrament. The space between the arm of his drill and the sink is a web of drying spit so thick that a scorpion could make its way across it. It would be best not look into the sink itself because you need to remain conscious.

The dentist sterilizes his instruments with *ouzo*. The licorice cordial does double-duty as an anesthetic. This makes sense, because I find it difficult to believe that anyone would allow this tooth person to shove a needle into his gums, unless he was drunk. But then, I do not believe he knows from anesthesia, so the issue is moot. I also find it hard to believe that in his role as dental practitioner this monk betrays his monastic habit and washes his hands. He has the air of someone for whom choosing which tooth to extract is a form of Russian – or Turkish – roulette. He may be seen without an appointment. If you're unlucky, he'll be there. On the one occasion I sought his help, I lost faith in the power of prayer, eased myself out of his chair, and fled to Thessalonica.

Oh, ye of little faith. I would have been better off blindly surrendering to the Athonite amateur than the pagan professional I encountered. Grateful for her pro bono offer, I did not ask for references, but somewhere between waves of pain, I caught the word "student". Not only did she pull the wrong tooth, but then she pulled the right tooth, and, lastly, the tooth she had left isolated without support. Having nothing to bite on, the lower molars eventually came loose. Then, through overuse caused by the need to compensate, the same thing happened on the other side of my mouth. On Athos, I would merely have died immediately of sepsis.

When is an icon not an icon and what does it cost?

Fortunately, only one person on the Holy Mountain practices dentistry as a hobby. On the other hand, the carving of icons is a not uncommon among monks. Technically, icono*graph*ers don't paint or carve icons; they write them. None of the three great monotheistic faiths permit the worship of representational paintings or objects. The lawyers of the Orthodox Church got around this by calling religious artwork "writing". Writing is venerable; veneration is not worship. Jews kiss the Torah and flames do not immediately consume them.

Down on earth, somewhere in the migration westward, the prohibition against images was temporized and transformed. Necessity might have been the mother of fudging. Christianity may be the faith of fishermen and its praxis a matter of, well, practice, but its theology isn't quite as straightforward as baiting a hook. The church recognized early that if it were going to embalm the more visceral faiths that it conquered, Christian theology would have to spin a more visceral cocoon. Since most people could not read, it resorted to painting a picture or many pictures, just as its predecessors had done, while the Divine Liturgy replaced ancient ritual and dance.

Icons are venerated (*proskynisis*), but never worshipped (*latreia*). The most anyone can say about how icons "work" is that they are not the paintings they seem to be but representations of people with qualities that have been found worthy of, well, veneration. Anyone who says much more about *how* they work – and many have – is like Br'er Rabbit trying to unstick himself from the Tar Baby. A primary purpose of icons is to make theology compatible with group history. To this end, there are icons of men and women who were definitely not Christian but who nevertheless were revered members of the tribe. The monks of Mount Athos have grandfathered Plato, Aristotle, and Socrates into the faith as too important to Greek identity to omit. Religion does not circle the world, looking for some culture to land on. It is inseparable from culture. It grows out of the soil in which its seed is planted as surely as does a tree.

The question of when a painting becomes an icon – if it ever does – headed the agenda of the seventh and final Ecumenical Council, in 787. Passions ran high: in the decades preceding the convocation, icons had been hunted like witches and hidden like saints. As Wellington remarked after Waterloo, the synod "was a close-run thing". In the end, the assembly decided for the iconodules (lovers of icons) and against the iconoclasts (the opposite). For the common person with common sense who cannot and does not accept the subtleties of calling icon painting, "writing", the rationale is another example of the brilliant disdain that Orthodoxy has for either/or thinking. Yes, until the icon becomes an icon, it is canvas (or wood) or paint, just as a cross is wood until it becomes a cross. At the moment that it does, however, while never ceasing to be wood or paint, it becomes venerable. It may be blessed, but it cannot give a blessing. You can ask the priest for a blessing through the cross; you can ask for the blessing of the saint that ineffably inhabits the icon.

With this kind of logic, it should come as no surprise that the Holy Fathers of the Seventh Ecumenical Council were only partially successful in putting the issue to bed. Twelve hundred years after the ultimate synod, the difference between veneration and worship still is not always apparent. In the unlikely event you perhaps forget to set your clock back one Sunday in the fall and get to a church in the world early, observe the different ways people express their devotion in front of the icon of the day awaiting them in the narthex. Some don't dare to touch the painted surface, fearing the fickle wrath of God or some disease left by the lips of others, while others literally slobber over it. Still others just walk past without so much as a hello. While this is nobody's business, when I was wearing my fanatic hat I often made it my business. And on Mount Athos others sometimes made my business their business. Such is the food chain of the pietistic.

During my sojourn at Esphigmenou during Great Lent, I refused to venerate a certain icon of the Mother of God in the refectory favored by all others *which*, I opined, while due a *kind* of veneration, was of a kind inferior to that due the neighboring icon of Christ, *which*, gentlemen of the jury, took one's words directly to the ear of the one whom one *worshipped*.

Nobody told me who squealed, but word of my heresy sped up the aforementioned food chain; I was hauled before the monastery council and asked, "Have you ever or do you now advocate the non-veneration of the Mother of God for failing to be the equal of her Son?" I submitted my rationale. What was I thinking? My Greek, while good enough to get me into this pickle of not necessarily conflicting interpretations, was not up to get me out. When I was a kid playing Cowboys and Indians, I was the one who wanted to be an Indian, but such independent behavior is not encouraged in a brotherhood. Like another of my childhood heroes, Joan of Arc, I refused to recant. They didn't burn me, but they did ban me from receiving communion on *Pascha*, the holiest day of the year, banishing me to k. p. While they announced the Resurrection, I gutted fish.

"I'd like the kitchen in robin's egg blue and the bathroom in cherry red."

Had Father N. of Constantinople, Paris, and Paros, clothed his models, showed them the door, and tried to make it as an iconographer, he would have discovered that Caesar and God had different ideas about the artistic life. Toulouse Lautrec might have summoned his genie out of a bottle of anisette, but writing an icon is a sacred act. A monk is supposed to fast and pray before and during a ritual whose forms, methods, and materials remain what they were in St. Athanasios' day.

At least one iconographer living in the world, the renowned Fotios Kontaglou, who is credited with the revival of Byzantine iconography after centuries of neglect, was hard put to deal with the dilemma of selling work he considered to be a sacred gift as a piece of "art" commanding a high price. At the same time, he needed to support himself and his family. One day, while watching men hauling bricks at a construction site, he asked himself, "Why should I be paid more than those laborers, who do so much more for the world?" Thereafter, he multiplied his hours by a laborer's minimum wage to get his price – one way to "live in the world and not be of it".

A carver monk will sell the labor of three years for a few hundred dollars. I'm talking about a cherry wood tableau of considerable size, replete with intertwined wooden filigrees of impossible intricacy and delicacy. He has the same disdain for business that he displays toward time. If it gets him enough to eat, what does he care if the purchaser resells the product of his soul and body for ten times what he received? Up to the present, the needs of the two worlds have been vastly different. Until the second coming of the Yankee Peddler (i.e., modern technology) there was little in the world that monks weren't prepared to reject out of hand. Now, trinkets from the late industrial age dangle before the eyes of the aboriginal monk, and he has no ready defense. To pay for these things requires not only a rethinking of one's philosophy but a retooling of one's workshop. But if monasteries do invest in modern woodworking machines (or, what is more likely, someone from the world invests in them), I do hope they operate them with a greater eye to safety than I personally observed on my first visit to Konstamonitou.

When I mentioned to one of the monks there that I was "kind of a carpenter", he proudly showed me an ancient band saw that lorded it over his workshop like Madame Guillotine. Eight to ten feet of its jagged blade was exposed, and no light glinted off the pitted surface. While I trembled nervously, my host gassed the sucker up, and the shuddering blade began to describe a double helix with teeth. While the carpenter-monk blithely went about his business in front of his rapidly oxidizing instrument, I readied myself to hit the hay at the twang of a snapped blade. I was particularly stressed because I had once shaken hands with Greek I met in a church in Toronto, who wouldn't let go of my hand as he told me about a carpenter whose right arm had been severed by the flying blade of a band saw.

"It was like a bull whip," he said. "The arm came zip!... right off! And, do you know where it is now?" He tightened his grip.

It is not good to rely on miracles.

Hard to believe.

Miracles are to beliefs as pictures are to words in their relative power to impress. Miracles failed to move the Israelites in the wilderness because, like beliefs, the power of miracles falls far short of faith. For forty years God wowed the emigrés with miracles in abundance; each time, after a brief flirtation with belief, their faith failed. We witness miracles and experience other wake-up calls every day, and most of the time they, too, produce at best a passing, heightened awareness. But this should not surprise us. The human being is the only creature that has so alienated itself from its own nature that it actually *needs* a God.

True belief is an oxymoron. We cling to beliefs, but the truth that makes us free us is self-evident. True faith is the simple conviction that if you take care of your business, God will take care of his, and if he doesn't, what business is it of yours, anyway? It is going to sleep and not worrying if either the promised manna or you will be there in the morning. We can argue about belief, but faith is indisputable. Belief is the fall-back position when faith fails – the candle we keep lit until the electricity comes back on. Beliefs don't change our lives, although we are not shy about using them to try to change others. Exclusive belief can actually be destructive of faith in God.

Beliefs eventually either dissolve into faith or point a finger at our faithlessness – like the words of the Jesus Prayer, which the monk says over and over until it becomes gibberish or silently enters his heart and sustains him. It is belief, not faith, which raises moral questions about why things happen and about good and evil: riddles that cannot be resolved and into which a good monk does not inquire. A monk will never receive his abbot's blessing to ask the horribly existential why – the radical question that suggests disobedience, which is faithlessness.

No monk has perfect faith. He constantly tests God, and in doing so is tested in return. Like his Israelite ancestors and those lost in the mist of unrecorded history, time and again he fails to discern the particular path chosen for him. Being human, it is not unusual even for a monk who has taken vows to forget the terms of this contract, like a disgruntled baseball player in mid-season. Father G., the reclusive Englishman who introduced me to the Orthodox Christian world and willfully avoided roads, also flouted or circumvented every order of his abbot that involved the acceptance of anything modern. He practically accused the *epitropos* who had purchased a refrigerator of heresy. He would never have admitted to compromising the sacrament of confession, but at the time we met, he hadn't confessed to his revered abbot for three years because he didn't trust him – an opinion in which he was encouraged and supported by his confidant, the worldly Father N. Yet, his abbot was the only one to whom he could confess that he couldn't confess!

In many ways, Father G. was the Perfect Monk, constantly reproaching himself for his failings and working out his salvation in fear and trembling. Perhaps he had forgotten that his abbot's beliefs would not invalidate his confession. Perhaps he could not see God's will in being saddled with his abbot (or his abbot with him). On the other hand, when I asked him to pray that the darkness be lifted from my benighted mother's eyes and her heart be turned toward Christ, his reply was as unexceptionable as my request is now incomprehensible: "I will not. I will pray only that God's will be done."

That was faith. But to wait on God's will is not always so. The sole monastic practitioner of the original craft of writing icons on *koliva* – the edible memorial to the dead – was a peripatetic. He was no talking dog: his work was of such quality that it deserved to be hung in a gallery, but if it made it out the church door, it was only to be consumed in the refectory. I had no idea where he lived. Either he found monastery life uncongenial, or it found him insufferable. I never saw him smile. Dirt seemed to hang around him like Pigpen, in *Peanuts*, and he had a gimpy leg. Whenever our paths crossed, I worried about the state of his soul compared, of course, to mine.

By the time I spoke to him, as we awaited the arrival of the boat to Dafni at Panteleimon's *arsanas*, I had seen him many times and he had seen me seeing him. He also knew my story. For all its emptiness, the Holy Mountain is a small community of less than two thousand. After maybe ten minutes of silence, during which I paraded my prayer rope, hoping to avoid conversation, he raised his thickly bearded chin and asked me when I would become a monk – that is, when would I take vows. The abrupt directness of the question, coming from an unexpected source, threw me. I did not think. I fell back on the answer I always gave to this question. I threw up my hands, shrugged my shoulders, and petitioned the treetops. "When God wills," I said in flawless Greek – as indeed it should have been, considering how often I had exercised that pious phrase. It always worked: a laugh, no further questions, and the hook came up picked of its bait. I smiled charmingly. I don't know if the iconographer spat, but he might as well have. Certainly, his reply, "So God speaks to you?" felt like spit.

There's always a will in the way.

At the penny arcade of history, my English friend and I were small fry in the game of imparting divine concurrence to our actions, or righteousness to our failure to act. In that river-bound arena known as the Garden of Eden, where archetypal man revealed the bloom on every neurosis that science has only recently discovered, Adam ate the forbidden fruit and laid the ultimate responsibility on a benevolent God. "The woman *you* gave me...." It's a wonder God waited until the time of Noah to wipe humankind off the earth.

To know God's will perfectly is perfectly impossible. To strive to know the unknowable is not. The greyhound that finally catches the rabbit makes itself useless, but it will spend its life chasing its perfection because it was born to do it. The monk sees his free will as Adam failed to see his – as a very great responsibility to do very little. So he guards the revelation he has had that God's will is not in the earthquake or the fire or the wind, but in the "still small voice" that discovered Elijah when he was lost and afraid. He sees it in what the apostle of love experienced on Christ's breast at the Last Supper when it was clear he wasn't listening to the master's words but to the beating of his heart. God's will is in what the *Hasid* learned by watching the blessed *maggid* (teacher) lace up his shoes. There are moments in everyone's life when we feel as if we are sitting in God's "lap", knowing where everything is and sure that wherever it is and however wrong it might look it is somehow right. The aim of the monk's life is to fine tune the instrument that receives the call to that experience – to wait patiently for his personal darkness to comprehend the light that lights everyone who comes into the world.

On the other hand, discerning the will of God has never been a problem for Americans, for whom manifest destiny was a God and Darwin-given opportunity for expansion across a continent as well as a profitable exercise of free will. From the Protestant pulpit, happiness was no longer one of the many virtues that shape life intermittently. Instead, it became the rightful and paramount object of human pursuit. Even an entitlement. This was the religious expression of the rebellious spirit of the Renaissance that we call the Reformation, and it has since been used by atheists and deists alike. The ancient Jews railed at God and expected no answer. The Catholic Church had its mysteries. But Protestants peevishly removed all the visible aids that drew worshippers into an unknowable God and saved only scripture, the words that could be manipulated to give any number of comfortable answers to "What would you *like* it to be?" After the Renaissance it was no longer enough that we lived and that the answer to why was implicit in the existence or silence of God. Whether our life was in our own hands or pre-determined, we demanded a meaning we could understand and with which we could agree. We could even choose our denomination and the place in which we worshipped, and change both if they did not make us happy. So much for the will of God.

Rodan meets Godzilla

Father G., my mentor on Paros, told me that the two elements of Orthodox theology that trouble converts the most are the veneration of saints and the Theotokos. In my case, at least, he was right. For someone who did not receive it in their mother's milk, belief in the intercession of others and the virgin birth require a level of humility not easily come by. If it is hard for an Orthodox to believe in them, imagine how it must be for someone to whom the whole religion makes no sense. And if non-Orthodox find the idea of saints and the Mother of God difficult to swallow, what must they think when they see people kissing what to them is nothing but paint?

While I was at Longovarda, I invited my mother to the scene of my most recent attempt to compromise her sanity. My aim in doing this was to show her that Father G. did not fit her profile of a religious "brainwasher". He might even be someone she could like. When I extended the invitation, it did not occur to me what a wonderful job I had done in portraying her to my alleged "Svengali" as his rival in evil doing – the archetypical Jewish Ogre Mother, whose lone reason for existing was to drive the inner monk out of her suffering son.

The spot that I chose for their rendezvous was the little, white chapel just across the road that ran between the charming fishing village of Naousa (pop. 600) and bustling Parokia (pop. 6000), opposite the monastery garden. On a beautiful May day, I escorted my mother, then in her late sixties but a world-class walker into her nineties, from her hotel to the meeting place – a distance of about three miles. We arrived there a few minutes early. Always prompt, Father G. appeared immediately after us, unaccompanied by a second and without any visible armament.

My mother is less than five feet tall and slight. Father G. is robust, broad-shouldered, and slightly over six feet in height. Introductions took place, weapons were chosen, and they took their places. Both aimed their considerable charm directly at the other. Father G. gave my mother a tour of the chapel. As he entered, he crossed himself and lowered his lips to graze the icons reposing on stands on either side of the door. I followed suit. He then explained the structure of the church, tiptoeing delicately across the theology of icons, incense, prayer, and anything else that might have caused her the slightest discomfort. After a few minutes in the cool interior, we exited and sat for a while in the miniscule courtyard, protected from the sun and the road by cypress trees, while my companions outdid one another in their praise of me. They agreed that my having graduated from Yale Law School indicated superior intelligence, but Father G. did not opine that my forsaking the life it promised was a step up, while my mother did not reveal to him the number of roofs from which she had been inclined to jump. When they parted, they shook hands with what I perceived to be genuine warmth.

Father G. disappeared up the path to the monastery. "Well?" I asked my mother, not without a trace of smugness for my role in ending the Cold

War. "What do you think now? Do you still think I was brainwashed? Do you still think he is my … 'Svengali'?"

"He is a very nice man," my mother admitted, and to her credit she had nothing but kind words for him ever after, and he for her. "But when you kissed that picture, I wanted to vomit."

One day, the Mad Hatter had a tea party.

The rebels of Esphigmenou granted me entrance to their lair in the first place only because they accepted my spiritual passport. Like those who have found that to visit Jordan while in Israel they must go by way of non-Jewish Cyprus, I was coming from a *kelli* whose inhabitants also did not commemorate the Ecumenical Patriarch. The monk who operated the *caique* that brought me to the *arsanas* in a driving rain must not have agreed with their politics, because as I stepped over the gunwale and unto the shore he had hurled my duffel bag some thirty feet through the air without a wide receiver in sight. Even with a few inches of mud to cushion the fall, the impact opened it up like a burst squash.

While I stoically retrieved the scattered and soiled contents of my bag, a middle-aged, shmooish monk shuffled over and proceeded to circle me like a one-man Pawnee raiding party. His thin, gray hair stretched tight against his head and culminated in a stiff, frizzy, rat-tail a few inches down his back. Having determined that I was unarmed and did not look as if I had mastered karate, he finally approached, stuck his face toward me, and sniffed me out. Tossing his head back suddenly as if a fly had settled on his nose, he rotated his arm like a softball pitcher before (literally) spitting "*Apo pou eiste!*" ("Where are you from?")

"*Nea Yorki,*" I told him.

"*Orthodoxus?*" he inquired.

I smiled modestly, eyes bowed, and replied "*Malista*"— a polite way of saying "*neh*". This slightly affected word was a product of my *Teach Yourself Greek* book, from which I learned other archaic words and phrases that were of marginal use in communicating but a great source of amusement to amusement-starved monks. Among the useful tidbits was *alas*, the ancient Doric word for salt, last uttered in public by Homer and which guaranteed me a guffaw. "*Aaaahlaaas, Ioanni? Aaaahlas?*" (Ho ho ho.) I also learned a rhythmic, important-sounding phrase, *Peran passis amphivolias*, that meant "beyond the shadow of a doubt". This proved to be an especial cause for great merriment to my hosts, who appreciated my great learning while puzzled by my greater ignorance. Apparently this phrase is from another kind of Greek called *katharevousa*, which is no longer in use, and which, I am told, was never spoken, appearing only in newspapers and diplomatic dispatches. After my initial embarrassment, I must admit I was not altogether unaware of the response my ingénue act was likely to produce and used this to my advantage.

It may have been that polite yes in a place where manners suggest "foreigner" that caused my pear-shaped inquisitor to raise his eyes and tchitch with his lips. It might have been the fact that all answers from *xenoi* are suspect.

"*Dhen einai Orthodoxos stin Ameriki*" ("There *are* no Orthodox in America"), he expostulated as if it were somewhere in scripture. Having proved to his satisfaction that I did not really exist, he turned and waddled away. In a sense I had to admire his canine decisiveness. In retrospect I can also appreciate his perspective, even if what he really meant was, "Outside of Esphigmenou there are no Orthodox – period!" We neither pick our prophets nor do we always recognize them. It took me years to discover for myself that there probably *are* no Orthodox Christians in America because any immigrant who wasn't a registered Protestant was one in spirit. American Jews, Muslims, Jains, Buddhists, Catholics, and Orthodox Christians are all philosophically Protestants. They weren't happy with the way things were and always had been and emigrating across the ocean was their protest. Of course, there were those who have tried to live here as if here were over there, and have welcomed extinction as long as they could stay who they were until they died. Which, as I think of it, also is a protest.

The shmoo's comment was revealing in another way. Did he say what he did because he visualized America as a spiritual wasteland, because he disliked Americans, or was it because he believed all Orthodox had to be Greek? Was he expressing – God forbid – an opinion? Monks are discouraged from having opinions. There is only God and the teachings of the church. They are forbidden to ask why because, "as the Fathers say", they will use it to challenge their belief in God. Eve seduced Adam with a why, and as a consequence monks cower in the shadow of women. Why, she asked, should she and her man listen to a God who talks to innocents about complicated abstracts they have never experienced and cannot understand? And Adam had no answer with which to satisfy that question because there was none.

This is not to say that Greek monks are any less skeptical about the concerns of the world than those in the world are about them and their priorities. Neither does having no opinions necessarily eliminate prejudice or intolerance. Xenophobia is part of the national consciousness, and Greek monks can't help being Greek. Greek monks hate what all Greeks hate – for instance, Turks and unripe olives. But, to Greeks, those hatreds aren't opinions but incontrovertible truth. As for the rest, having retired to battle the grayness in their souls, there is no reason for them to see anything external to its workings in shades other than black and white.

The greatest danger that opinion poses to a monk is that it puts him squarely on the lip of the spiritual quicksand in which one judges others. Once the seed of judgment takes root, it is almost impossible to dig it out, infecting everything it meets as it gathers evidence of its own righteousness. And the consequences of judging don't wait for a Judgment Day. Whosoever judges their spouse will find themselves outside their marriage. Whosoever judges their friends will find themselves without friends. Whosoever judges their neighbors will inevitably wind up outside the church.

I wish I had said as much to the guest master at Esphigmenou who, prior to the Easter Massacre, had accused me of harboring "satanic delusions" when I told him that during the night a rat had fallen out of the ceiling of my room and landed on me. I don't know what good it would have done, since a few months before he'd accused another American I knew of the very same thing when the very same thing happened to him. But it might have made him reconsider his evaluation and think exterminator before exorcist. On the other hand, that it was a repeat performance might only have confirmed the shmoo's opinion of Orthodoxy in America.

It was for Socrates' suggesting that opinion severely impedes a person seeking the truth that embarrassed Athenians put him to death. It was because the monk of St. Catherine's expressed nothing but opinions that Kazantzakis gave him the gift of doubt. Sifting useful kernels of real judgment from among the chaff of opinion is called "discernment". Discernment – learning the fine distinctions between good and not so good, real and unreal, worthwhile and worthless, etc. – is a lifelong quest, the highest of monastic virtues. It is more desirable even than patience and obedience, which only contribute to its cultivation. If, as they themselves will tell you, patience and obedience are practically nonexistent among them, how can Greek monks ever acquire discernment? How can anyone?

Someone asked this of Nasruddin, the Hindu "holy fool" – a title given to people in many countries, including Greece, who are not quite all there, as if their obliviousness to worldly cares is proof of a blessed soul.

"Nasruddin," the man asked, "what is the secret of life?"

"Good judgment."

"And how does one acquire good judgment?"

"Experience."

"And how does one acquire experience?"

(Pause.)

"Bad judgment."

When an abbot asks his monks to think, he is teaching them to make judgments of this kind – to distinguish the good cholesterol from the bad. *Skepsis*, the word he uses, is the imperative of a Greek verb meaning "to reflect". One of the daily scenes on Mount Athos is an abbot admonishing a monk who has done something thoughtless with a pained "*Skepsis, pater mou. Skepsis.*" As he does so, he points to his own head. After all, the abbot is accountable before God for the monk's soul. He who thinks invariably entertains doubt. The *gerontas* (old man) does not mean that his charge should doubt that water flows downhill or that God can't make it flow uphill. He wants his monk to mind the little things – drops of inattention, opinion – because eventually they will erode his soul, "precept by precept, line by line". What the abbot wants the monk to doubt is the value of his own will. He wants the monk to know that he is as ineffective as the first man was told to be – that his gift is to keep watch, not to create. Or as the Hasidic Fathers say, to "give your soul back to God in the same condition as you received it".

"Well, bless my soul—what's wrong with me?"

The blessing of an abbot is more powerful than a Papal edict or a Security Council veto. A monk quite literally can do nothing without his abbot's blessing except go to the Turkish toilet. The abbot does not rule by justice, but by fiat. As the sole branch of government, subject to no checks or balances, it is within his power to grant requests by *oikonomoia* – the "law of the house". Which he is. You do not have to give a reason for your request, or any reason at all, even if it is for something contrary to rules, local traditions, or Sacred Tradition. If he grants it, his nod lifts all doubt of impropriety from your soul. I once asked my abbot's blessing for an egg on a fast day, when eggs are *verboten*. I could have asked for permission to hang-glide, and, if he said yes, I would have been off to the nearest cliff top, secure in my knowledge that his blessing would protect as I drifted out of sight over the "wine-dark sea". This was only an egg. The abbot said yes to my impertinent request. Admittedly, at this point, I got a little legalistic. I then asked if I could boil it. Another nod. And finally, I asked him if I could eat it. He paused for a moment, no doubt searching my eyes for the reason I was putting obedience to the test of absurdity natural to someone trained in the law, then waved me away with his hand. Of course, I interpreted this as consent, and given the fact that a Greek who wants you to approach him will wave you away, I believe I had some kind of twisted precedent on my side.

In exchange for relinquishing responsibility for their temporal lives, monks get the time to wrestle with their souls. If you think such an arrangement differs little from the army or prison, just take a look at the rules of any school, club, business, etc., and the implied trade-offs therein. If a monk acts without his abbot's blessing, he isn't sacked, expelled, or fined, but has a chance to 'fess up and repent to his abbot at any time he is moved to do so. Like most rules we invoke to give some order to our disorderly world, the need for a blessing can be abused and paralyzing for either or both parties, and discourage the exercise of free will necessary to make the mistakes that eventually may lead to discernment.

The Blackness of the Monk

At its heart, *Moby Dick*, that marvelous book about everything under the sun and above the sea, is a painting in black and white: it's about the either/or thinking that is the *bête noire* of Western Civilization. Chapter Forty-two is a treatise on "The Whiteness of the Whale". It's a hopeless task. A mystery. Plunging into it is like trying to find your way through a snowstorm. Is white intolerable enlightenment, or blind ignorance? The albatross of fair winds is white, yet so is the man-eating polar bear. The lily is white, yet so is the death-cap mushroom. Angels wear white? Well, so does the Ku Klux Klan. As did the Crusaders, those self-proclaimed swordsmen of God. Wedding dresses are white, but so are shrouds. White is all we know, which also is nothing.

There is no chapter about blackness in *Moby Dick*. Why? You make white by taking things away; black is the result of adding all you've got: one is kataphatic, and the other is apophatic. Blackness is the all-color, the most difficult to find and create – as unfathomable as the deep into which Moby Dick sounds before he breaches into the light. It is the descent of Christ into hell before his resurrection. It is Ahab: black clothes, black hair, black eyes, riding a black ship with smoke-blackened sails, free will run amok, taking upon himself the vengeance that is God's alone. Is black the sum of all knowledge or the absence of it, the impenetrable night? We know black. We are afraid of it. It also comforts us.

All Orthodox monks wear black. Why? Most Catholic monks don't. Anglican monks don't. Is this just another example of Orthodox perverseness? To wear a color that comes with a bad press? Does black symbolize poverty? Identify the sinner? Does the monk wear black to his marriage with God because the world wears white? Does it have something to do with heat retention? The early monks lived in the desert: cold at night, not so cold during the day. Was black plentiful? General Issue? Was it cheap – the reason early Fords were black?

Ultimately, there is no difference between black and white. To be wholly one or the other represents no real option. It's like having a right brain without a left. Like science without religion and vice-versa. While it is only natural to constantly flip-flop between the intuitive and the rational, since we are unable to occupy both spaces at any one time, if you find yourself stuck at either end of the spectrum, take that as a warning. That is *not* natural. Something has driven you there; cut you off from the fullness of life. What could be more symbolic of the age of industry, than a dirty, foul-smelling, smoky whaler? Is *Moby Dick* a commentary on the attempt of technology to bend human nature to its will? It could be. And what happens in the end? It's you or me, either/or, and both are taken down.

Melville fled to the anonymity of the Customs House when he felt he could no longer escape civilization. For ten years I dressed in black, and lived among men who also dressed in black. But for the ten years before that, when I was engaged in pursuits quite the opposite of what most would call holy, I also dressed in black. At different times in my life, I have favored blue, red, and green, and even, for an aberrant moment, orange, but these were only interludes among a definite preference for the all-color. And the reason was pretty much the same. Black provides a boundary: a buffer between the wearer and the world behind which he or she feels not only safe, but a little invulnerable, as if nothing can come in or go out unless he wills it. The option of surprise is on his side. Black is a mask. Bikers used to wear black. It was scary. It made others feel uneasy. Their faded blue denim jackets were only billboards for illiteracy and violence. Since color has come into the world of the motorcycling angels, the whole thing has gone to hell.

Black is the color of impending doom: black looks, black clouds, Black Monday, the Black Death, Black Bart, Blackbeard, the Jolly Roger, the outlaw's hat. It is the color of expanding space and the holes in space. It is the color prized in a mythical tulip, the mania for which led to disaster. It is also the color of "my true love's hair". The wearer of the black feels that his life is his own. The wearer of black has time to decide. Black is "No." Black is human defiance – a shield. Black sets the monk a little below the white clad angels, but because absolute black is a (physical) impossibility, he can change the focus of the eye of the mind in his heart. Angels cannot change. (Lucifer was an archangel.)

Absolute goodness, if it were attainable, would be as boring and meaningless and I will venture to say, as purposeless, as absolute evil. Adam and Eve couldn't take it. The *Pequod*, loaded with sinners, catches up with Moby Dick because while he is speedy and powerful, he is utterly predictable. But the black *Pequod* goes down with the white whale.

I've read that men like games and danger, and women are the most dangerous game. What man doesn't want a woman who combines the Virgin Mary and Mary the Magdalene? The black and the white. The animal and the spiritual. The adorable and the passionate. Black attracts women even as they fear it. A white clad monk would provoke as much interest as an angel. Where is the "bad boy" within? Women want to build a nest, maybe; but when it's not going to lead to that, don't they also want a built-in "out"? A reason why it could never have worked? What honest, church-going woman isn't contemptuous of the notion of carnal sin, yet sees Christ as her paramour? So when they see a priest, or a monk, wearing the black, doesn't the hate-love within them come into play, and they feel, perhaps … tempted and … alive … by what they're told they cannot have?

The way to a monk's stomach is through his esophagus.

In the absence of electricity, paraffin lamps are in common use throughout Mount Athos. There are also paraffin stoves, little camping affairs placed in the *kafeneions* (cafés) strategically situated around the buildings. In the hearts of Greek men in the world, the *kafeneion* occupies a place not unlike Mount Athos. It is a sanctuary in a world of trouble, where men smoke, drink, and swing their "worry beads" (*combologia*). It is where they can boast of their conquests and momentarily forget the cruel joke Nature has played in which they, who always want sex, can't always have it, while women, who allegedly don't always want it, can have it whenever they do – theoretically, of course. It is where they have exercised their skills at the honorable game of backgammon forever. Not by treaty, but by some unspoken agreement, in Greece, women do not cross the threshold of a bona fide café. They may stand at the open door and drag their men out with their screams, but, like the unordained at the Royal Gates, they know that if they stepped inside they would wake the ghosts of Greek men dead. Old habits die hard. While an abbot may discourage his monks from spending too much time in their humble cafes, at Konstamonitou sometimes Father Bartholomew and I returned to our cells with only a few minutes for prayer before bells or wood summoned us to another liturgical marathon.

The use of semi-modern stoves in cooking does not extend to the kitchen with its dozens of mouths to feed. For many reasons, this was my favorite place in any monastery. Standing among the huge cast-iron pans and cauldrons, I immediately felt like a living participant in the Middle Ages and not merely one who lived in buildings constructed at that time. To watch an Athonite cook going about his business raises images of a medieval hall after the hunt, or of torture rooms deep down in the dungeons. Machines that could have lowered a drawbridge for Ivanhoe or raised Braveheart to the rack maneuver enormous cauldrons into place over wood-burning pits. Indifferent wine spigots from musty kegs and evil-tasting *raki* trickles out of huge wooden vats of putrid fruits and vegetables, while monks sprinkle powdered magic on goat's milk (from male goats, naturally) and transform it into wheels of delicious *kasseri* or *kefalatiri* cheese. We know *mezithra* as a grating cheese, but if you haven't tasted it soft and hot you have only seen the butterfly's empty cocoon.

The soil on Mount Athos is so rich and the water so plentiful that you could drop a car in the ground and it would be even odds to produce an automobile tree. The gardens give everything asked of them, sometimes in quantities so prodigious that they can be a dubious blessing. Working in their black habits under a blazing sun, monks lay out and tend extensive beds of onions, garlic, cabbages, and melon vines, with rake, hoe, and shovel, and buckets of sweet water from underground sources that have been doing their thing for a thousand years. At harvest time, the trees groan under the weight of over-laden branches. At Konstamonitou, during the persimmon season, pyramids of the delicious, sweet, red/orange fruit were stacked in the window alcoves of the refectory, literally blotting out the sun. A luxury in the world, a plague in the monastery. Waste not, want not many, many trips to the *mairos*. Sometimes size joined quantity to add to our peculiar kind of misery. In the early autumn, two succulent, meaty, one-pound tomatoes decorated every place setting at every meal for weeks. At Bourazerei, I saw two monks, arms extended, backs bent, straining to carry a single cabbage, and it wasn't because they were weak from fasting.

Because the monks have no way of preserving produce, they either devour it in season or it shows up later as firewater. Some practice canning, but not many, and those who do probably got their diplomas from the same school as the dentist. The Carpatho-Russian-American abbot of Prophet Elijah canned tomatoes in an imperfectly sterilized manner that really put my faith to the test. With all due reverence for the protocol of hospitality, I could not accept his kind offer of a plate of what I was sure had become deadly "love apples" in which the citric acid would have been hard put to keep abreast of the botulism.

They don't can food, they don't clean windows and they don't do floors, and they can't possibly eat all they grow, but monks don't condemn all they don't eat to the *raki* barrel. At Konstamonitou as at the other monasteries there were the virtual cats for the scraps left at the end of the meal. For the salvageable food there was a cage in the pantry constructed of chicken wire to keep out the rats. Our dependence in the world on refrigeration for everything is more a comment about us than on the possibility of getting sick. You don't make cheese in a refrigerator, and yogurt and sour milk are the preferred forms of that beverage in most countries. Bread just got hard. Nobody seemed to mind. They just crumbled it into their soup or dipped it in their tea.

Winter makes the monastery kitchen a doubly desirable sanctuary. In the pre-church darkness I usually could be found lingering there with my back to the crackling fires, soaking up the delicious heat. At Timion Prodromos, one chilly morning, I witnessed something that did temporary wonders for my sagging faith. As I stood in the kitchen avoiding church with my robe tucked into my belt, my back to the stove, and a glass of hot tea resting between my frozen hands, the vessel suddenly exploded with atomic violence. I couldn't have blinked fast enough to protect my eyes. My hands held the air where the glass had been as if it were still there. I was not wet, nor was water visible anywhere. Not a shard of the glass that covered the floor in a radius of ten-foot had touched me! I have since learned that an explosion is quite likely if you don't put a metal spoon inside a cold glass ahead of the boiling water.

It was the not being touched part that defied explanation. There's probably a scientific reason for this as well, and I have heard of magicians who can sit in a box with exploding dynamite and come out unharmed; but again, why is a question asked only by monks who are already on the way out. That morning, I was content with calling it a miracle and departed immediately for the church.

Baby, it's cold inside.

Is there anything that makes us more aware of our species-wide helplessness than the weather? Masking our prayers as science, we make hopelessly incorrect forecasts for the week to come, the next, and the next. We design clothing to protect us from the cold and slather on sunscreen to stop us from burning. We build machines for tracking and predicting storms, and people still die in them. The temperature of our world goes up or down a few degrees, and we are all dead. Our hubris aside, the only certain role we can play in the weather is to be in awe of it. To watch the barometer go up and down and batten down the hatches or wet down the sails. To look at a red sky in the morning and repeat the sailor's warning. To stare at hundred-foot waves, rivers of bubbling lava, torrents of mud, avalanches of snow, jagged gashes in the earth, whirling fingers of windy death, and, sometimes, lavish slabs of polychromatic sunset.

Ambrose Bierce describes peace as "a period of cheating between two periods of fighting". This is not the raving of a recognized curmudgeon. Of the last four thousand years only two hundred and eighty-six have known peace. Peace in nature is even more fleeting. An instant of beauty can be followed by instant and violent death, and the constant impact of weather on life is immense.

Mount Athos in the winter is a wonderland. I spent a lot of time wondering how cold I would be if the heating failed. I had arrived with considerable experience in this area. Within two minutes of landing on Paros the Christmas Eve of my ill-fated assault on Longovarda I had learned the fruitless phrase, *"Kanei krio"* – "It's cold." Every day, the wind screamed through the electrical wires outside my window like Jimi Hendrix on a tortured E-string; at night it tested the latch and slipped under the door. Many were the mornings when I had to dismantle a large ice-sword dangling over my door.

After two months of my catechumenate, I became hypothermic. I wore every stitch of clothing I had brought with me all the time, but it was no use. I slept in all my clothes and under five blankets and still froze. If I shifted my head on the pillow, the warm spot was ice within seconds. Lying in bed every morning, the wood having sounded for church four hours before dawn, I knew what the supine Snoopy felt as he contemplated the icicle that had him trapped in his doghouse, waiting for him to make a move: "I think I'm going to lie here for the rest of my life." Was it worth getting up? Or would it be better to play dead until I actually was? But the church contained the only sizable public heater in the entire compound, and eventually that persuaded me to throw off my useless covers.

While I cannot attest to what was going on behind all the angels' closed doors, the only private source of warmth to which I had access was Father N.'s smoky den, and my frequent visits to our Walter Winchell were not always occasioned by my concern for his health. To keep warm, we moved around a lot. I helped Father G. in the garden; when we could we took long, long walks into the neighboring hills. A night in the bakery was a few hours in Heaven. But this only happened every two weeks.

When I had first come to Paros, the previous spring, I had brought a bright, red sweat suit and injected some discipline into my days by rising early, running down to the shore opposite Naxos – to the great puzzlement of farmers already at their ploughs – and plunging in. On this trip, I also brought my gear but received no blessing to run. Father Hierotheos, the acting *igoumenos* (abbot), told me that if I needed any exercise besides work, I could do prostrations.

Longovarda was not exactly a young man's monastery. The youngest of the four priests was eighty-five years old. The abbot was ninety-three. For reasons of health he spent most of his time at a modern convent in the mountains, where the nuns kept his room at a temperature that would boil water. He rarely left the hummock of pillows and comforters piled onto his bed. It was to this man that I made my initial confession – the one that would relieve me of all the sins I had collected over the previous thirty-two years.

Confession is a monk's therapy; like therapy, a lot depends on whether (a) the seeker wants to be healed and (b) he believes in the cure. Since the confessor is only a conduit to the ear of God, confession supposedly works independent of his abilities. Don't kid yourself: a bad confessor can put you off confession just like incompetent therapists can put you off talking to them. That wasn't directly relevant in my case, however, because, although my two monastic companions didn't trust him, my confessor couldn't understand English. It would be like talking to a wall. Father G. would translate and, I imagined, bear the onus for the substance. In the convent church, in the presence of the abbot and the trusty Father G., I unloaded all I had accumulated while walking up and down and lying down and doing things in the earth. Everything: all my now-illicit relations, names included when I could remember them. Was I proud of my former life? I couldn't stand it, but you bet I was! Hold on now. "Judge not that ye...." Aren't sins as necessary to a prospective monk as a J. D. is to a would-be lawyer? Without falling, how could one repent? And you think I went to law school for nothing? I knelt before the quivering *gerontas*, and he placed his *epitrakhelion* (stole) over my head. He mumbled something while I wondered if he had ever heard the kind of things I had dropped into his ear and if that had something to do with his shaking. Did I believe I was absolved? I know I stopped thinking about what I had done. Is that absolution?

Stavrovouni, the stony aerie on Cyprus that I once called home for six wintry months, had a small fireplace in the refectory, but, the doors had to be wide open for the fire to draw. Here, too, physical exercise was the key to warmth – difficult to do in a place not much bigger that the head of a pin already crowded with angels. Sitting on sun-warmed stone like a lizard was the other option. Naturally, neither were available at night, when a chamber pot under my bed was the only thing that could get me to lower my feet to the icy marble floor. *Kanei crio!* Even worse, I discovered that the bloody cracks in my fingers were not stigmata (as I had hoped), but chilblains, which succumbed without prayer to the Vitamin B supplied by a kindly pediatrician from Limassol.

One might forgive a reasonable person for assuming that, by contrast, Mount Athos was perfectly equipped to deal with the uncompromising cold of winter. After all, a dense wood covers ninety-five per cent of the peninsula. Logging companies do carry away most of it, but lack of fuel isn't the problem. It's the technology and the buildings themselves. The stone walls of the huge, undermanned monasteries keep the cold out no better than the castle walls in Poe's *The Masque of the Red Death* barred the Grim Reaper from joining the party. But on The Mountain, warmth did not depend on constantly moving around or attempting to enjoy life as a reptile.

Simonopetra introduced central heating into the Holy Mountain in the early seventies. Until then, the main source of heat in that house had been Russian stoves – heating chambers built into the walls, about two feet cubed. If properly tended, this stove can produce enough heat and residual warmth to keep a room toasty for twenty-four hours. Unfortunately, and especially as they get older and earthquakes do their damage, they can also produce enough fire to sneak through cracks and ignite the straw in the bricks used in most monastic construction. Burning unnoticed, these fires are almost impossible to stamp out. The last straw that persuaded Simonopetra to modernize was a blaze that destroyed a considerable part of the monastery. A similar mishap also was responsible for the charred buildings at Panteleimon, where, however, they still use their ancient stoves.

The residents of Bourazerei, where the nightly, common prayer rule was fifty thousand stand up Jesus Prayers, were *fanatikoi*, the extremists whose company I enjoyed before it dawned on me that, while Christ might indeed be wherever two or three were gathered in his name, the church was more likely to be where the *most* people were gathered in his name. Bourazerei is on the north or windward, side of the ridge. The winter of my residence, the *skiti* was in the process of converting from Russian stoves to central heating. A good part of one wall of the main building had been torn down and the inside gutted to allow the installation of the new boiler system.

If you are saying to yourself that there cannot be much heart in saying the Jesus Prayer fifty thousand times in four hours, remember that the goal of saying the Jesus Prayer is to eventually flood the heart with wordless prayer. Standing supposedly ensures that one does not fall asleep. After a few weeks of this pious exercise, my heart may not have been filled, but I could no longer get into my shoes. I tried lying on my bed with my feet in the air in a forlorn effort to get the blood running out of my feet and back up into the rest of my body. I even tried praying for deliverance – a most unascetic request in a place that considers trials to be blessings. I tried rubbing my swollen limbs with lemon juice. No surprise: no success.

I was too much the self-venerating martyr to complain openly, so I just showed up barefoot for church, hoping my brothers would secretly applaud my imitation of the classical penitent. The abbot, a far more practical man than I, noticed the elephantine condition of my feet, hooked me toward his throne with his forefinger, and sent me to Prophet Elijah for a pair of boots. Prophet Elijah was about an hour and half's walk from our *skiti*. You may ask how I managed to get there when I couldn't get into my shoes, and to tell you the truth, at this distance in time I have no answer. But I must say that the Jesus Prayer, spat out at warp speed, can warm the body like a car heater drawing from a high-revving four-cylinder engine.

Then again, how did my abbot know there would be boots at Prophet Elijah? A hidden telephone? No. Our abbot did not speak English and the other did not speak Greek. Crushing as it may be to my ego, I can only think that I was not the first person in the past thousand years whose feet swelled under such circumstances and had sought relief, since a monk's feet are the only part of his anatomy to which he gives more than passing care. He stands at work, in church, and in his cell, and any place he ventures on the Holy Mountain involves a significant amount of walking. There may not be a shower in plain sight, but every monastery has a number of basins prominently displayed where a monk can find cold-water comfort for his aching feet.

The American abbot sized me up like the shoe salesman I hoped he would be, and then disappeared into the cavernous storerooms of the pocket-monastery built for thousands. He reappeared shortly, holding his solution up with both hands and, I like to think, a bit of a smile. No one had worn the Cossack boots that he produced since the 19th century! Those enormous, hard leather smokestacks, sheepskin-lined, came up to my mid-thigh and gave me a footprint that would have had King Kong shaking in *his* boots. I clumped back up the hill to Bourazerei. Standing up for prayer or keeping warm ceased to be a problem. The boots stood up and I stood in them. No longer constricted, the warmed blood rose through my upper body, and I passed many an all-night vigil peacefully asleep on my feet.

While I was at Prophet Elijah, the abbot also offered me a few bars of olive green soap, stamped with the Imperial seal and the date – 1875. I didn't have a real need for them, any more than there is a point to warning monks that peanut butter can affect their ability to reproduce, and I had no one to whom I wanted to send them as a "Wish you were here". But where else in the world could I have been given something as venerable as those boots and been told to use them? Or, had I been so inclined, could I have washed with soap that was a hundred years old? It was like being allowed to walk out of a museum clad in the armor of some 15th century knight just because you told the curator you were afraid you might get mugged on the way home. Imagine if I had taken them to *Antiques Road Show*? Or put them on eBay?

Aside from providing warmth and rigidity, the boots had another use. When I finally left Bourazerei, I took them with me. I walked through the snow to other monasteries where, head down in a welcome bowl of soup, eyes slyly up, I waited to see how long it was before a resident monk came in, terrified and babbling about what he had seen. While I kept my head bowed piously and my feet out of sight, he would mime the size of the fish he hadn't caught, and describe the mammoth tracks "the creature" left in the snow. Simple pleasures. *"Aaaaahlas, Ioanni?"*

Why don't they ever listen to me?!

Konstamonitou, my monastery, was one of the finest examples of the classical monastic approach to heat. Every cell boasted an upright cast-iron wood stove with a vent in the side. A Norman Rockwell kind of stove. A grate supported the little logs that lay down their lives that we might live in relative comfort and allowed air to circulate above and below. The grate made the stove quite efficient. That is why it was there. The Greeks of Konstamonitou, however, appeared to believe that there was something demonic about these little thermal regulators and refused to use them. The result was that while the monks spent nine months of the year leading their mules up into the hills to chop and collect firewood, what they brought down was consumed at a rate prodigious enough to take a hundred and fifty loaded freight cars over the Rockies.

Now, here was a place where I felt I could be the one providing enlightenment – and, possibly, enheatment. Technological Man of the World instructs innocent Man of the Spirit in the use of what is second nature to him. My initial efforts to illuminate my peers, however, delivered in short declaratory sentences and gestures, met with a uniform look and gesture that said either, "Don't be ridiculous," or, "You are ridiculous." I have trouble with the cases in body language. Still wishing to help the monastery (and only incidentally prove that I was right), I ascended to the abbot's room to get the ear of the One Who Counted in All Matters. I knocked obsequiously on his door and heard a tired command to enter. I pushed. I pushed again. The door opened about six inches. I leaned, and it opened a few inches more. Part of my problem was that I weighed all of 140 pounds, a condition that had resulted from my having perhaps too great a belief in the enhanced spirituality of the thin. When I did squeeze inside the abbot's lair, I saw, or rather waded through, the other reason I'd had such difficulty entering.

A volcano's worth of ash sloped gracefully from the royal stove down to the doorsill. On one side of the stove sat the abbot, his head resting in his hand. In the meager light, with his face framed by his thick black beard, he might have been the Renaissance painting of Saul brooding in his tent as he waited for David to arrive with his harp. On the other side, a monk furiously fed the cast-iron Moloch with wood snacks.

My well-rehearsed attempt to explain how the flame-driven wood-chipper could be converted into a benevolent, purring, heat-yielding friend was accepted with a tolerant nod. I even drew a diagram on a napkin, and, for emphasis, rolled it into a ball and theatrically threw it into the stove, where it flared for a moment and then joined the rest of the ash. The abbot asked me if I wanted to speak with him about anything else. I shook my head, backed out of the room with a bow, and retreated gracefully to my own abode, virtually kicking the virtual cat that might have sat on my doorstep. I adjusted my grate, stripped to my T-shirt and jeans, and consoled myself with images of the others choking and freezing while I slept (and prayed) (relatively) naked.

"I've got [its] love to keep me warm."

Heating the rooms was a problem. Trying to heat the church, the ceiling of which was lost in acro-darkness, was an exercise in faith. True to its outlaw image, Konstamonitou also was one of the leading houses on The Mountain in adhering to the monastic philosophy of making public displays of conspicuous waste. As if to say there will always be enough and so what if there isn't? It's not the end of the world, and the world will end. This profligate attitude is a very curious companion to the parallel habit of never allowing anything to *go* to waste. Recycling is as natural to the Greeks as if they invented the word, which they did. Yesterday's blown-out tire is tomorrow's rubber sole.

The lonely church stove was a very large oil drum set down in the center of the nave between two rows of age-polished *stasida*. The huge drum did not have a grate. Younger monks constantly streamed toward it from the rear of the church like the animated brooms in *The Sorcerer's Apprentice*, bearing logs from the mountain of wood on the portico in a futile effort to placate the monster's appetite. The heat rose as if it were wired to the roof. At frequent intervals during the long night services, older monks arose and shuffled toward the middle of the church, where they turned their backs to the furnace glowing red through the black metal, raised the hems of their cassocks, and tried to absorb a little heat through their nether parts. Younger monks appeared out of the surrounding darkness, made furtive grabs at the warmth, and then scurried back into the frozen land beyond the shadows before their reputations were ruined. There they shivered in silence while the cold made its way up from the floor through their shoes and eventually to their brains with a fiendish, slow inevitability that parallels the asphyxiation of crucifixion.

The younger monks almost never sat in the *stasida*. Those were for the elderly whose legs had already gone ahead to announce the imminent departure of their souls. The *stasidi* is a marvel of subtle construction. Whenever I was in danger of being warmed too much by my consumption of Jesus Prayers, I would stare at – excuse me, meditate on – the *stasida*. The seat that swings up, thus allowing one to stand on something other than the icy marble floor, is too narrow for comfort and too high off the floor to provide a firm rest for one's feet. While it is difficult to sleep in such a contrivance, monks have great perseverance, and many were the black, woolen prayer ropes I had to rescue from the floor and wind about the dangling wrists of their somnolent and sometimes snoring owners.

Holiness doesn't smell like that, does it?

With all the alternation of heat and cold, as well as the consumption of a diet high in roughage, is it any wonder that the toilets in Konstamonitou were constantly in use? The monks referred to these facilities as "Turkish" toilets, and, for once, Greeks had no problem giving credit where it was doo. Of course, what kind of skill does it take to poke a hole in the ground? No cistern – a coffee-can and a bucket of water. In some commodes, a raised footrest flanked the hole on either side, automatically positioning one's rear to achieve the desired end.

The Turkish toilet is a very practical convenience for those who wear untrousered garments. There is usually one Thomas Crapper upright in every monastery, but its purpose is to show tourists that monks are not barbarians. The advantage of the Turkish toilet is lost in modern variations, which feature a flushing system that sweeps across the enameled basin like a tidal wave. But while the smell in the new model is not pleasant, in the earlier one, it is much worse.

Does this discussion take you aback? Where life is simplified, and much of the talk is about food and the growing of food, where the diet is a restricted one, and old age is all around you, concern for the workings of one's organs of ingestion, digestion, and excretion can be of inordinate interest.

Monks do hand wash themselves. They also may brush their teeth, but not after receiving Holy Communion, lest they flush some of the divine elements lingering between teeth down the pipes. They also wash their clothes. They also sleep in their clothes. Laundry day at a monastery finds most of the brothers bent over stone cisterns, scrubbing their black robes and black-ish undergarments with hard green laundry soap. The fact that the water comes from a huge cauldron, heated by a wood fire that can take hours to bring to a boil, creates instant community. As there are no dryers, a monastery on wash day can look like the backyard of a Brooklyn tenement.

Monks may be careless of their bodies and personal hygiene, but the uncared-for appearance of many old-style Athonite monasteries is in large part due to there being so few monks and so much to care for. In the newer, younger, and more populous *koinovia*, where there is adequate manpower and spirit, the brothers sweep and swab the long stone hallways every day. Where grime persists most likely is where the sweaty imprints of countless hands have seeped beneath the surface of wood and stone. Since there is little communal pride within the older communities, the declining *idiorrhythmic* houses are not so salubrious. Lack of help has persuaded even the relatively flourishing *koinovia* to shut down whole wings except for the chapels, which the monks open, dust, and liturgize once a year to let the particular saint to whom it is dedicated know that he has not been abandoned.

About garbage, they are not so fastidious.

From Stavrovouni Monastery, the view of Cyprus in any direction is extraordinary. Perched twenty-three hundred feet above sea level on the easternmost peak of the Troodos range, the monastery is a full fifteen hundred above the neighborhood. Every day I was there began with the rays from the rising sun bounding toward me off the cloud-tops like a dog with the morning paper, before the packed vapor drifted away to reveal a world so far away and so visually unpopulated that we might have been survivors from the ark looking down at an earth emptied of life.

In the years when he had been alone on the mountain, Father A. had rescued a chapel below the monastery from serving as a dumpster, to which it had been condemned by the Turks. The priest also made a point of sweeping the tiny courtyard every morning before any other task. But what happened to the refuse of daily life? The detritus from the kitchen, the plastic containers, and cardboard boxes? I could not recall ever seeing a trash can, even for the wrappers and cigarette butts that festooned the floors after Sunday's crowd of worldlings had departed.

Since my head was regularly unavailable to common sense following the liturgy, I might have been convinced that angels descended with dustpans and brooms while we slept had I not been in the refectory one day when the holy man of the mountain shuffled in with a scoop full of rubbish in his hand, made his way to the window, and heaved its contents over the sill. After he had shuffled off, I peered out the window toward the sea, far away, glittering white and yellow on blue in the late afternoon sun. I lowered my gaze. The mountain fell away sharply. Along with a moat and a drawbridge constructed twenty three hundred feet up from the sea, it had deterred resolute plunderers for over fifteen hundred years. If only they had waited below, and been fond of trash.

Clinging to the side of this natural fortress for hundreds of feet were orange peels, papers, plastic, and every other kind of the very rubbish that Father A. had found intolerable when it defiled the chapel of Constantine and Helen. All things shall pass, but not all things are biodegradable.

"Louie, this could be the beginning of a beautiful friendship."

If you suspect that because monks do not bathe they might emit a rather strong smell, you would not be wrong – unless you were a monk. The theory of relativity tells us that a person who may smell rank to someone who bathes every day may not offend one who does not. After a few weeks of getting used to my own stench, I hardly noticed that anyone else smelled of anything. Almost anything. Because the acrid odor of incontinence was not a scent that as yet enhanced my own person, this parasite of old age was something else. I did not consider it my business to discover what people in the world – say, someone I might sit next to on a plane – felt about the odor I exuded. I, myself, had not been partial to the sour stench of layered sweat in the days when the shoe was on the other nostril.

The amount of time spent at dinner rarely reflects the preparation that goes into a meal; so, too, one really good bath quickly wipes away the accumulated dirt of many years. In 1980, I flew Royal Air Maroc from Athens to New York for some r-and-r. Because of the airline's need to jump through some curious contractual hoops in order to maintain this particular route, our Boeing 727 put down in Casablanca, where all hundred and fifty of us were put up at a four-star hotel for two nights. No charges were added to the fare of seventy (70) dollars.

What we had to put up with! For one thing, the distance from the door to the bed of "my" room almost qualified as a pilgrimage. Once there, I made a face worthy of the world-weary Ecclesiasticus at the emperor-sized, gold cloth-covered, and thoroughly sybaritic pleasure field on which I was expected to sleep. When would the rest of the world discover the pleasure of a good, hardwood board?

It was the bathroom, however…. Oh, the bathroom! They could have filmed *Titanic* in the tub. I resisted manfully for about five seconds, but the lure of apostasy was too much. I filled the huge basin with hot water, climbed in, and gingerly settled back as the unfamiliar liquid crept up my body to my chin. I closed my eyes. Like fingers of eucalyptus oil, relief spread across my face and coaxed open a smile. I took a quick peek toward my feet. They were still a good three feet from the lower end of the tub.

Soap having had almost no effect, I began to scrape the grease from my skin with my fingernails. I used a wet towel like a shoeshine rag to get at my virgin back. The water turned so dark I could no longer see my legs. I drained the tub, filled it back up, and erased a little more of my history. I loaded my shiny locks with complimentary shampoo, ducked under the water, and discovered that the stuff on my head was composed of individual strands that squeaked as I drew them through my fingers. There were bald patches on my calves, worn bare by the friction of cloth where the sun refused to shine. As I left the bath, I felt twice as naked as when I had entered. Once in the other room, I hailed a cab heading in the direction of my bed. The coolness of the linen sheets caressed my new vulnerability, and I felt not a trace of guilt.

The next morning, we boarded an eagle-like 747 to New York. My humility got the better of me, and I insisted on being the last one into the cabin. By the time my bearded, black-robed self piously passed through the hatchway, all of the seats in Economy Class were occupied. The cabin attendant beckoned to me. If she hadn't been a Muslim, she might have said "The first shall be last, and the last shall go First Class." But she was, and she didn't. Good thing I had taken a bath. And, as it turned out, not solely for the sake of my fellow privileged ones. To the customs officials in New York, however, smelling nice apparently wasn't enough. To them, my dark garb and hirsute condition did not indicate that I was a designated bearer of holiness, but rather a likely bearer of smack. A thorough search revealed neither.

My beard was another matter. I trimmed it occasionally and washed it whenever I showered, but the brambly thing remained with me until the summer after I left seminary, when I took a job as a sailing instructor at a sports camp. For the first few weeks, hand on tiller, I must have looked like a reincarnation of the pirate, Edward Teach, minus firecrackers sparkling under my chin. But I had to face it: when the inner life no longer supported the advertisement, my gaunt, bearded presence felt like a fraud. Early one morning, before the pop song that daily changed the expectation of a beautiful day into a compulsory fact had knifed into the collective pre-conscious, I returned to my room following my daily, naked ride on a little sunfish around the mist-covered lake – John the Baptist freed of his camelhair. There, I allowed my hands to execute what had been in my mind for a week. First scissors, then a razor … then another razor. For the first time in ten years, I saw my face. I hardly recognized myself. I traced the long-forgotten line of my jaw with my finger. I felt great. I went down to the dining room for breakfast, loaded my tray at the buffet, and ate in solitude. Nobody there recognized me, either.

The summer provided another kind of education. Not only had my social skills withered to a mumble, but living in a world devoid of conflict, I had not rubbed against anyone psychologically for ten years. At times, I was the repatriated Rip Van Winkle; at others, someone who grabs a tow-rope and is dragged through the snow on his nose. My body was not used to the kind of constant activity for which a summer camp exists, and my mind did not think in a way that nourished or was nourished by that activity. Words and ideas and fads had been born while I was bowling in the mountains. The swimsuit-clad bodies of women, while teasing me out of my slumber, looked only vaguely familiar.

And yet, I pitied the poor rich kids at the sports camp. So many things they had to deal with! So many choices! Parents! Peers! Teachers! So little choice! So little time to make any choice. So much pressure. Go here, go there, listen to the bugle, listen to the bell, have that damn song wake you up to tell you every day had to be a beautiful day. Tournaments, races, other competitions. So much less freedom than the monk who, once having surrendered himself, has no one and nothing pressuring him but his own responsibility to keep track of his soul.

The western wall of the Monastery of Great Lavra—first among the Athonite monasteries in size, antiquity, and prestige. It's clear that turning the other cheek wasn't the only option.

The Monastery of Grigoriou. The Jewel of the Riviera. The *arsanas* is just left of center. The telephone wire is the breadcrumbs that have led many a lost monk back to his monastery.

Terraced gardens at Grigoriou. The topography of the coast south of Dafni is not hospitable. Further down the coast at the "dread" Karoulia, home to the most eremitic hermits, it is worse.

Two levels of balconies on the landward side of the south coast monastery of Grigoriou. The supports appear sturdy enough, but what fastens them to the wall?

The *skiti* of Bourazerei. When I knew it in the 1970s, it was a dilapidated farmhouse. Transformed by EU money, now it is a retreat for the Archbishop of Athens and All Greece.

A monk getting building supplies from a shop in Karyes. Most likely, he is an inhabitant of a *skiti, kelli,* or a *kalyve.* The major monasteries do not use Karyes for their supplies, but have it shipped directly to the *arsanas.*

PART THREE

LEAVING THERE

They set the slave free, striking off his chain
` Then he was as much of a slave as ever...
His slavery was not in his chains,
   But in himself...
They can only set men free...
   And there is no need of that:
Free men set themselves free.

James Oppenheim, "The Slave"

The sun is setting. A visitor leans on the rail of the rickety, wooden balcony hanging out over the water. A warm breeze is his only companion. He has no concern for his safety. He may be smoking a cigarette. His last, he swears, until he leaves. Hold out till tomorrow. Piece of cake. He grunts. He watches the yellow globe turn orange, then red, then disappear and briefly blaze orange one last time before sizzling into the "wine dark" sea. Perhaps out of a feeling of fellowship with the men who have shared this same insubstantial ledge over the centuries, he takes a long last drag and then flicks the glowing butt into the black, where it tumbles end over end before vanishing silently into the sultry and meditative night.

Dinner was ample and nourishing. He has even begun to like the unpretentious fare and the undemanding atmosphere in which he ate it. He stood through *apodeipna* – the service that closes the day – and though he still didn't understand a word, and the chanting was garbled and not all that beautiful or haunting, he no longer finds it strange that this world revolves around the church *typikon* even as the monastic cells circle the *katholikon* rising out of their midst.

He hasn't shaved since he's been here; as he rubs his hand over the stubble, what was a token act of respect now feels like the beginning of liberation. He's a movie desperado out in the wild. He has not, however, given up soap. A cloak of melancholy drops over his shoulders. *Why couldn't it always be like this? What's so great about what's out there? What besides stress? Is my will only free if I choose what imprisons me? Here, I feel as if somehow I'm on ... parole.*

The image of his wife or significant other or even the vague remembrance of a total but beautiful stranger suddenly appears on the other side of the looking glass and he realizes that, if it were not for her, he just might never leave. *Do we really love each other? Is life all a matter of bargaining this for that? Maybe these people aren't so crazy? I can't stay, of course – that is crazy. I have ... I've got to get back. But what will it be like now? Have I changed at all? I need another smoke.* He checks with his conscience and shrugs. *Not the whole thing* A few puffs and the glowing ember gracefully arcs end over end toward the sea below. A draft of air swirls from under the balcony, catches the butt and lifts it slightly, carrying it out over the water before the wind loses interest and returns to its cave.

So will I, too, go out like a light. [CENSORED]!

The breeze enters through the open door; it fans out, wafting up and down the corridors between rows of cells. It is dark now. A mallet strikes wood. Again and again. Behind a wooden door with no lock on the outside and nothing worth stealing within, a monk lies on a micro-thin mattress and stares at the ceiling. As the sound approaches, he feels his body tense; but as it fades away he thinks, *A few minutes more. Just a few....* In the smudgy flame of a paraffin lamp, his silhouette is a distant mountain range on the wall. Canada? The Himalayas? *Anywhere but here.*

He feels the greasy black woolen prayer rope pass between his fingers. Was he – was *it* – doing this in his sleep? Sleep steadies his head on the pillow and brushes his temples, luring him back into her embrace. Words tumble from his dry mouth like the guard called out at midnight. *Kirie Iisou Kriste, eleison me, Kirie Iisou Kriste, eleison me, Kirie Iisou Kriste, eleison me.... zzzzzzzzz.... Lord, have mercy on me... zzzzzzzz.... a sinner.* A woman glides into his noesis. She might be a fantasy. She might be the woman who drove him here. Or a hometown girl whose open bodice caught his eye as she was bending over her laundry and filled him with lust and shame both. He may see his family in the world. Or an ongoing argument with a brother. Or an act for which he did not ask a blessing.

The monk struggles. *What am I doing here? I love him because he loved me first. But what about her? When she said she loved me, it felt so ... so how? Christ! I can't even remember!... And this bed is so hard. Maybe the world isn't all that bad. It's all a blur. And what if ... if I am wrong?*

Something – the sting of habit, perhaps – startles him into instant wakefulness. He slowly raises himself off his bed. He feels a twinge in his back and stops abruptly, his face twisted in pain. *What does a monk do?* he reminds himself as he gropes for the bottle of aspirin. *He falls down and he gets up; falls down and gets up. But isn't that*

what they do out there? He starts to cross himself, then stops.
   God, I would love a cigarette!

Maybe the twain can't meet, but what about east and west?

There have been movements to secularize churches or spiritualize the world since people first noticed that there was a space between the earth and the sky and inner drives they could neither understand nor control. There are those who see God in everything and those who see religion as a social movement. There are animists, and there are communists. We know that we have two sides to our brains, and each has a different function. To Caesar the things that are Caesar's and to God the things that are his, in our persons as well as our public life.

One of the reasons that we find love so confusing is that the reasoning side of our brain, concerned with progeny and survival, is often in conflict with the emotional side, which can find no rational basis for loving but loves anyway. We can accommodate both, but no matter how much pressure we exert, we cannot make them one. So, how does one "live in the world [of the flesh] without being of it"? Or live in the other world without discounting the flesh? Or is being human always to live with this question, unanswered?

Jesus preached a co-existence of the two. Not a commingling, but a co-existence. Like his own two natures – the human and the divine – each never without the other, yet always alone. Like our eyes, each of which forever give us two slightly different views of a thing, but which must work together to give us perspective.

Nietzsche said that whoever separates body from soul knows nothing about either, but he regarded the body (including the mind) as the senior partner. Monks have an opposite view. They believe that the dominant spirit *requires* incarnation to be able to comprehend the divine; that it is necessary to live a passing existence if we are to experience the possibility of eternity in the same way that one must vocalize the Prayer of Jesus before it can take its place in the heart. This does not make them any less subject to the laws of desire than anyone else whose bodily needs constantly squawk for satisfaction. Scripture tells monks flat out that they are in the world and will have troubles there, but that he in whom they believe has overcome the world.

While the monk's primary work is prayer, he does not believe that he gets a free lunch just because he prays. The need to do physical work is his covenant with the world; it symbolizes his spiritual poverty and his descent from Adam. According to Tradition, it was through Adam's ambition and disobedience that he forfeited the right just to *be* and was forced to *do*. When he tried to shift the blame to she who made him complete, his "helpmeet" became the object of his desire and his enemy. Eve then took his place as the one who knew what she was, while his disobedience condemned him to forever prove himself: to earn his living by the sweat of his brow. To measure his manhood by his ability to "perform". A woman's trials are of a different kind, not the least of which is men, the weak-brained, strong-backed creature she outwitted and whom God condemned her to forever obey. The punishment that both continue to share is that they can never again be one flesh or one spirit.

Just as some parents punish their children without explanation because they believe that the child must know why even if they don't, the monk truly believes in the justice of his punishment because of what he is and who God is: God is whole and he is not. At the same time, it is part of the monk's *askesis*, his spiritual athleticism, to guard against becoming so fond of work and its product that he ignores the transcendent wonder of all life and its Creator – like the master bell maker in Melville's story, "Belladonna", so absorbed with perfecting his creation that he gets his skull crushed by the clapper.

And this is where the monastic viewpoint parts company with that of the world. Monks are grateful for their existence, but they do not accept the human condition – however comfortable, intelligent, sensually satisfying, or sophisticated – as a final one. Monks have pledged themselves to the eventual triumph of the spirit in the unknown world that is to be. "Have no other gods before me" does not distinguish between work, things, and women as competitors for adoration.

"How is one to live in the world without becoming of it?" In a monastery an accomplished artist works in the kitchen, a writer finds himself planting garlic and onions in the monastery garden, and a talented cook washes bottles. A monk with a green thumb balances himself on a scaffold with his brush in green paint. This apparent misuse of talent occurs neither because monks have a mechanical aptitude that stops at the winch nor because abbots are blind to talent and ability. Many monks are extremely clever with their hands and at making do with what they have. But to help the monk resist the strong pull of the world into which he was born, it is traditional for his abbot to give him no work for which he might be suited or to which he might become overly attached. Repetitive manual activity occupies and exhausts the body, freeing it to open the mind to prayer – his true vocation. Therefore, the monastic ideal of work is a low-tech, monotonous job, like sub-gourmet cooking, gardening, cleaning, or painting: one for which the monk has shown no great fondness.

Monks don't compete for these jobs and not just because of the lousy pay. Writing delicate icons secures a monk no more status than taking out the garbage. Show a hint of pride, and the iconographer is out there picking onions. The communal life also teaches the monk that there is no job someone else can't do, and the more obvious and emphatic that teaching is imbedded in his daily life, the more likely he is to absorb it. This includes prayer: he is merely a vessel for prayer, in which quality is less influential than quantity, creativity less virtuous than obedience, and ability less prized than tenacity, just like in the simplest manual labor.

A monk prays because he is suffering in an alienated state. He needs a spiritual guide – often the abbot – because the logic of wisdom implies that those whom God chooses never know it, while those who imagine they have been chosen risk repeating the plunge of Icarus, who flew too close to the sun on man-made wings and fell into the sea.

This is not to denigrate the importance of a monk's ego. Since surrendering oneself to God-in-one's-abbot presupposes something to surrender, a strong ego is as important to living a true monastic life as it is to making one's way in the world. If we were constantly aware of our true insignificance in the scheme of things, why would we do anything except grub for worms? Without an ego, too, how could one recognize, like Anthony the Great, that hell is not a place, but simply is "where *I am*"? It would not surprise me if many have turned to religion just because it gives them a non-judgmental mirror in which to discover who (or that) they are: something their clueless parents did not or could not provide through the grace of being able to love unconditionally. While the fortunate child gets the chance to explore who he or she is, most only get to observe their parents, piling up impressions that the latter are powerless to prevent. I know that for me the very word "father", as it describes monks, priests, and God, was by itself a great attraction to life in the church and a means of sustaining me in it. Add to this the notion that, no matter the deference paid, a priest or a bishop is no "better" than you are, and you've got the makings of a relationship that's hard for one seeking such a thing to resist.

The detached view that anonymous medieval and Byzantine artists brought to the creation of religious art literally allowed them to gain a perspective outside the demands of ego: to find themselves not in their work but in the gift they made of that work. Orthodox priests, too, receive their special powers to administer sacraments solely through donning their sanctified vestments. When they pray for the consubstantiation of the bread and wine or hear confessions, it is only as a vessel of prayer. Character and personality are irrelevant to this aspect of their ministry, which enables them to carry out their duties without agonizing over whether they are "good" enough for it. When they hear confession, they rarely dish out penances or try to exact promises of better behavior. Standing in the place of God but not being God, who are they to do such a thing and to what end?

In his life in church, in the *trapeza*, in the workshops and in the fields, the monk learns that while we are all given individual talents, only the soul is unique. How far this is from our post-Renaissance veneration of individual creativity and reward! How close it is to describing the industrial reality of the assembly line ... but not quite. For while anonymity in his work debases the production worker by crushing the ego that is his sole means of knowing who he is, in his drive toward *theosis* the monk makes of his ego a conscious, if often unwilling, sacrifice. (If one consciously could will oneself to give up one's ego, wouldn't that be an exercise of it?) Ultimately, ideally, and even ironically, it is when he allows himself to experience the love that constantly overflows from the Holy Trinity is when he loses himself and is most likely to acquire the elusive discernment of himself as fully in God and fully man. The three Persons of the Trinity are not people, but hypostases: fatherhood, sonship, and the mystery of what goes on between and around them. Their relationship teaches us to love by loving. To renounce conflict while allowing the tension that is inevitable between us to work to the good. When lovers say they lose themselves in each other sexually, isn't it similar: the experience of a love that is not really "theirs" as a possession but something ineffable and ecstatic (literally, "outside substance") that passes through them and surrounds them? At least for a moment?

"What's it all about, Alfie?"

As far as the world at large is concerned, monks contribute nothing to the world – an assessment with which most monks, who see themselves as witnesses rather than doers, gladly would agree. Well, what discernible "good" does a monk do ... as we understand good? If his goal is only to save his own soul, then he's as selfish as anyone working on Wall Street, and his life has about the same meaning. But the monk prays not just for his own soul, but for those of others, because while his soul is unique it is not alone. He prays for those who will not pray and in the stead of those who cannot pray. Like the thirty-seven *tzaddikim* of the Hasidic tradition, the monk's prayers just might be saving the world from collapsing into meaninglessness, but again, who knows? Does belief in God require the world to have meaning? Only if we think his ways are our ways. Does everyone need his or her own life to have meaning? To leave its "mark"? Does anything *have* meaning, or is it only something we *give* it? Socrates said that the unexamined life isn't worth living. On the other hand, Saul Bellow opined that "the examined life makes you wish you were dead." For some, God *is* meaning. For others, an unnamed faith in existence is all.

Many believe that love is the meaning of life. In much of the world, however, love serves only the will to survive; children are economic assets or liabilities, and marriage is a contract to benefit families and prolong the line. Sex that confuses these goals generally is forbidden, and sex that violates and jeopardizes them is often punished by death. Where wealth created leisure, love also could afford to become more romantic. Eventually we came to view marriage in pursuit of wealth or power as somehow tainted, preferring to ignore the ugly lesson that when marriages fall apart it's most likely for lack of one or the other or both.

What Father N. read in his Paris garret was something quite different. John's first epistle is neither pragmatic nor romantic: "We love God because he loved us first." This is an explosive revelation for anyone who is used to thinking of love in either a sensible or an emotional way. According to the disciple, we have a debt that we can only repay with love that we do not regard as a debt. As we contemplate this antinomy, we realize that this single verse tells us that something approaching unconditional love is a real possibility. It tells us that *being* loved is secondary; that we love because God taught us that, as we are made in his image, we are love as he is love; with no expectation of that love being returned. The kind of love that exists between a parent and a child and makes the Prodigal Son the summation of the New Testament. "Home is where they always have to take you in."

These days, does anyone doubt that children need to be loved in order to love? But the love provided by parents rarely suffices because, even if they can't say why, children rightly intuit or perceive that much of that love has conditions. So the love they return also has conditions. When Francis of Assisi said, "It is more important to love than be loved," I believe he meant this: If you can love unconditionally, then, it will matter less to you if you are or are not loved in return. You did not love expecting a reward; you experienced love in the giving of it. Ironically, if your love carries expectations, you won't know you are loved even if you are. If you are lucky enough to find yourself inside and around love with another, any word for what you are experiencing will sound inadequate. Sounds a little like true fasting, doesn't it?

The inability to love others of their own kind may be one of the reasons so many have found their bliss in what they imagine is loving Christ, unfortunately forgetting that Christ said that love of God and love of others are the same. The Jewish sage, Hillel, responded to a man who baited him to teach him the Torah while standing on one foot by reciting the Golden Rule; that to love one's neighbor as oneself is what truly matter; that the rest was commentary. The sacred scriptures of twenty-one independently grown religions affirm this in very similar words. In love, we recognize that there is no essential difference between us and anyone else; and yet, love requires us to see others as unique and completely apart from our self, putting their welfare ahead of our own without any reason other than that we do. It might be what Christ means when he says to follow him one must hate their parents. Or what causes a soldier to lay down his life for his friends. Marriage is doing this on a daily basis. How difficult is *that*?!

Nature's neither neat nor nice; technology isn't either.

In our culture, with its emphasis on immediate pleasure and eternal youth, it is difficult to realize that for most people, for most of history, life has been short and relentlessly brutal. Nature seems to care for creation only to provide food or slave labor for others. The individual is nothing. Neither is any particular species – three hundred disappear every day because they cannot change to meet changing conditions. We humans are not exempt. Earthquakes, diseases, famines, floods, and even wars are all ways of picking the winners. In the course of human history, hundreds if not thousands of proud nation-species have disappeared. Every war ever fought has been for the control of finite natural resources that affect our ability to survive individually, tribally, or species-wide, whether it was the face that launched a thousand ships or oceans of oil in the desert. There is no hiding from Nature's way, hoping to fool ourselves into thinking we'll never be gone. Nature doesn't care how we play with the truth.

Nature knows what it needs.

For the most part Nature wants us to have babies, although sometimes it doesn't. Like a God that is absent from history, Nature only regulates the quantities it takes to give its children a shot at survival. Nature doesn't care if we try to remake ourselves. What is the point of supporting a creature that is struggling to change when millions of new humans are born every day cranially wired for current needs and requiring no transformation? A ten year-old knows more about computers than I ever will.

Nature also doesn't care if you don't get along with your spouse. It wants you to have some kind of relationship only long enough to conceive, incarnate, and rear babies, and it's got a whole bag of tricks for doing it. It has no need for you to look attractive past the age of conceiving. Nature makes all babies cute so they will be lovable and parents won't kill them for disrupting their lives. After all, babies have to have their shot in a million to give something back. Even so, cuteness hasn't always been enough. The ancient Spartans disposed of physically imperfect newborns, and some societies still regard being female as a fatal imperfection.

Nature also is extravagant. All day, every day, all over the world, it puts five million sperm in a life-or-death competition with each other with only one winner. Among the animals that live to be prey, infant mortality is horrific. Predators pillage nests, big fish herd little fish, and snakes swallow sheep. A wolf carries off a calf; the cow mourns for a moment, then goes back to breeding more food for wolves. Wars, floods, earthquakes, volcanoes, tornados, plagues, famines, avalanches, landslides, tidal waves, blizzards, droughts. The blessings of sun and sustenance are forgotten, snowed under by suffering and pain. Is it any wonder that practically since our appearance on earth, we have sought at least a divine explanation of events and at best hoped for divine protection from them?

But the deity that won out in the West is not a God that rewards what we would call good or punishes our notion of evil. He rewards Jacob for stealing his brother's birthright, and the ten virgins for withholding oil from the lamps of the importunate; he doesn't let Moses cross the Jordan, and destroys a poor man for trying to steady a cart bearing the Ark of the Covenant. This is a God that favors the strongest army and the CEO with the most lawyers, and blesses the wide receiver who kneels in the end zone after date-raping a coed the night before. And why? We leap to the defense of one who we say is omniscient and omnipotent; make excuses for him as if we were his parents; try to explain his uncharacteristic conduct as if we knew what was characteristic of God; and say that transgressors will receive their just desserts in the afterlife. But "… my thoughts are not your thoughts, neither are your ways my ways, saith the Lord." Which is probably why Jews, long-practiced in reconciling hope with reality, prefer to answer questions about God with questions about God, and Orthodox Christians try to slip to the side.

.   God is the Great Why that justifies Nature with no attempt at justification. He does what he does because he is that he is, and he is as inscrutable and capricious as the Nature that would have created the need for him even if he didn't exist. We have no access to his "mind", but by giving him a heart we find our solace. If we praise him, is it not also to establish our familial right to blame him? There are very few "natural" deaths, but we blame God for taking someone "before his or her time" as if he had broken some arcane promise. We need no prompting to fear him, but would we love him if we did not believe that he truly loved us first? If human beings had expected God to be any different than he is, we would have dropped his worship long ago. We can't explain evil, but we can't explain mercy, either. It keeps us doubting. And it keeps us going. Museums are the temples of religions that had their gods "figured out".

The world of technology isn't any nicer than Nature. In fact, it imitates it. How could it be otherwise? Technology is dependent on economics, and all the reliable indicators and theories of economics were tested in Nature. It's why capitalism, which finances technology, is so cruel. Like Nature, technology holds gladiatorial contests every day. It weeds out what doesn't work, what doesn't work as well, and what no longer works. To justify employment, a man or woman must produce. Whoever persists in old ways and hangs onto methods of production that were cutting edge only minutes ago becomes useless. Beating a slave to death for falling down on the job may now happen only in movies, but it remains a pretty good metaphor for our more sophisticated times.

Technology, like Nature, needs no moral excuse to accomplish its aims. Utility takes the place of morality in both worlds. Modern technology has made the small farm and the big family obsolete. In the 18th century, industrialization brought hardship to hand-weavers and marginalized a venerable craft, but there was no good economic reason to continue to make rugs by hand if a power loom could make a hundred in the same time. The hand-weavers had to decide whether it was more human to starve than to survive, because ordinary consumers look at price before value. The old stuff became art, and hand-weavers posthumously became artists.

Weird as it may sound to those who see religion as the source of our ethical conduct, monasticism has no conventional morality. A monk would say that it is not because it is *morally* "good" that we treat others as we would like to be treated, but since God willed all things into existence and declared all he created to be "good", respect for others is perhaps all he can know about that will. If all God created was good, then everything that happens is the will of God, including allowing things to happen that we would not call morally good when plugged into the ethical systems we have come up with to regulate society.

"You say potato, and I say … potatoe."

Although some people have approached technology as an art and prayer as a science, technology for the most part is science, while prayer is all art. However essential it might be to discovering a place in creation where a person can live inside his skin, prayer, like art, does not appear to contribute to our survival. Yet the way most of us *use* prayer – what I call "industrial" prayer – has more in common with technology: it is a means to an identifiable, specific end. You pray, and you get some kind of answer. If you don't get an answer, or if the answer is not what you wanted, it must be because you screwed up somewhere – in your life or in your prayer. Tinker with either or both, and maybe you'll get it "right". In this kind of prayer, the game is ours to win or to lose. We are the source of our own victories as well as our losses, our virtues as well as our sins: inept judges of good and evil. Even those to whom the notion of prayer is ridiculous can at least understand this prayer of cause and effect.

By contrast, the Jesus Prayer, the Prayer of the Heart, in which the heart "swallows" the reasoning function of the mind, appears – like art – to have no discernible use. And a world conditioned to cause and effect, process and product, and visible proofs of success, finds this very difficult to grasp or to justify. The great king, psalmist, and ladies' man, David, described noetic prayer as *theosis* in his mystical description of himself: *"I pray, I am a pray-er, I am prayer."* Noetic prayer is like a good stroke with a pool cue. It is an unthinking state that allows the practitioner to focus on the object of his prayer (ball) without making any discernible petition (vector calculation). Unlike the pool stroke, however, which produces either a satisfying "plunk" as the object ball drops into the desired pocket or a string of curses, nobody knows whether such prayer is effective or not. Or whether practice does anything, much less make perfect. It's a matter of grace. (As are some of my more spectacular pool shots.)

With this kind of prayer, who can even say what "effective" means? It might be John the Apostle listening to the heart of Christ and not hearing his words. Or Seraphim of Sarov describing the marvelous effects the "Spirit of Peace" has on others. The monk prays to Him that Is in the same way that he loves Him *because* He Is. He wants nothing from him except to live in him. So, too, he loves his brother simply because God created him in his image. He does no harm to others because in harming others he harms a part of himself. I can't say for sure, but I do believe there are some monks whose heart is so in touch with the heart of all that they truly do feel the world's pain as if it were a pin in their shirt and not a nail in a distant and indifferent wall. There are people in the world with similar gifts.

But even noetic prayer shares some qualities with familiar worldly behaviors. It is active, not passive. The monk works to put himself in a position to pray the way a mountain climber assaults a peak to see the sun: neither can be sure of what he will experience when he gets there. There are similar dangers. The sense of being more spiritual than thou that can accompany prayer shows that noetic prayer is as susceptible to abuse as nuclear fission, admittedly without the immediate possibility of destroying anyone but whoever has his finger on the trigger. Constantly denying the flesh can be as destructive as perpetually giving into it; obedience without accountability can be as damaging to the soul as corporate power.

There is nothing intrinsically holy about being a monk. Neither is the pursuit of knowledge (or technology) for its own sake a guarantee of wisdom (or actual benefit). To think otherwise would allow scientists to wipe their hands clean of the ashes that fall from mushroom clouds. In Biblical terms, the tree of knowledge from which Adam ate is clearly distinguished from the tree of (eternal) life from which he disqualified himself by his disobedience. Where raw knowledge is god, death is the ultimate human experience.

Because the monk believes in the co-existence of the divine and the human, both in the natures of Christ and in his own person, he does not fear death in quite the same way that one does who believes it all ends with the grave or who believes in an afterlife but for the most part avoids thinking about it. It is a monastic proverb that a monk treats his body as if it were going to last a thousand years and cares for his soul as if it were going to leave him that day. He awakes with remembrance of death on his mind and maintains it throughout his day, with the Prayer of the Heart constantly telling him that, though he no longer has to fear death as annihilation, only the mercy of God can absolve him of his sins.

Doesn't that seem a little contradictory? If he is unaware of the judgment that will be passed on him, shouldn't he still fear death? On the other hand, if he knows that God will ultimately be merciful, why should he care how he treats others? The monk lives his life as if he cannot depend on the limitless mercy in which he believes. He may believe that simply the willingness to accept divine judgment is the truest test of his faith.

To die, to sleep – perchance to be cloned.

Humans are almost certainly the only creatures that think about death before it happens. Everyone is stuck with death. Even Christ, on his cross, asked out and was refused. When Paul says that Christ destroyed death by his own death and resurrection, what he did was remove the "sting" of death – our anticipation that we will be no more, or will be in a place or as a thing we would not want to be.

In the effort to make death more palatable, every religion promises either another kind of life or another chance at this life; some are more specific than others, but there's no first-hand testimony that any of them deliver on that promise either as a reward or a punishment. The fear of death and the inability to accept seemingly pointless suffering keep all religions in business. But institutional religion is where one begins one's religious education; hopefully, not where it ends. "Love without fear is nothing," says one of the Hasidic Fathers. "Fear without love? At least that's a start." Why? Because fear is innately human – intrinsic to our survival, "reptilian" – as is blood love; but love of The Unrelated Other is extrahuman.

Fear of God is not simply awe, as some cozy apologists interpret it. It is real, honest to God, fear. The kind that keeps all animals on their tiptoes. Only if you believe that someone can harm you, can you understand mercy. And if you look for this mercy in spite of what that other can do to you, then you understand faith. "Perfect love drives out fear." Even the fear of death. Which is why no one can love perfectly. But we can try. To try is to journey – and what else do we do with our lives?

A religion without love and acceptance has no good reason for being. Fear without love can create a screaming need to believe while yet in this life that one is "saved" in the next. At its extreme, the belief one will benefit from the next world can foster an impatience to end this one. Poverty and impotence that does not feed on hope breed despair. Where people feel excluded from the possibility of a technologically better life, or where statelessness has deprived them of their identity and even a squeak of a voice in this life, millions have thrown and will continue to throw themselves into the arms of regressive religions that promise a life that looks like this one, but much, much better – one they can understand, like industrial prayer, where their blind obedience will reap material rewards, the cost of which is only their miserable existence.

I cannot tell a lie. It was my religion's fault.

Guilt is the confession of our failure to love. First, our failure to be obedient to our higher nature – which we will call God; but also our failure to be our brothers' keeper. Guilt didn't begin with the Bible; the Bible only confirms its existence. Cain asked why God did not love him as much as Abel instead of realizing that as he was the image of God, he had it in himself to love his brother. Guilt is the mark that Cain bore as he wandered the earth, the sign of the mistakes and follies we would like to see heaped on the back of a scapegoat and sent into the wilderness never to return. But final expulsion of all our sins, (*amartias*), is a thing only "devoutly to be wished". In the Old Testament, the Israelites had to cast their misadventures into the wilderness every year. In the sacrament of confession, Christianity offers the chance to do it daily until casting them out becomes a habit; because whether we call it that or not, to sin (*amartanoh*), "to miss the mark", is the human condition.

When a marriage or any kind of commitment fails, it is inevitable that we feel at least a little pricked by guilt, rage, or both, and it is no different when we fall out of love with a religion to which we have devoted a good part of our being for a considerable part of our life. We thought we had it all figured out and now what? As in any relationship that goes south, there's a good chance we will feel betrayed. But if religions expect more from humans than we can deliver, we have similarly unreasonable expectations of them. Institutions like the church inevitably are fallen angels, who, having fallen, do not have it in their nature to improve without an upheaval so vast as to destroy them: it is not within them to change without changing what they are. Unlike corporations, which must constantly find new products, improve on their existing products, or prevent others from making better products or go under, religions are stuck with one product and must continually remind us of our need for it. They can fiddle with the packaging, but if the product changes, so does the church. For three hundred years after its birth, Christianity struggled to increase its market share. Because tautologically no religion can ever admit it is "wrong" or that any other faith is "right", when Constantine turned Christianity into a de facto monopoly, he probably sounded its moral death knell. Like any institution that suddenly finds itself powerful, the success of the new faith led it to take ungodly measures to secure its future. It anathematized doubt, murdered its opponents, and repressed those of its own that were not part of the power structure.

And we, the human element, the alleged Faithful of any worship, are co-conspirators in this rotten development. We accept the corruption of religion, and therefore of ourselves, because in the balance it works for us. I can't think of any religion that has overthrown an existing social order. When Catholics tried it in South America, Rome excommunicated them for their efforts. But because we forget that the need for recurring personal separation from what (and often who) we know, parents included, however painful, is as much our responsibility as unconditional love, we often support much that we personally view as duplicitous and even wrong.

We may be uncomfortable with the kinetic nature of life, especially when linked to our inability to personify change, but any relationship, whether with ourselves, with others, or with God, that does not evolve becomes idolatrous. Aboriginal peoples fear having their picture quite literally "taken" because it imprisons them in a moment outside the unstoppable rhythm of life. The cosmetic industry thrives on trying to recapture what anyone with an interest in truth would tell us is no more. We treasure photos and films that prove we still are what we ceased being some time ago. We cannot admit that constant motion might be all there is, which we quite willingly agree is the lot of every other species, as if we stood aloof from evolution.

Whatever life is, whatever our faith or lack of faith, at the end of our lives very few think we got it "right". The terror of having spent our short span of existence on the "wrong" road is as powerful as the fear of divine retribution and is its own vengeance. Some yearn for a chance to do it over again, while others want absolution for this intolerable probability; for this, there is nothing to turn to but religion. Psychologically, therefore, we cannot afford for our religious institutions to be fallible. Annihilation literally is as unthinkable as that there ever was a time when there was nothing. We must believe that there is "something else", even if we have no faith that there is.

"We're staying together for the kids' sake."

At some point in their lives, many have said, say, or will say, "I am fed up with my religion and *all* religions. I can do better myself. Haven't the established faiths degenerated into shibboleths that allow the cultures that support them to target their enemies? Don't they really serve only the interests of the few? How are they different from other businesses? And hey ... I didn't choose to be this."

Religions – mainstream or charismatic – must plead guilty on all counts. And I'll throw in a fourth: whether through ignorance, apathy, venality, or hypocrisy, those claiming to speak in the name of God, clergy and laity alike, have turned off hosts of others from embarking on a glorious adventure, the search for "rebinding" internally, with others, and with the world. Paul wrote that faith consists of only believing that God *Is* and that he rewards those who merely *seek* him. What is true of the search for perfection is true here: the greyhound that actually captures the mechanical bunny becomes useless. Martin Buber said that the proprietary use of the divine name so affected him that it delayed his writing *I and Thou* for fifteen years.

But while it is easy to sack a religion, and to hate it for what you believe it did to or hid from you, it is not so easy to sack the notion of God. Or at least some kind of intelligence, for instance, that is capable of producing the spectrum of species on display at a dog show. It is one thing to believe that life evolves, but a soup-to-nuts belief would seem to require the same amount of faith that goes into a cradle-to-grave-and-beyond belief in creation.

Bearing this in mind, yet armed with our Protestant right to pursue our own happiness and convinced of the corruption we are leaving behind, we bid ye olde religion farewell and set out on romantic, spiritual journeys that take us as far away as possible from what we have known. Some hope to find themselves while others seek some escape from that same wearisome self. But who can "do" religion by oneself? Or in the company of only a select group of like-minded others? Is religion possible without the same kind of indiscriminate community that humbly sustains us throughout life? That, incidentally, provides the variety of experience basic to evolution?

In the early days of the church, one's parish was where one lived. There were no "magnet" churches, or churches for the spiritually gifted (whatever that is) or those who think they are. Those who thought they were saints walked the streets with sinners. They didn't form exclusive clubs. No matter what technology promises, there is nothing new under the sun when it comes to the inner workings of the human being. In the search for meaning in a very distracted life, meaningful religious experience can only rest on the "height, length, breadth, and depth" of what has been common to humanity through the ages in the company of others.

Divorce isn't always a wrenching and acrimonious split. Like kids leaving home, some people respectfully outgrow their religious roots, just as there are divorced couples who continue to love each other. When an abbot recognizes that a monk of long standing and experience has reached the stage where he might benefit from a separation, he is still reluctant to release him into the wilderness for fear of his forgetting what he has learned from his brothers. People in the world who strike out on their own, or who search for a church – or a particular church within that church – that measures up to their personal notions of righteousness, run the same risk. But is there anything to act as a check for them? From the number of churches and individuals that are their own church, apparently not.

It can't get any better, and it can't get any worse.

Despite our defiance, death has been surprisingly unsympathetic to our attempts to push it into the inconceivable future with creams, potions, diets, and exercise. To burn and then hide it in urns or dispose of it in a cemetery that looks like a golf course. Since the Renaissance and the Reformation shifted the focus from the greatest good to personal happiness, however, personal death began to assume a greater importance than it ever had when it was clear and generally accepted that most people existed as fodder for others. While Copernicus and Galileo risked their lives to prove that we were not at the center of the universe, our newly released egos disagreed, and the span of our own life became the central act in time. No longer satisfied with our role as passing spear-carriers, we began to believe that civilization peaked in the infinitesimal era of our personal zenith and went downhill as we did. It was therefore as logical for generation after generation to assume that it was living in the "last times" of the world as it had been for those Thessalonians in Paul's day, who passively waited for Christ to reappear out of the sky and swoop all of them up into his kingdom.

Thus far, we have not been able to bend life to our will, either. Life has its own inexorable parabola. A Jewish legend says that when we are born we know everything, but an angel touches our lips and we forget. So we begin life knowing nothing about life, instinctively fearful of it and relying on others for our support. We grow toward it, we acquire more and more information, we respond to more and more stimuli. For a few wonderful years, we know (*gnorizo*) the world we live in intimately and implicitly. We breathe in the roses and catch them at the precise moment they release their fragrance. We are knowledgeable statesmen; we dare to criticize the arts; we can name all the new bands, dance all the latest dances, run down the rosters of every team in every professional sport; we read all the new books, speak the new slang, go days without sleep, revel in the latest technology, discuss politics with urgency, argue the new philosophies, have sex many times in a night and run a marathon in the morning, and never think of death as other than accidental – a mistake that will always take us "before our time". We are the makers of the True Renaissance that only we understand. We proudly identify as part of the generation that has brought the world to the apex of civilization. We are surfers on top of the wave. We are the world and we represent all others on it. We co-host the earth with God.

And then we fall away. We are no longer the ones that make the tastes, fads, and understand the present. We say we appreciate contemporary music, but we can't hear it, so we don't like it. Athletes who are only names to us represent cities in which we have no interest. Hip words sound wrong in our mouths and become shibboleths, with us on the wrong side of the river. We become irrelevant to an ever-advancing world. We miss the wave, or go over the top, or stand stranded on the beach as the tide runs out, not quick enough to see the wonderful, ever-new wave rolling toward us – sunlight sparkling on the crest – as anything but a mounting menace. We try to interpret the present according to the past and inevitably, we fail. We are reluctant to give up the power that knowledge gives us, mistaking knowledge for truth. "All I really know," remarked Will Rogers, "is what I read in the papers."

Few grow old gracefully. We may be natural-born misoneists (a nice Greek word meaning "haters of change"), but our relationships with people, places, and things tell us that such hatred is a waste of our fleeting time. Our bodies betray our expectations. Wrinkles defile our youth; liver spots won't go away. We walk fast and call it "jogging". For safety, we drive in the slow lane. We are the impotent butt of jests on a hundred billboards that glorify the young. We still lust, but now we must pick our spots and pray our bodies won't let us down. Intellect gives pleasure where once we held out for passion. The same mind that keeps us young makes us foolish. We are bewildered at how everything else grows old. We imagine we dance like kids and look ridiculous even to those who would like to think we look great. If we have not had children, we may realize that without them, faith is difficult. Too late. With irretrievable irrelevance come visions of death, life after death, and even annihilation, that overpower our egos. We fight back: we exaggerate the importance of our own existence even as it becomes a burden. At some point, we see the crab slip away and come to terms with the empty shell or slip into the uncharted bliss(?) of senility. The illusion of free will, so necessary to our sense of being, bows before the reality of genetics.

Losing one's grip on the world can produce moral Ludditism even as we enjoy technological improvements in our living standard. Along with the comfort of nostalgia comes complaining. All that's good happened in the past. Things may be getting better, but people seem to be getting worse. We become captives of our beliefs, and then we keep those beliefs captive. We no longer trust others at the very moment we most need to. We build walls around our outmoded ideas and ourselves, and we pity the new generation we can never be. A pleasant sense of righteousness tempers our fearful bitterness over the loss of cherished virtues; it allows us to weep at the present generation's failure to keep commandments no generation has ever kept, while we talk reverentially about values that we, in our own love of material comfort, have trashed forever.

Is the present just another "last times" like all the others? Or is something happening now that is both qualitatively and quantitatively different, like the difference between a slight tremor and the lethal grinding of tectonic plates inside the earth? Population growth and the increasing speed of communication are forcing us to make more decisions for a greater number of people based on more information than we can possibly absorb and use wisely. No matter how you believe it happened, human beings were built to maintain themselves and to reproduce, and it never got further than that. Belief in a "last time" helps to ease the pain of no longer being able to contribute in either way.

But modern technology is developing ways to do away with both the need (and opportunity) to work and to have progeny. It has even found ways of eliminating direct male participation in reproduction and is busy designing the same fate for women. It can alter the nature of foods, fool Nature into thinking winter is summer and day is night. Agro-businesses claim ownership of the winds that disseminate seeds.

Thanks to discoveries and inventions, we continue to push back the age at which we can expect to die, but technology isn't satisfied with this. Its implicit promise is the death of death itself while we are still in this life. The sudden inability of humans to control the machines and processes they create has already induced a feeling of license and free fall that cannot continue indefinitely. Technology may finally pull so far ahead of the ability of our species to evolve as to bring about the true "last times".

With no more death would go the fear of death; with no fear of dying, the question of the existence of an afterlife would become moot. If Ponce de Leon had found the Fountain of Youth, would there still be a church, Catholic, Orthodox or otherwise? The death of death, engineered by technology, would be the death of belief in the distinction between God and man.

What then? That ninety-nine per cent of all inventions ever invented have been made in the past fifty years is largely due to the fact that not only are there more of us, but more of us live to an age when our brains have matured and there is enough time to pick their fruit. Physically, we can do things unheard of a generation ago. Just look at the records for speed, strength, and endurance in various sports, with or without steroids. But as creatures that still live and die, we are nowhere near adjusting to the doubling of our life span or the break-up of the vertical family that technology also has helped bring about. Who knows the consequences when endless life and an unlimited amount of leisure become commonplace? Maybe we will learn what the monk knows, however we may disagree with the conclusions he draws from it: that in our current model of incarnation, to know what it is to live it is necessary to die.

"May be the last times, I don't kno-ow."

He may not engage with the world, his heritage may not be our history, and his eyes may be focused on a perhaps impossibly distant future, but the celibate, apparently passive, monk would not be fully human if he did not manage to create his own prickling nostalgia. His "simpler times" is made of tales of a more heroic age, when half-naked men lived in the desert, sat for years on the tops of pillars, or willingly bared their necks to the downward sweep of scimitars. In contrast, while the modern world has had its share of persecutions and heroes, it is shockingly poor in unalloyed Christian martyrdoms. The millions of believers who died under Stalin perished among tens of millions destroyed for who knows how many other reasons. Modern monks read about the fatal witness of their predecessors in the *Lives of the Saints*, but do they really understand who those people were or why they did what they did? I have never found their tales enlightening, nor am I envious of their gruesome deaths (shudder), or even their courage. While at one time I nodded in mandatory amazement at their legendary valor, nothing has ever convinced me that martyrdom is a legitimate vocation. In fact, what is the difference between a saint and a suicide bomber, except that the bomber takes others with him? Christ didn't die for a principle, a cause, or a religion; he died for us.

The monk may look to the past and indeed he may appear to live in the past, but he knows a secret: as Christ is the same today, and yesterday, and yea, even tomorrow, so is he. He never feels irrelevant because whatever happens, however infinitesimal he is, wherever he is, he knows that without him, creation would not be creation. He is important to the world simply because he is, in the same way that the earth is good simply because it is. Without the millions of sperm that die, the one would not have a chance to make its contribution. What happens to the world is not his concern, which is to keep himself free of sin (*amartia*) – the energy that works to defeat the Divine Plan. The perennial advent and disappearance of the "last times" does not depress him. He may not push for Armageddon, like some weird millennialists, but the "last times" must happen before the new age comes. His struggle is to maintain his belief in his way of life while in that life: to wake up every morning with a heart filled with doubt and the remembrance of death, to eat the manna that is each day that he breathes, and in the evening, to lie down knowing he has done his prayerful best concerning God, himself, and – even if inadvertently – humankind.

Just as you are unlikely to find Pericles or Solon in the present government at Athens, the Orthodox monks of today are not the famed desert-dwelling ascetics of yesteryear. But monks throughout history are all fathers and brothers because the *tropos*, their way, has remained the same. That *tropos* is mystical prayer, and the enemies of prayer have not changed. The monk sees the threat of the material world overwhelming him as necessary to his personal struggle. In the relentless march of progress, he hears the galloping hoof-beats of the definitive "last times". He welcomes the challenge, believing that God is all-merciful and will take account of his weakness and inability to resist. Moreover, it is a popular conceit among modern monks that the onslaught they face is so much more soul-threatening than that with which their ancestors had to contend, that God will acknowledge whatever little effort they make to preserve their vows. Certainly, the curvaceous, dark-haired, dark-eyed beauty in a lingerie ad, pouting her lips from a billboard, presents a different kind of enticement than the mental images St. Anthony wrestled in his secluded desert. As I heard one abbot wheeze, "The days will come when simply calling oneself a monk will be enough to merit salvation." I have also heard a Hasidic *rebbe* say that mercy will cover whoever remembers the Hebrew alphabet.

Which reminds me of a story – neither Hasidic nor from the Desert Fathers. Two geezers are discussing whether there will be baseball in heaven. They agree that whoever dies first will return and tell the other. So, one dies and few days later appears to his friend.

"Well? Is there baseball in heaven?" the friend asks.

"I've got good news and I've got bad news" is the reply. "The good news is, yes, there is baseball in heaven. The bad news is you're pitching on Thursday."

Father V. would have laughed.

"I love[d] to go a wandering along The Mountain['s] tracks."

In spite of dire warnings and premonitions, Mount Athos – perhaps in utter innocence, perhaps subconsciously envious of the business model that runs the world – has set sail on the corporate sea. A number of the *koinovia* now are under the combined, ultimate spiritual direction of a single elder – a C. E. M. (Chief Executive Monk) who is responsible to no one on Earth. Not even shareholders. At the final audit, he will be responsible only for the souls in his care and to God. I find it a little sinister that the organization of monasteries should mimic the corporation. I can see no advantage to it, and it creates even more distance between the spiritual head and its extremities. Isn't a corporation a "fictitious person"?

This kind of cooperation is new to the Holy Mountain, where monasteries have been places of physical isolation and individual activity within a small, closed community. Intramural activity in every division was confined to participating in the feast days of neighboring cloisters, small *skitis*, and even smaller *kellis*. Just moving around Mount Athos was a commitment of body and soul; to descend the narrow *monopatis* that led into the deeply forested valleys was to play with the possibility of becoming terminally lost. As an American friend of mine noted, while soaking his blistered feet, "All the paths here are *up*." In those days, however, mobility was not a monastic priority. According to Tradition, a monk's cell was his lifelong teacher. Even if he thought about changing his mentor or his house or leaving, period, the journey was a physical hardship. This is no longer the case.

The modern monk thinks nothing of asking for a blessing and then disregarding the decision of his abbot if it isn't forthcoming. The most common reason for a monk to move is his concluding that where he is staying, his *topos*, is threatening his spiritual life, his *tropos*. It will not come as a complete surprise that abbots, like modern parents, are reluctant to jeopardize their authority by insisting on something that they are increasingly powerless to enforce. The result is that monks not only float around Mount Athos, but they also float around the world. After all, the behind of a monk can fit in the same airplane seat as that of a businessman.

There also are abbots who don't just watch their monks go – they go themselves. These men believe that it is not enough to tend their own flock; they feel called to preach the Truth to people outside the Holy Mountain. Modern travel facilitates the spread of the delusion that the way unmarried, celibate men live in seclusion can be interposed over life in the world. For all they may have learned about inner peace from a lifetime of waiting, these abbots are as untutored in the ways of the world as the average visitor to Mount Athos is in the ways of the monk. A 10th century recluse just might not be the leading authority on the evolution of the marital state from the days when the wife was chattel to where there is not only more or less equality (whatever that means) between the sexes, but where sometimes there are not even two sexes involved.

In a pond as small as the Orthodox one, it is easy for someone to believe that he has become a sturgeon, and that others prize his roe like caviar. This is especially true when his business card reads "Mount Athos". He has no idea that his demand for a proper, fuel-poor fast from people who need energy for an eight-hour workday, a stressful commute, and a family, might provoke a hostile reception from some while his new disciples risk becoming unfit for the world in which they live and wouldn't care if he did. Hasn't there always been opposition to the One and Only Truth? Haven't the faithful always suffered?

The customer base for these wandering abbots consists of homesick Greeks, or converts appalled by the materiality of the American Orthodox churches; who identify the message with the messenger and form cults of personality. This development is anathema to a healthy church. Ironically, a universal faith cannot afford such people not because their beliefs are particularly heretical, but because they and their followers have no doubts whatsoever concerning their beliefs and their imperiled righteousness. If they don't secede completely, they set themselves up as parishes within parishes and feed on those who do not conform to their non-conformity.

Not every abbot works the lecture circuit; nevertheless, technology allows him to be present in the world, to broadcast his message to anyone who has a Walkman. How is this harmful to monasticism? Remember, the faceless, unaccountable, international business conglomerate began life as customer-friendly, idiosyncratic retail stores. A monk depends on communication with his abbot – not so much to hear what he says, but to watch him lace his shoes. When instruction is no longer hands-on, the lessons that can come only from the person of the teacher disappear. Like an absentee parent, the cyber-abbot may imagine he is still in touch with his community but this is a delusion (*plani*). "He doesn't talk to us anymore," said one monk of his *igoumen*. "He talks to his microphone."

One little taste can't hurt, can it?

Even as some monks try to take Mount Athos into the world, the modern world is moving inexorably toward the Holy Mountain. It finds a willing host in the monk who believes that either his calling or his obedience to his abbot makes him invulnerable to temptation. When he goes out in the world, he would have to be sense-deprived not to be aware of the comforts of even relative opulence and the rewards of commerce. Returning to his spiritual spawning ground loaded with contraband that no dog could sniff out, this accidental tourist may think he has nothing to declare as he sneaks an alien spirit through Customs. But the traveler monk is a latter-day Trojan Horse. He may try to absorb what he has seen before it absorbs him, but as they sang about American doughboys when they returned from France, "How can you keep them down on the farm, after they've seen Paree?"

As if breathing second hand smoke, monks don't even have to move from their monastery to experience technology and the ripples it creates wherever it drops. Along with their brethren who have gone abroad, strangers and visitors exude it like host-seeking pheromones. Through increased contact with the world, monks unwittingly adopt its measure of worth. They begin to understand money in a new way. Handcrafted icons, once sold for a song, now command a price that would finance an opera. Money has become more important, not because essentials have become more expensive, but because monks perceive more things to be essential.

Modern technology does not need to destroy Mount Athos. It doesn't even need to convert it. It just wants it to learn its language. A spoken and written language is still our basic form of communication. Music may be more primal, but language is low-tech, relatively easy to learn in one's youth, and gets ordinary things done. Indeed, conquerors bent on destroying a culture often have begun by forbidding the use of its language. Those who accept the new tongue soon find themselves thinking in that idiom, inadvertently giving their approval to the images and values it was created to serve. You may recall that under the Ottomans many Greeks renounced their faith for economic advantages. The increasing presence of technology is a given. As God said of Adam after his creation had acquired an awareness of good and evil, will it be long before monks "become as one of us"?

I speak from my own experience. I like to write. Writing is a very solitary craft. Like monasticism, sometimes it is a solitary confinement, and sometimes it is communion with all that has ever been, is, and will be. I like writing with my computer. I can move paragraphs around, create parallel versions instantly that I can edit at my leisure and not worry about my spelling or, to some extent, my grammar. I began using a computer for its obvious advantages, but I had to adjust to the computer's language to get it to work for me because it had no way to adjust to mine. Now I approach the process of writing the way my computer wants me to. I can still lose myself in my writing, and those moments are so ecstatic that when I return to Earth, my lips often flap when I have to talk with real others. I am sure mine isn't a singular experience among writers. But it is not just advancing age that is to blame for my increasingly lousy spelling and disorderly composition, even as it allows me to run across the bridge between mind and fingers where I used to crawl. I know that my memory also has suffered from relying on my new master; every advance in technology everywhere does the work of a part of the brain that we already know to be underdeveloped or underused. As for the empty part, which acts as our RAM, the more we fill that huge interior space with raw – and often inaccurate or premature – information, the less we will be able to make sense of it.

Are we thereby perpetuating childhood at the expense of maturity? Sam Johnson walked the streets of London nightly, composing and correcting ideas, images, and conversations in his mind, which he later wrote down as page upon page of flawless "fair" copy. Austen, Dickens, Hardy, Eliot, Sand, Balzac, Dostoevevsky.... Prolific writers, all. Do you think they had time for laborious revisions? How many of us can even remember a phone number for more than a few minutes? Do the lightning abilities of my computer free me to use my mind for more important things? Or are they removing a seemingly insignificant but essential part of a process that will eventually cause my creative hard drive to crash, like the corruption of some tiny .dll file hidden deep inside a program that deprives it of its essential logic and integrity? Instead of enhancing the creative process, will it isolate it and then, perhaps, replace it or switch it off? I don't know, but please don't turn off the electricity. I do know that I can't go back.

I also like to bake. I learned to bake bread in a 17th century Greek monastery. When I took this skill into the world and started a business, I tried to do everything the way they had in the old days. I kneaded my breads and scones by hand in batches so small that I occasionally wound up doing ten bakings a day. In addition, I built all my equipment – kneading trough, balances, cooling racks, delivery trays – out of wood, using only the most primitive hand tools. I tongue-and-grooved with a linoleum knife and a screwdriver and fashioned dowel out of hardwood toothpicks. I did not build a bee-hive oven, but I seriously considered it. I had a nice, little business, and had I known anything about business, might have been able to make it into a nice big business. But had I done so, I can assure you, I would not have been mixing two-hundred pound batches of dough by hand.

Lastly, I like to make my own furniture. For years, I remained faithful to my historical approach. I was determined to become as independent of outside sources of energy as possible, and as I worked, I imagined disasters in which I would be the only one not affected. I took considerable pride in this demonstration of what I saw as "living in the world but not being of it". But as I moved from living what I thought of as a monastic life in the world into the world of work, I no longer had the time to hand-cut tongue-and-grooving or patiently figure out the precise compound angle of the corner of a kneading trough. I also initially believed that seven thousand dollars a year was all I would need to live adequately. Within two weeks, that became fifteen; by the end of the month, it was thirty. And this was without girlfriend or wife! I look at some of the things I made during that period, and am amazed – both by the quality and that I had the time and patience to spend six months on a single piece. Now I use power tools. Much of the thrill of creation still remains – of transferring a vision into wood, of fashioning parts and then miraculously finding they fit together; of seeing and touching exactly what I had imagined – but the process is very different, and my limited contact with the world, which allowed me to do it "my" way, is a thing of the past.

The world into which technology pulls us is a world it has redefined. If he wants to, sure, a monk can use technology and still find silence somewhere for at least a few hours a day. But "precept by precept", at some point he will find himself over the line he thought he could draw in the sand because there never was a line at which it was possible to stop in the first place. Not even with a "v" chip. Monasticism requires denying the world – not the place, perhaps, but definitely the world as a mindset. Why should a monk ever be in a hurry about anything? Yet many are, no doubt without being aware of it. You can no more be a little monastic a little celibate.

History speaks and what it says is not reassuring to the defense. The offense is relentless. Can Mount Athos, where the wheel is a relatively recent invention, survive the assault of a power that is far advanced in the ways of the world, and whose premises and values – no matter how well disguised and attractive – are so at variance with the contemplative life? How can it possibly compete for the souls of those within its precincts? Every impregnable fortress has eventually spawned a weapon that in the end got it pregnant. Guns, starvation, battering rams, tunnels, disease.... Walls didn't save the Trojans, who fought for their way of life. What of Athonite monks, who either think it cannot happen or passively await a Babylonian captivity when they will be marched out of their fastness like the ancient Jews from Jerusalem? Or those who may bemoan the siege and sigh but see it as proof of the impending arrival of the not-unwelcome "last times"? The Turks took Constantinople by dragging their ships over land left unfortified because the Byzantines considered it impassable. A gossamer wall of prayer and a veil of celibacy held together by faith is all that separates monks from the world. "The City will fall when ships sail on land," was the prophecy. Who ever thought *that* could happen? When it fell, Hagia Sophia became a mosque. What fate awaits a fallen Mount Athos? Or is the Holy Mountain "too big" in the Orthodox scheme to be allowed to fail?

"You really got a hold on me."

Athonites have hailed the infusion of new monks into communities that not long ago threatened to go the way of the Shakers as a rebirth of their calling. But is this truly a renaissance, or is it more like the smoke that billows from the tailpipe of a clunker a few spark plugs short of the junkyard?

Monasticism will always have an audience. The desire to flee one's being, place, or fate is a natural response when people can't accept the confusion and inequities of life. It is a place of refuge for some, of escape for others, and for others it is the best drug you could ever take – if properly abused, a cheap and almost constant high. It is where you only have to make one decision, and someone else takes care of you for the rest of your life. Many of the same qualities attract volunteers to a life in the military. Just as the stock market is at times bullish and at other times bearish, so in some ages the solitary life exerts a greater pull than in others. In times of disillusionment and hard times, monasteries prosper; there were six thousand monks in Mount Athos as recently as the Great Depression. Science has no answers when the world makes no sense. When the world seems to make sense, men lose sight of their mortality, and there are many empty seats in the refectory.

Reading the front page of any major daily any day is enough to cause anyone to want to make for the mountains. While news of thousands of people dying in an earthquake somewhere in the Far East still may not ruin my cappuccino, a fall in rice futures might. The increasing encroachment of more and more people, the eternal insecurity of relationships, and the remorseless demands for payment of the bills that are the price for the privilege of battling through each day at some point can become Just Too Much. One cannot face reality all the time and live, any more than one can face the face of God, and some people need more than temporary diversions. It might be a belief in another way, with other premises and conclusions. A few need to immerse themselves totally in that radically different way.

Monasticism in some form is no more or less vulnerable to the threat of extinction than any other activity or need of the human beehive. Still it surprises me just how many men and women I know who have toyed with the possibility of living far from the maddening crowd, even if it has not been in the context of a recognizable faith. And how many people – some of whom looked at me as if I had gone off the deep end in the days when I had gone off the deep end – at some point in their lives came to appreciate my experience more than I did. Never mind that by that time I was the one who couldn't imagine what *they* were about.

If the recent monastic revival reflects a rejection of the ways of the world, it is a more sophisticated world than that which either inspired or expelled men in the past. Many of the new monks are educated men in their twenties and thirties, to whom the monastic life, with its regularity and non-competitiveness, is more appealing than the increasingly fast-paced world outside the walls. Whether refugees from the advance of technology or treading water in its wake, these men hope to resurrect the life of silence. Paradoxically, the culture of computers with which they come equipped denies the value of any one place over any other and the ability of anyone anywhere to hide from its persuasiveness; even in the world of capitalism, fixed assets have become liabilities. And isn't it ironic that a life unrestricted by place is also the way of terrorists, some of whom – to our astonishment – also are educated men?

Where does God go when the sun goes down?

At the beginning of my journey in black, applying logic where faith would have served me better, and disregarding logic where it legitimately confounded faith, I truly believed what a monk told me: that it was impossible to be an Orthodox Christian without being a monk. Father P., the revered Athonite *pneumatikos* who shared his cherries with me, took this a step further. "You cannot be a monk," he said, "except on Mount Athos." I heard this dogma from those who know the place only from its awesome reputation as well as from those who lived there. No doubt they have adopted the opinion of a wandering abbot-friar. But monks who live outside the Holy Mountain do have a feeling of inferiority, like Americans that don't live in New York (or weren't born in Brooklyn). Mount Athos is more than a home for monks. It is the second holiest place in the Orthodox world, next to Jerusalem. It is where prayers keep the sky from falling.

Those were strange and fearsome words I had heard. Did the *pneumatikos* mean that Greek monks truly believe that without Mount Athos there can be no monasticism? How can the truth of a way depend on a place? If it is possible to be a monk only on Mount Athos, it would appear to be a frail way of life indeed. As if you couldn't be a monkey outside a zoo. Except in some extreme cases, countries do not automatically disappear with the capture of their capital. But maybe the edict is not as crazy as it sounds. The temple built without hands does not imply that there is no need for a mortar-and-concrete temple at all. Even the new virtual world requires a palpable server somewhere. I don't know for sure, but my experience tells me that to maintain a *tropos* does require a *topos* – that to maintain a Tradition and a ritual does indeed require a place, even as a people require a state for the sake of their own identity and to gain the respect of others – even if they don't live there. Like Moscow and Jerusalem to Russians and Jews in their Diasporas. And The City to Greeks. Without roots, what it is to be human retreats into the seat of all selfishness, estrangement, and eventually despair, that is, the mind – which is what happens when we activate our computers and live in a virtual reality.

History suggests that without Mount Athos, the Athonite off-shoots that have sprung up in the American desert would lose a good deal of their spiritual cachet. But who knows? A lost Mount Athos might just provide Orthodox monasticism with its own Constantinople. An unrequitable love. Some unrealizable hope to keep it going. And someone to hate and blame.

These are the interesting times. The ones that crack history out of the textbooks. Filled with doubt, fear, and anticipation while the various parts of a serious upheaval jockey for a fit. Theory pulls practice after it or practice pushes patiently until those who enjoy its benefits find a theory to justify what already has happened. As an abstract idea, Progress could never compete with Tradition for a monk's allegiance. But when new things, inventions, or discoveries precede their apologists, existing philosophies can absorb them only just so far before something has to break. The history of any worldly empire, from ancient Persia to the Soviet Union that fell apart under the pressure of flagrant economics and smoldering nationalism, testifies to an old New Testament truth: "You cannot put new wine into old bottles."

Unless a dummy pours boiling water into it, a bottle doesn't break without pressure. So, too, very little history happens suddenly. There is usually handwriting on some wall that goes unread either because the reader's focus is elsewhere or because he is willfully blind. In most cases, computers give ample warning they are going to fail. Empires fall decades before a conquering army turns their cities to dust. The collapse of our failing businesses and relationships catches us by surprise only because we would not or could not read the signs. Standing on a path leading out of Karyes on a rainy day five years into my journey in the Orthodox world, it was decided in me that the cloth from which I was cut was not black. The seed was sown. What did it matter that I continued in that life a few more years? It would quietly remain there, perhaps unnoticed, nevertheless germinating; one day it would burst. Three years after I paused on that path in the place no true monk would ever want to leave for a minute, I found myself rudely plunked down in the sand at the foot of the exit slide with no way of climbing back up.

Moving between two worlds is not like changing jobs within one of them. Priests and monks talk the same language, but monks and people fully in the world do not. My exit was scary as hell – comparable only to the feeling I had on my arrival some years ago at the Mexico City airport, which is easily the most foreign place I have been. And yet, I could not stay in the monastic life when I knew that my reasons for being there were gone. In the way that leaves cut off from their roots quickly wither, if you continue to live a life in which you no longer believe, you will soon believe you are dead. I tried to keep contact by entering seminary, but it was a halfway house.

Whether monks welcome technology or fight it, at some point, enveloped in the white noise of the modern world, unable to resist or accommodate it, they may give up the ghost and decide that their lives are irrelevant. They may be embarrassed at how far they have been left "behind" by a world that through its insistent images and promises will not allow them to forget this. Will they adapt to the realities of a world with which they feel they can no longer co-exist? Will they claw their way further into the past as they try to maintain a semblance of equilibrium? Or will the cold wind of technology blow more people their way? Could the technology of the Information Age in the end create *more* monks?

Location, location, location.

The monasteries of Mount Athos are no longer self-supporting agriculturally. Financially, they never were, although in the past huge contributions coming in from the faithful, the skeptical, and the scared made this consideration moot. Monks have talents, and some monasteries now do their own publishing, but few monks have the kind of abilities that translate into broad, marketable skills. With the infusion of modern sensibilities and methods, the costs of maintenance have increased geometrically.

Houses that have relied for their provision on rents from properties in the world, collected from resentful tenants they never see, are particularly vulnerable. Monastic ownership of land outside the Holy Mountain is both old and extensive. At one time, the Great Lavra owned two large and populous islands in the northern Aegean. Some monasteries own apartment blocks in Athens and Thessalonica. The perception that the land was a gift from a tyrant for some kind of suspect collusion, and therefore a monastery has no right to rents is not new, while living off others' need for housing seems downright hypocritical. It just takes someone to do something about it. As I've mentioned, the Greek government and tenants occasionally have seized monastic property, often without payment.

A lot of money went into building Mount Athos, most of it coming from well-heeled patrons. The family of Athanasios, founder of the Great Lavra, was extremely wealthy and well-placed. Since it was all for the glory of God, it didn't seem paradoxical, but in these less fervid days, the wealth that once tempted pirates now looks like a diamond ring on the hand of an avowed pauper. Unless you see monks as pious curators of that which is not theirs, the possession of treasures, like the ownership of land, might even appear to undermine their reason for being and cause a cynic to opine that one needed money to be poor. But if the treasure is not theirs, whose is it? In another time, who would even have thought to ask such a question?

While monks are protective of their privacy, they have not been great guardians of the land that has created it. If an Orthodox Christian commits suicide, he forfeits burial on sacred soil, but in their handling of their natural resources, the Athonites may be doing just that. Logging contracts could eventually destroy the Holy Mountain. Trees are not like manna. It takes years to replenish a forest. It may be that because it is a part of the monastic ethos that every day could be the last that monks seldom consider the possible consequences of their immediate actions. Or perhaps they believe that the handwriting has been on the wall for so long that it has become meaningless graffiti. Or perhaps they don't care.

But even if Mount Athos weathers this latest storm and doubt gives place to some new kind of stability, its fate may not be in the hands of those who live there. It is possible that the Greek government will not let it live. This may be heresy to those who see the Holy Mountain as essential to Greek identity, and therefore, eternal; on the other hand, overcoming cultural identity is implicit in the future of technology, whose driving force is built-in obsolescence and whose enemy is nostalgia. Nothing goes on forever. Mount Athos has done far better than most. When the "last times" finally do come to *Agion Oros*, it may be less about the monks or how they support themselves than a matter of tourism and real estate.

Monks almost invariably have built their homes on the most aesthetically pleasing corners of God's global acre. Theoretically, to a monk beauty is irrelevant. Physical beauty is a pagan value – passing, distracting, and an attachment. Isaiah describes the "man of sorrows", the prototypical Christ, as distinctly lacking in beauty. In my days as a fanatic, the contemplation of natural beauty once made me weep because I thought of it as no more than a tiny taste of the divine, all I was worthy of in this body.

That monasteries occupy places of natural grandeur is at least partly a consequence of the Christian usurpation of pagan temples built by people who were very much in awe of nature and found it prudent to appease their gods by acknowledging their comeliness. Then again, let's face it: deep down, theory aside, who doesn't like to live in a beautiful place? The Franks might not be returning, but the lovely isolation of Mount Athos cannot but appeal to a popular need to get away from the material world that has inspired a flourishing industry that caters to such yearnings. For some, a few days of peace and quiet is the anteroom to a new life. For most, a few days of deprivation satisfies their hunger like a few good chocolates.

But this is only the tip of the iceberg that may sink the Holy Mountain. The commercial potential of the place is enormous. The ink had not yet dried on the Treaty of Lausanne, when there was talk about how nice it would be if the government turned it into a casino. Working both ends of the room, lobbyists proposed that those artifacts that foreigners hadn't already stolen or monks hadn't sold could go to the Byzantine Museum in Athens. But this was pressure from the outside; transition is more acceptable, with less recourse to rescission, when it is one's own hand that does the binding or the loosing.

Which is not to say that the lobbyists have given up. There have been rumors of efforts by Greece to acquire Mount Athos and turn the twenty major monasteries into luxury hotels. And why stop there? Why not a theme park – say, Monastoland? Or the definitive Club Monk, with *kalyve* love nests, hot tubs, and aerobic hikes through the rugged terrain? As the dispossessed are led out onto the Trail of Tears, spin-doctors no doubt will assure them that their new home will be "just as good" and it's all "for their benefit". Like the tempters of legend, they may whisper that the ascetics richly deserve some comforts for spending so much time alone in the service of humanity. Every so often, a Greek government floats a trial balloon to see how the public would take the dismantling of its heritage. So far, there has been enough popular opposition to deflate it.

Mount Athos? The Holy Mountain? A… a Disneyland? Impossible! you say? Remember, *yiayias* excepted, Greeks do not have a high personal regard for monks, and they have a real ambivalence about their Byzantine heritage in general. Hellenes do not remember the Middle Ages with the unmitigated pride and affection that they have for the glory days of the demigods. To many, it is a reminder of four hundred years of servitude to the Turks. I imagine that most Greeks respect monks more for fighting in the War of Independence than for their way of life. To many, monasteries are old buildings inhabited by old men whose indolence is an affront to modern economic life as well as the heroic past. As a counterpoint, the Acropolis, empty of life but full of much-adored ghosts and glory, still dominates Athens.

Thirty seconds thumbing through the pictorial offerings of any kiosk in Athens would tell a blind man that not all Greeks carry their religion out of the church and into the street. For the moment, however, and whatever their reasons, even to non-monastic and, shall we say, worldly Greek Orthodox Christians, Mount Athos is a symbol of the resilience of the eternal religion they confess and a place to find peace from the cares of domestic life. For Orthodox women up to, and to a degree even including, this generation, it is the Holy of Holies beyond the veil. Although Tradition excludes them from setting foot on the sacred Athonite soil, the exclusive domain of the most honored representative of their sex, its existence in some way enhances their life. There are even C. E. O. – Christmas and Easter Only – churchgoers who despise monks and the life they lead and believe knowledge of their religion passes from generation to generation by osmosis, who will tell you over a cigarette and an ouzo they would die for *Agion Oros* and so would every other Greek with them. *Ya sou.*

The Greek government has already taken steps to make Mount Athos more accessible. A modern highway across Chalkidiki cuts the time from Thessalonica to Ouranopolis in half. From what I have heard, this has made some monks very nervous. Others, perhaps in the grasp of self-delusion concerning the good will of their countrymen, or content to let others make a decision they cannot bring themselves to make, greet the possibilities of increased contact with the world with more than a little enthusiasm.

A number of years ago, the *Epistasia* rejected an offer by a group of Italian businessmen to finance a funicular railway that would link the *skiti* of St. Anne's with the sea, several hundred feet below, because it would both increase the ease of secular infiltration and the temptation for monks to leave home. If the Trojans had been as perceptive when the retreating Greeks offered them the big wooden horse, *The Iliad* might have had a different ending. But, the Trojans were not without their victories in the early going, and the funicular affair was only one battle in a long war against an enemy that is as determined and probing as water.

Secularism, the faith of technology, does not always have to introduce something utterly new; it can "improve" what is already there. In 1981, Greece joined the European Union. The European

Union is an economic association with increasingly political ties among its members. For the past twenty years, the EU has been donating funds to the monasteries of Mount Athos for the restoration of dilapidated buildings and the preservation of antiquities that would otherwise have been lost to neglect. What it expects in return is still unclear. This aid from the EU is not the same kind of support the Roman Emperor in the East once lavished on the Holy Mountain. That personage gave his patronage on the condition that the monks pray for him and wash away the unavoidable sins connected with the pursuit of his political objectives. Living "in the world", he paid others to be "not of it". Some rulers even fled to Mount Athos in an attempt to avoid temporal or eternal death. Somehow, I do not believe that the modern financier looks for that kind of return, or envisages a life of retirement among bearded, unwashed men, unless an external audit of his ethics or accounting practices suddenly gives him religion. With the increased logging of irreplaceable trees, and no direct financial support from the Greek government, the monasteries may soon find themselves sitting at a table and playing for their lives with a very small stack of chips and no one to bank them.

"Open the door, Richard."

The European Union is an unabashed apologist for capitalism and democracy. Its cornerstone is the premise that economic collaboration can eventually bend cultural differences to its needs. At this point, a continental monoculture has already formed around technological language and a common currency. The old, locally sensible way of doing business in the Mediterranean world increasingly is a thing of the past. No more lengthy, healthy siestas in the middle of a brutally hot day. No leisurely demi-tasse of coffee as part of the ritual of doing business. No more body language to enhance the ancient art of haggling, because no more bodies. No more church holidays when no one works. In e-commerce, customers do not meet those from whom they buy. And the Internet makes no allowance for how hot – or whose feast day – it is. If you can't reply instantly, you lose.

Saintless Protestantism has the fewest feast days of all the Christian confessions – days when people don't work. Along with less down time, computers, and SUVs will come the Protestant spirit of laissez faire in all things that carried the United States to the top of the heap. In line with the breakdown of national barriers, the EU insists on religious pluralism and the eventual disestablishment of state churches – the most powerful psychophysical lynchpins of national identity and unity. To protect workers against discrimination in the pursuit of economic happiness in whatever country they choose to work, the EU also forbids people to reveal their religion on its identity cards.

The era of free trade in religion is poised to begin. For the first time, individual Greeks will have to exercise their discernment about how they worship. It will be a shock to Greek parishes and priests alike to wake up one morning and discover that the state no longer supports either of them. The salary of the priest will have to come from the pockets of parishioners, as will the upkeep of church property. Will the laity be willing to pay for what they regarded for so long as their birthright? Remember. Ninety-eight per cent of Greeks call themselves Orthodox, but regular church attendance in Greece is about two per cent. That is not high. The relationship of the priest to his flock has to be different when he depends on them for his living. There is a good chance he will discover first-hand the shocking and compromising imperative to become a fund-raiser. And who will support the church hierarchy? And what will happen to that hierarchy the first time a bishop feels the unfamiliar power that a parish can exercise though its purse, as the Ecumenical Patriarch did a few years back when he challenged the democratic spirit of the American congregations on whose kindness he has always subsisted? It may be that in Greece the only Orthodox who survive will be the Old Calendarists and other sectarians, who have always had to fend for themselves.

Greek homes will now hear the knock of the door-to-door religious salesman. The profusion of Evangelical and especially Pentecostal storefront missions in the barrios of Roman Catholic countries and the ghettoes of urban America indicate that after centuries of willful ignorance, Protestant missionaries have finally caught on to the importance of integrating faith and culture. However, the culture they are wooing is not the traditions that are indigenous to the particular country, but the civilization that has formed around universal technology. It is no longer ghost dances or days of the dead with which the people identify (and which the Catholic Church cleverly managed to ingest in the past), but exuberant electronic music, larger-than-life video screens, interactive electronics, cartoons, and tolerance of individual fashion and behavior to which even the Catholic Church – to its credit, disgrace, or the power of its instinct for survival – finally is awaking.

In pushing not only for the disestablishment of national churches but favoritism toward any particular faith, the EU is imitating the hated Ottoman Turks: it most likely will pressure the Greeks economically until pragmatism prevails and they choose to abandon this part of their identity. With the probable dilution of the Faithful by economic necessity and the unrestricted exercise of free choice in religion, will there be enough Orthodox to justify the economically unprofitable existence of the Holy Mountain? Will this finally create the climate of indifference necessary to toll the funeral bell? And with that, will the whole notion of identity – as expressed through family, tradition, and worship – quietly disappear, perhaps to resurface generations later in a hopeless search for roots, or not at all?

While the monasteries, with the predictable exception of Esphigmenou, have accepted aid from the European Union, it is not yet clear how that affects the Treaty of Lausanne. Remember, one of the goals of economics is to make the way straight for manufacture and trade by making all parts fungible. Along with cultural amalgamation and religious pluralism, will there also be an attempt to erase gender distinction? If this is true, and Mount Athos is under the economic thumb of the EU, what is to prevent its political arm from insisting that women be allowed to enter the garden from which they have been banished for half the Christian era? That would certainly settle the monks' vegetarian hash very quickly. *Kafeneions* no longer provide refuge for Greek men; is Mount Athos next?

Once Greeks become aware what the EU is up to, the monoculture, however intimidating the power it represents and whatever the consequences it portends, will not have its way unchallenged by the people who beat back the King of Kings at Marathon. After the bishops who attended the Council of Florence in 1439 tentatively agreed to a reunion with the Pope, the Orthodox laity practically stoned them. And what other country has made a national celebration of the inclination to say no? October 28 is *"Okhi* Day", the day in 1939 – exactly five hundred years after the Council of Florence – when Greece again refused to capitulate, this time to the Axis Powers. There is the possibility that in trying to *force* acceptance of its pronouncement concerning identity cards, the European Union may jerk the collective knee and provoke serious resistance, for Greeks are among the most independent-minded people on earth. However, there is no rush. Technological culture has effectively usurped its former bosses, established religions and independent states. It has all the time left to the world to absorb both into its own amoral, corporate immortality.

All religions are separated by a common faith.

Underneath their dress clothes, religions are the same because the religious impulse cannot help but be the same the world over. All believers face the mountain, the desert, and the swamp in front of them with equal bewilderment. "Why do the wicked prosper?" ask both Jewish and Zoroastrian scripture. The fact that Buddhism has no gods and Christianity has God hides the far more important truth that the process of karma parallels the Christian Pilgrim's Progress: the intuitive chain of original sin, present faith and works, and future judgment. Buddhists call their religion a "path", and Orthodox Christians call theirs a "way". What's the difference? But because of its strong ties with culture, and the walls built around cultures, religion as a discipline has never effectually recognized that the moving force behind all of its thousands of manifestations is one and the same. Without the spirit – the freedom it promises and the constraints it imposes – the best religions would simply be parochial codes of ethics, and the worst ones would be attempts at bloody appeasement. The culture out of which a religion grows – while giving it the particular flavor that we find at times exotic and at other times repulsive – tries to capture the spirit and make it serve a particular people. In other words, it feeds Fay Wray to King Kong. It vitiates the common source.

When language was shattered at the Tower of Babel, it took with it the possibility of a universal religion that would have been one mega-idolatry: a very real, universal, subjective approach toward religion that literally objectified and enslaved God, pushing aside the spirit. In the mitosis that followed the crash, only the universality was destroyed. The quality remained. But now each little piece that survived was hostile to every other; they could not recognize their common source – like those pirates who attacked Mount Athos and wound up fighting each other in the fog.

The idea of mercy aside, however, where are we today that is any different from pagan days? How do our competing faiths differ from the gods the ancients took out of their saddlebag at night and set up on a rock to protect their camp from what they didn't know and what they feared, which often were one and the same thing? Or the kind of belief that was spawned purely by the *need* to believe? And the kind of god one could service with industrial prayer. Make the harvest good. Give us victory in battle – against other creatures … (you created). Go, Raiders! But our brutality to others who essentially are like us should be no surprise: when you make an object of God, who is the Great Other, in this way – like a bobble-head stuck on the end of your need – aren't you doing the same to *all* others? And denying the autonomy and mystery of God and of all others? You may say you respect other beliefs, but there isn't a person who hears this rot who can't smell the hypocrisy; after all, for you to be "right", they have to be "wrong". Doesn't it astonish you that so many religions can claim to be the sole spokesperson for God?

Because a religion has been around for thousands of years testifies only to its success in reflecting the aspirations of the culture from which it springs and the success of that culture in staying around. Will technology put the capstone on the Tower of Babel and utterly objectify religion? Will its aversion to traditions usher in an age of universal Pentacostalism and reduce established religion to a cultural vestige? Or will it provoke a religious retrenchment and regression such as we are currently seeing, ironically, primarily in the Arab world and the United States?

You *can* go home again – but not by the same road.

A good part of this book is devoted to getting to Mount Athos, admittedly with many stops on the way. I would like to say this was by design, but it wasn't. In a sense, it had to be. Look back at the initial epigraph: "Man is a rope connecting animal and superman – a rope over a precipice.... What is great in man is that he is a bridge and not a goal." For the pilgrim, "getting there" is a physical reality, the exhausting effort out of which rises the spiritual dawn. The pilgrimage plays a significant role in every religious tradition: the *hajj* is the ultimate earthly experience of Islam; without the exodus from Egypt, and the forty years in the desert, there would be no Judaism. Hindus and Buddhists journey to sacred places and receive counsel from those they consider holy. I don't think I'm going too far out on a limb to surmise that a large part of the attraction that the latter two faiths have for Americans lies in the fact that Tibet and India are a lot further from the United States than either religion is from Christianity. The existence of a distant goal creates the possibility of a physical journey that is longer than a once-a-week walk to the corner in a suit and tie or a dry-cleaned dress – a feeling of earning your faith.

The pilgrimage of the Orthodox Christian monk is a journey from the womb of the mother to the bosom of the father. From the material to the spiritual. From prejudice to discernment. From self-interest to service. From willfulness to grace. From Alpha, the beginning of human awareness of the immanent divine, to Omega, what we can never know. On the way, he falls into potholes, stumbles over obstacles, and explores blind alleys, seeking eventually to reach a place where he *knows in his whole being* the right thing to do in any given situation and to distinguish the truly good from masks of evil.

"Leaving there" is equally important. Ephemeral as peace, we are merely sojourners on the earth, "as all ... [our] fathers were". As a species deeply involved in our environment, physically, emotionally, and spiritually, we are neither built for nor entitled to more than a transient rest. I have no lasting regrets about leaving the monastic life, though I felt the same pain that at least for a while inhabits any relationship gone south. How I could have entered it in the first place is often as incomprehensible to me as it may be to you. Perhaps my donning the black was necessary: I needed it to effect a life-saving change of behavior; a shot at maturing in spite of myself. For all that I possessed two of the best educational union cards one could hope to own, at the clip at which I had been going nowhere, who knows what would have happened if I had stayed in the world, repeating circles in the sand, sinking deeper and deeper each time around?

In one of seven letters attributed to Anthony the Great, the writer says there are three ways of coming to God: one is born with love for him, one hears or reads of the rewards and punishments attending belief and unbelief, or one gets hit in the head enough times that he finally gets it. I am quite sure that bashing my head on that steel bridge post was the only way I could have made my "decision". Having done so, in monasticism I found a haven. I lived the life of a monk for ten years and knew nothing of what was going on in the world. I read no books that dealt with anything outside the existence I had chosen. It was only by accident that I knew who was president of the United States. I missed everything and I missed nothing. I was very happy. Remarkably peaceful. Unimaginably healthy. For this privilege, I paid a price. Without the friction, tension, and relationships of ordinary life, I made no psychological progress for more than ten years. There was some compensation: I did avoid any possibility of contracting AIDS.

I know that what started me on my way out of Mount Athos and the life it represents, on the day I stood in the rain on the path leading up and out of Karyes, was the inescapable certainty that *if I could not pray in the subways of New York with the same peace I found in a monastery, whatever I found in the monastery was worthless.* Looking back, this was without a doubt a ridiculous stipulation, but that was me. I could not even have told you what that sententious sounding syllogism meant, unless it was an unwitting expression of love of "the other", which I doubt. I think it was an expression of longing, if not for my old life in its entirety, then at least some of it. Others on The

Mountain might find the fullness of life there. Do I doubt them? Probably. That's also me. On my return to the world, I did not have quite the same feeling of revulsion for my adventures with the spirit that I once had for my dalliances with the flesh; but for years I did cringe in the presence of any reminder, and I certainly felt that my singular devotion had been just as misplaced. For solace, I told myself that if the church took something from me, it was only because I acquiesced to the theft. Sometimes this worked; sometimes it did not.

The technology of the Information Age has no interest in pilgrimages that aren't upgrades. Its ultimate illusion is the global village, where no one has to go anywhere but can go everywhere, where the telemarketer who calls you by your first name is your friend, where the shoemaker in Beijing is a neighbor who will never knock on your door and you will never see suffering in the street. *Agape*, unconditional love, is not an abstraction, but an experience: you can't love all people; only people. But how can you love someone you cannot see? Or have mercy on them when you can kill them by pressing a button, not knowing (*gnorizo*) what you have done? On the other hand, you cannot live in the world we have inherited and ignore technology. If you can, you are living in a world far more distant than the one I found. But if technology and attitudes, and the things it demands and creates, are all you've got … why are you?

C'mon, did you really expect a conclusion?

If we look at monks as humans – something many have difficulty doing – we may make good use of the mirror they provide, see through the surface distortions, and discover someone very much like us. The monk spends his day falling down and getting up and falling down and getting up. Is ours – with our risks, fears, joys, loves, successes, and mistakes – any different? Are monks hiding from life because they live within walls? Look at the walls that you erect to ward of things and people you don't want to deal with. Are monks slaves to dogma? Examine your own long-held, no-longer-if-ever-examined opinions. Monks have no freedom? No security? Look at the ground on which you stand and what the future looks like beyond your next paycheck. Are they isolated? Consider the chasms between us that grow wider and wider daily as modern technology isolates us through the illusion of bringing us together.

In reality, we are a lot closer to being a monk than we are to being Donald Trump or Bill Gates. For most of us, the life of the billionaire C. E. O. is hopelessly out of our reach, while living a life in harmony with what surrounds and inhabits us is only a breath and a bit of doable will away. This is what we may take away from our stay on the Holy Mountain without paying customs: something that may allow us to see our own world in a different, though kindred, light.

A visitor from Alpha Centauri would be probably more familiar with the modern landscape than our parents or even the us of our childhood. People walk in the streets with earphones on their heads, oblivious to their surroundings, or avoid others entirely in cars that are as luxurious and isolating as Howard Hughes' penthouse. With the increase in information, we imagine that we are getting more and more in touch with ourselves and with others. But don't kid yourself – a distant relative is not only a telephone call or a five-hour plane trip away. Those thousands of miles are still thousands of miles, allowing people we think of as close to become the facile projections we may not know that we need them to be. Even now, few die among those with whom they lived. One of the reasons we need social security is because for many of us our own families can provide us with none.

When I look out of my window or around the room in which I am writing this, I can find nothing that says I have control of my life. I depend for my heating, my lighting, my clothing, transportation, communication, and my food on people I don't know and the fictitious people they work for. I know they don't care about me, and I have less and less opportunity to engage in any kind of dialogue with them. The only time they call me is if I owe money or to say how much my business means to them. My money, the measure of my worth, is on a little piece of plastic that activates a chip in a computer controlled by somebody, somewhere who I am blindly obliged to trust and placate. To try to get through to a real person on the phone puts me in touch with my inner Kafka. Because a machine counts my vote, I'm not sure if I have a say in who governs me or how I am governed. I am asked to believe in myths that by contrast make the Virgin Birth appear quite reasonable; I often catch myself wishing for miracles. I need nothing but my senses to know that in its unregulated pursuit of cheap labor and broad markets, globalization is eroding the safety, health, and quality of my life and of those around me.

From my window on Mount Athos, I saw the woods, the sea, and the sky. A monk shouldering a hoe on his way to the garden or coaxing a mule over a rock-strewn path. A priest opening the doors of a church. I heard the sound of a brother, his robe tucked in at the waist, repairing the roof over my head, and the beat of the *symandron* calling us together to pray. By now, you know it hardly was utopia. But where was I more the master of my fate?

The easy way to dismiss something perceived as a threat to one's viewpoint is to label it as not worthy of consideration. But prejudice is its own punishment. It allows us to be blindsided by both facts and mysteries. Understanding often requires becoming uncomfortable: willing to be surprised. These are not two of our favorite situations. We may not be sympathetic to another view, we may not be able to find a place for it in our own life; but only as we try to understand others will we perhaps understand ourselves and be able to make ourselves understood.

What I'm getting at isn't like two religions, each claiming possession of the One and Only Truth; or two competing scientific theories, one of which must be wrong. Philosophically, they may be completely incompatible, but religion and science are two ways of seeing the world that must coexist as long as there is no incontestable signature to creation. Each adds a dimension necessary to the advancement of our species. Unfortunately, both continue in their efforts to subsume – rather than accept and attempt to understand – each other. Once it was religion determining the boundaries of science. Now, science tries to explain religion. Good government and self-government cannot afford to let one party obliterate the other. We cannot afford to poke out one of our eyes.

The Puritan dilemma that has dogged our steps since the introduction is still with us at the end: "How is one to live in the world without becoming of it?" How is one to raise the bar above basic individual survival in a way that benefits others? To develop and live a communicable morality, one that is neither wholly absolute nor only relative? To use the incredible bounty we have inherited and the inventions and discoveries we have made in such a way that we do not do irreparable damage to anyone or anything? John Winthrop and his people did not succeed in doing this. They chose to abandon the world, no matter that they prayed for it. They wasted no Christian mercy on Indians, and their utopia, Massachusetts, became a repressive, bigoted theocracy. They forgot what is essential to any faith or community, religious or secular; and that is compassion.

Thomas a Kempis wrote in *The Imitation of Christ* that he would rather have compassion than be able to define it. Compassion is as much a part of a human being as muscles and a brain. It exists in the no-man's land between the impersonality of beliefs, where we stumble around and finally recognize that we are all in the same boat, ultimately dependent on each other because where it matters most we are ultimately ignorant. Those who worship material progress won't find the answer. But neither will those who look to the sky for the First or Second Coming. "The duty of a true believer is to treat your brother as if there were no God," observed an Eastern European *tzaddik*. That observation could have come from anywhere and anyone. The Messiah is always here.

A refurbished *kalyve* on the north coast of Mount Athos between Iveron and Great Lavra. When I was there in the seventies, most of the *kalyves* were in disrepair.

Stavrovouni, the magnificently-situated monastic aerie on top of Cyprus—twenty-three hundred feet above the surrounding countryside.

Inside the Monastery of Longovarda, on the island of Paros. When Longovarda was built in the seventeenth century, thirty-seven monasteries flourished on the island.

The Best of the West (My mother)   The Beast of the East (Father George)

EPILOGUE

BEING AS NOTHINGNESS

Well, he never returned, no, he never returned,
And his fate is still unlearned…

Jacqueline Stiner and Bess Hawes, "M.T.A."

What compels a person to return to the scene of the crime? If we need visible proof that years have passed, a mirror is a lot cheaper. I went back to Mount Athos a few years ago. I hadn't been there since 1984. This time, I was not traveling in black. My present connection with the Greek Orthodox Church is as an *ecclesiarch*. In a monastery, this is the person who pounds on the *symandron*; whose obedience it is to see that the church is ready for services and that the chanters don't stumble over each other in their haste to display their wares. My job description as an *ecclesiarch* in the world comprises the preparation of the church for services, participating in them as a tonsured Reader, and riding herd on a host of teenage altar boys who are there because if they weren't, their parents would be most unhappy with them. Whereas once I would have been appalled at the boys' behavior and their lack of interest in their family's faith, I now can appreciate their boredom with doing something that parents and clergy have done their best to ensure meets so few of their needs and none of their wants. Yet even with all its headaches, politics, and distractions, I find being involved in a large parish and a Sunday parent far more satisfying and invigorating than living alone with others who are living alone. I also assist the priest at baptisms. Up to now, I have done about five hundred of them. It's a rare double: five hundred baptisms and five hundred mediations, not as yet recognized as a great achievement. Baptisms are something else that keeps me in church. All those little people, all different, all with their whole lives ahead of them.

What brought me into the Orthodox Church hasn't gone anywhere: through the Personhood of Christ, I continue to be aware that the holy and the human are contained in one being. I worship with humane people and with bigots, liberals and conservatives, rich, poor, and those in the middle – a mix I would find in any group anywhere doing anything and who test whether I can put into practice attitudes and behaviors I casually acknowledge as truths. If pressed, I call myself a Greek Orthodox Christian agnostic Jew. I am an agnostic, because while I have been granted imperfect faith, I have neither the *chutzpah* nor the hubris to presume to know who God is or what he wants. I am a Jew because I always will be, just like a Greek always will be a Greek.

On this trip, I flew into Thessalonica, rather than Athens, because it is no longer necessary to get approval from the office on Academy Street for a stay on the Holy Mountain. Now a Pilgrims' Bureau in Thessalonica takes care of the whole operation from the soup of answering your original inquiry to the nuts of issuing your passport. At the airport, I struck up a conversation with a young Greek woman at the baggage carousel. She told me she wasn't all that happy with the European Union's insistence on deleting religious affiliation from the new identity card. Given her age, I expected that shift toward equality would have excited her. She explained that if her card did not read "Orthodox" she would have no chance of landing the job at the bank for which she was interviewing that morning.

On this trip, I also would not be traveling alone. In Thessalonica I rendezvoused with David, a good friend of mine from California, and the enormously bright and funny priest-monk, Father S. David is Jewish. His father is a rabbi. Naturally, David is synagoguophobic. Father S. is a very modern Greek monk whom I had met while he was doing a few months of graduate work in the States; now he was living in Greece as a convent's resident priest.

Although I had never heard him discuss women, I imagine Father S.'s situation presented him with a number of challenges he had not foreseen when he took up the habit. In addition, he was very fond of the life he had tasted in the United States and had an eye out for any chance to re-cross the Atlantic against the desires of his bishop, short of outright mutiny. Unfortunately, on our arrival, Father S. told us he would not be able to accompany us to the Holy

Mountain. His bishop had vetoed the expedition; perhaps he had envisioned his prize priest-monk stowing away in a container ship carrying purloined icons to New York. That evening, Father S. took us to his favorite sweet shop in Thessalonica. On the way, we passed a McDonald's. Our guide said that during church fasts, the chain now offered something called a "MacLent". It was probably a vegi-burger, he continued, making a face that conveyed the impression that both he and God shared a single opinion of its worth. He hadn't tried it, he added unnecessarily. At the sweet shop, on the other hand, he was not at all reluctant to sink his fork into a huge *katafaiki*, the Greek pastry that looks like shredded wheat dripping with honey. His pleasure was obvious and unstereoptypically monastic. After the olive, sugar is the main staple of the Greek diet, which may explain why, according to another one of those surveys that have you wondering about just how they got their funding and their information, the average Greek tips the scale at sixteen pounds excess avoirdupois, making them the most overweight people in Europe.

The next morning, we took care of the necessary administrative chores. I had kick-started the process months before with a letter to the Bureau requesting specific days for our visit. In the reply, they still wanted to know what kind of work I did. This time I wrote "mediator", confident that this, my Biblically-approved and actual profession, would get me through the needle's eye as surely as if I had never cut the nail on my pinky. There are still daily quotas on Orthodox faithful and on heretical applicants: a hundred from Column A and ten from Column B. Father S. took us to the Pilgrims' Bureau, a single room on the second floor of an unassuming office building. Two young civilians with short hair and stubbled cheeks looked up as we entered. Our guide greeted one of them with open arms, and they immediately launched into a conversation to which David and I were mute spectators. It took us about a minute to get the necessary documents from the other man, and then another fifteen to pry my silent monastic away from his chat with his pal. We would now receive our Athonite passports at Ouranopolis instead of Karyes.

David and I caught an afternoon bus, our object being to stay in Ouranopolis and avoid having to rise at five A.M. to catch the early morning monk/pilgrim special. In retrospect, this concession to comfort was quite unpilgrimish and deprived me of the pleasure of showing my companion how right-on I was about the various species of traveling monk. The Chalkidiki bus station was the same as it was back when, down to the DNA of the dust on the windows. Cramped, chaotic, and improbably efficient, it had long ago tailored its *typikon* to the rural population it served, and technology had yet to show it could improve upon what was. At the rear of the station, a small coffee bar offered Greek coffee or Nescafé in paper cups. Nescafé is to Greeks what Spam is to Hawaiians: a despised American convenience food for which less materially fortunate cultures have developed an unfathomable esteem.

Two minutes before its scheduled departure, our bus pulled up to the curb. The driver jarred to a stop and left the motor running as he leaped out and opened the rear door and the undercarriage luggage compartments. Passengers climbed through the one and baggage tumbled into the other. Slam! Slam! We were off. On this next generation of Daimler bus, the windscreen extends to the roof. There was no room for Christ at the inn, and now there was none in the bus. Instead of a wall-to-wall icon-screen, the safety of the passengers was in the hands of good tires and brakes. There was a threat of air conditioning, but it came to nothing.

The country that we passed through on our way to Ouranopolis had not changed much, though "they" had repaved, widened, and in some places, straightened the road. Remnants of the old, winding street lined the new highway like an Andy Goldsworthy project. Though this was a destination bus, it served as local transportation to towns and villages that have no public transportation of their own. At three o'clock, the universal hour of release from scholastic labor, bunches of uniformed school children swarmed on and off. The kids laughed, punched, shoved, and shouted each other down. Women returned from neighboring towns with their shopping. The driver delivered parcels station-to-station and sometimes to the door. A ticket inspector got off and another got on every few stops to make sure that no one rode for free. *Almost* free was the ten-dollar fare for this three-hour trip.

Every village we passed had at least three hundred and sixty five churches, and the women on the bus, old and young, in worn black dresses and very short skirts, crossed themselves at each one. Good brakes and tires are for men. Smoking was not allowed. This does not mean that Greeks were inhaling the sot weed less than on my last visit. Just not on public transport. Now, however, smoking was merely a noxious habit; not the devil's incense. Furthermore, I have to admit, after my years in the healthocracy of northern California, the presence of a pack of cigarettes on a café table was "curiously refreshing": a comfortable reminder that nothing changes at a snap of the fingers.

The still life was not exactly the same, however. Almost every table at every café, taverna, or restaurant, displayed a mobile phone next to the smokes. Greek men treat their phones *like* cigarettes: they don't light them, but first thing they do when they sit down at a café, or get behind the wheel of their car, is to make a call – or at least appear to be making a call. In the streets, thanks to invisible headsets, so many people seemed to be talking to themselves that it looked as if the national mind had snapped and created a nation of perhaps not so holy fools. On the two planes I took, passengers appeared determined rather to fight than switch off their phones. Admittedly, none of these asocial habits is particularly Greek.

Along with mobile phones, the multiplication of cars is the other obvious fact of contemporary Greek life. In cities that have wonderful transportation infrastructures, SUVs, the weapon of choice, nearly scrape the walls on both sides of streets where two cats couldn't pass without touching. Where the money comes from to pay for these expensive vehicles in a country not known for its prosperity is perhaps proof that this is indeed becoming one, global community – ubiquitously mired in debt.

Butcher shops now open on fasting days, and signs no longer make it a no-no to blaspheme on public transport. On this trip, I noticed people begging in the streets who clearly were not beggars. Their misfortune seemed to be no longer a social concern, but like almost everywhere else, was accepted as the inevitable detritus of soulless economics. One of the unrecognized benefits of monasticism, and of considerable significance should monasteries disappear, has been that along with providing a lair for the lazy, crazy, homosexual, and socially maladjusted, monasteries historically have been places where families could dump children they could not afford to feed. In Israel, Syrian outcasts populate most of the Orthodox convents.

Arneia appeared prosperous: a new football stadium, a school, and streets stretching into occupied suburbs. It was the first time I had seen it when I (and the bus) hadn't been in an early morning fog. A stop, but no refreshment: this wasn't the through bus. The road after Arneia boasted new blacktop. Otherwise, it had not been altered. As of old, it dropped like a snake to the coast and the seaside town of Stratoni. I did notice that the clusters of crosses that once issued vain warnings to drivers at almost every curve were no more. I heard they were offensive to modern sensibilities and bad for tourism. In some places, the feeble light of a single vigil lamp continued to burn like a wrecker's fire on a reef. A crash is no longer an event; a death is no longer worth a memorial.

The bus driver pulled into a residential street in Stratoni and deposited a large box on a doorstep. We passed Ierissos without seeing it. The same kind of cookie cutter, expensive villa/resorts that neutralize the rest of the Aegean mar the last few miles of the road into Ouranopolis. Ouranopolis itself was an eye opener. Whether it had changed or not I could not tell, since on my previous visits I had shielded my eyes as if it were Gomorrah. Ouranopolis is a charming little sea-front town: an esplanade, trellis-covered restaurants, and narrow streets winding up into the hills. No smell of cooling brimstone; it isn't likely that the reconstituted me would have found anything objectionable even had it been there. The pornography that is so publicly available had not by-passed the kiosks of Ouranopolis, but the town could hardly stake a claim to notoriety based on that alone. Besides, it was at a kiosk that I discovered the miracle of the phone card that bought three or four reasonable international calls for two and a half dollars. It was October, and it was late in the day; we saw no naked bathers.

Doctor Johnson noted that imminent death can wonderfully order the mind and pull it out of the quicksand of reverie into which it would most willingly disappear. Moving from one world to another can have the same effect one one's perception of reality. The massive, square tower at the water's edge, no longer was the 19th century folly of a nostalgic, eccentric Englishman, created by my lazy imagination, indifferent to the world and its history, but actually was what it looked like – a 14th century edifice.

David and I found a Spartan room in which to spend in the night. It was painful to watch our landlord, an elderly man crippled by disease or injury, lead us up to our room on the third floor of a cinderblock of flats. For what our accommodation lacked in amenities, the view of the Sigitikos Gulf, turning colors in the rapidly descending twilight, was more than adequate compensation. Our host said that for no additional charge we could leave our luggage with him while we were on The Mountain, and he would meet us on our return.

The Ouranopolis office of the Pilgrims' Bureau opened at eight thirty in the morning. Amid the anticipated chaos, the shouting and the arms waving wildly above the mass like longshoremen at a shape-up, everyone entitled to an Athonite passport got one. The boat that was to take us to Mount Athos was a substantial vessel, a smaller version of the cavernous car ferries that ply the Aegean. Trucks loaded with construction material trundled onto the capacious main deck, while we climbed the stairs with the other passengers. It was a beautiful autumn day, and the capacity of the sundeck was severely tested. (Not that those "maximum capacity" signs are any less of a wall decoration on ferries than they are on buses, but often with severer consequences.) The crowd surprised me, since it wasn't a feast day, and it was out of season. David took two seasickness pills.

At nine o'clock, we ported our helm and backed away from the quay. The engines shifted into "forward", and we headed south. Leaning on the railing, watching the years slide backward by, we met Jack, the Anglican Bishop of Sheffield. Just Jack. Not even "His Grace, Jack". Apparently, the Church of England is less formal than its elder sisters. With a slight nod, Jack drew our attention to a well-groomed, white-haired, Orthodox prelate, who, while traveling without retinue, had conspicuously exposed a little patch of the purple episcopal garment he was wearing under his black robe. Jack wore a plaid shirt and slacks.

At Giovantsa, we off-loaded a truck laden with cinder blocks that came within inches of going straight to the bottom as the ferry drifted slightly away from the quay. There was little commotion. Near misses don't raise more than an eyebrow among people used to sustaining direct hits. From the first view of the *arsanas* of Zografou, directly ahead as we rounded a headland, it was clear that somebody was pouring a lot of money into Mount Athos. Skilled artisans had sandblasted and finely squared the stone tower in the port into the pristine look of the newly-built. Dochiareiou, the third stop, was a skyscraper under construction. A tall, red crane towered over the walls, its horizontal beam maneuvering blocks and beams into position. A thick, gray, plastic wrap, which covered a good quarter of the monastery that was visible, flapped noisily. There was a feeling of great busy-ness, even though few workmen were visible and almost no monks.

Further along the coast, the burnt-out shells at Panteleimon were still burnt-out shells. The green roof of the main building looked spanking new, as did a few of the outbuildings. What we could not see was that Ukrainians had driven out the Russians and taken control of the old *Russikon*! Would it now be called the *Ukrainikon*? Since Mount Athos is a sovereign state, and each monastery also is essentially sovereign, and the monastery did not legally *belong* to the

Moscow Patriarchate, there was no court to which the ousted abbot could appeal. Time may be at a standstill on the sacred peninsula; not so the winds and the tides. The once-dominant ethnos was now without a major holding anywhere on The Mountain.

For the moment, the monks and the restorers appear to be companionable bedfellows. It seems that preserving the old simply because it is old has become important to a world that otherwise regards anything (or anyone) old as being expendable. What will happen when the monks realize that the aim of their new pal is to shore up the old buildings and not necessarily the way of life? That's an awful lot of prime real estate being kept off the market for the benefit of a handful of men who contribute almost nothing to the economy.

I have no answer, and David couldn't possibly have helped me. We never discovered whether the pills he took would have prevented him from getting sick when the ship yawed, because you could have balanced a drachma on the deck. What we – or rather he – did discover was that two of those little tablets floating around in your blood stream can make you oblivious to your surroundings for about forty-eight hours. For the next two days, I sometimes felt like I was leading a comatose bear about on a chain. Poor David! To come all that way to fulfill a desire of many years and to have one's petard hoisted by a reasonable desire to avoid pain. There's a lesson in there somewhere. Along with a monastic chuckle.

The quay at Dafni was the same. What was missing was the ancient wooden *caique*, waiting to take small groups of intrepid pilgrims further down the coast. The vessel that now plied that route was the one that had previously been on the Ouranopolis to Dafni run. The wood from the *caiques* had most likely helped someone to get through the winter. The gentle hand of progress had ripped out the interior of the old Customs House but passed over the rest of the little frontier port, like the Angel of Death ignoring the marked dwellings of the Israelites. It is now possible to buy pizza at the gateway to Karyes: an inauspicious portent of things to come? I wondered if my old *kafeneion* at Konstamonitou now sported a Coke machine.

The maroon bus was gone. I imagined it rusting somewhere on The Mountain, the paper icons shriveled or faded, the evil eye sightless, beyond the need for prayer – too much like work to attract scavengers. If it hadn't been a total loss, the engine, like that of the dismantled *caique*, was probably powering something else, possibly a generator. In the two modern tourist buses that had replaced it, there was no room for an icon screen. A small cross hung by a rope from a ring in the roof, allowing the curious to gauge just how far over the bus was leaning toward the afterlife as it negotiated the treacherous curves. Perhaps just such an experience had inspired some anonymous craftsman to key a four letter expletive/directive in the end of my armrest.

The bus crept upward, leaning into the horseshoe curves and throwing the sun to the opposite side every few hundred yards. As we climbed, smoke from the chimneys of buildings unoccupied for centuries announced a new prosperity. Nothing else seemed different, except that the road was worse. In two places, sledgehammer rains had reduced it by half, and we tip-toed within a foot of eternity. We recovered and edged over toward the safety of the cliff side just in time to allow two pick-ups to speed by.

A week before our visit, the heavens opened up as if God had reneged on his promise to Noah and was bent on erasing life. A monk drowned. The details leaked out: he had been driving a small car; the road slid out from under him, and he and the vehicle plunged into the sea. There are no radio stations to announce road conditions at eighteen minutes past the hour, although I can easily see a Radio Karyes in the near future. When a road gives way on The Mountain, it only concerns those who make a living transporting people, or others on foot who aren't in much of a hurry ever. As if he felt it his duty to take our minds off our peril, the Orthodox prelate we'd seen on the boat humbly announced to the rest of us that he was going to stay at Bourazerei, the impoverished *skiti* of shivering memory that is now the honorary property of the Archbishop of Athens and all of Greece. The implication was that he had an invitation.

"Are you a bishop?" Jack asked, gently blending mischief with compassion.

"Why, yes; indeed, I am a bishop," announced the hierarch, crammed into his proletarian seat halfway up the bus. "From Finland." His eyes lit up. Finally, someone had acknowledged the rank he had tried so hard to disguise. "How ever did you know?" he asked. Without waiting for an answer, he continued: "Do you know that the largest manufacturer of mobile phones in the world is in Finland?" Perhaps this was a sales trip.

We passed over the divide and growled down the far side of the ridge. The gray, pocket monastery of Saint Andrews loomed on the left. To the right, a large white "H" stood out from the middle of a dark red asphalt dish, like the letter on a cheerleader's chest. As had been rumored by Father Simeon: a heliport.

At Karyes, Jack wanted to extend his visit an extra night, so we looked for the building that quartered the *Epistasia*. I knew where it was without knowing how. Like a bee finding a favorite flower, unseen but functioning indicators unerringly took me to where I had last seen it sixteen years before. Here, at the heart of the heart of Orthodox Christian monasticism, I felt a perverse thrill in exercising my animal senses. Small pleasure. Brief pleasure. The office was closed. The sign on the wall said it was open from nine to one. When *would* it be open? A passing monk gave us the answer: a shrug of his shoulders and a superfluous *Dhen xero*. "I don't know." It didn't matter. The passports we carried are something you could hang on your wall at home. Nobody checks them. Unless the bearer is a woman or a wanted felon, once you are there, you are there. Maybe the essentials were still intact. Although cars lined the street of the capital, there was still only one street.

Jack, David, and I took off in the direction of the monastery of Iveron, on the former *idiorrhythmic* coast. Bourazerei was on the way, and emboldened perhaps by the Finnish bishop's confidence in his own expectation of a warm reception, Jack expressed a desire to see if he could get a room there for the night. I was the man for the job, I assured him. Hadn't I spent a miserable winter there? I knew *exactly* where Bourazerei was. We strode down the dusty road, the dark blue band of the Thracian Sea visible in the distance. Ten minutes became twenty and then closed in on half an hour. I began to lose a major part of my confidence, thinking that somehow we had already passed the *skiti*. After all, way back when, my desire for silence had relegated my excursions to backcountry trails and not the road the dust of which we were currently ingesting. Did Bourazerei even front on the road? I couldn't remember. With every curve we rounded, I willed the hoped-for skyline into being. Then, there it was. Only it wasn't the ramshackle, tree-dwarfed dwelling I'd been expecting. A spanking new, pink brick building, trimmed with limestone, rose above the surrounding conifers.

No sign directed us anywhere. No names; nothing to indicate that this was the place we sought. Even when we knocked down the broom that someone had shoved between the handles to keep the wooden gate shut and mounted the stone stairs on the other side, I could not be sure that this was where I once had stood in my Cossack boots, snug and warm and asleep in the freezing and scantily-clad church. We came out onto a flagstone driveway. To the right was the padlocked main gate, which we had fortuitously bypassed, or I believe we would still be ringing the bell. To the left was about a billion drachmas worth of new construction. It looked like half the financial aid supplied by the European Union had set down right here. And for the benefit of the man whom the previous lessees had determined was a heretic! Talk about Italian revenge!

No monks were in sight. One came around a corner, saw us, and turned on his heel as if he had forgotten something that was even more important than avoiding us. I called to his back; without turning to look at us, he pointed toward the reception room as if he had been a voice-activated signpost. Sitting on a plush banquette in the path of a cool breeze and sipping our *raki*, white confectioner's sugar from the *loukoumi* powdering our trousers, we inquired after the Finnish bishop. Oh, yes, the guest master told us. He had come by, but no, they had not allowed him to stay.

"We are a poor cell of only twenty-three monks," he explained, his hands wringing each other with the pain of disappointing weary pilgrims. "We are not able to take care of guests."

I picked up my lantern and my cane, and I groped for the door. On the way down the rutted road toward the sea, Jack told us that there was a good chance he would stay at Iveron for at least two days. His leg was beginning to swell up. Three weeks previously, in Australia, a scorpion had played darts with his calf. Bishop Jack was a trooper. With Jack walking stiff-legged and me having to guide what was available of David with my hand, we didn't resemble the Three Musketeers, but we could have made a fortune in alms if we had been anywhere people had money that wasn't tied up in capital improvements.

The guest quarters at Iveron were ... adequate. No revolution here. Dorm rooms, narrow beds with primitive springs, bare light bulbs. One of my spies has told me that Iveron does have a commercial-grade washer and dryer in the monks' laundry. When, on our way out of The Mountain we ran into Jack on the boat, he told us that after David and I departed, they had moved him to where the special visitors stayed. In the piped-down hyperbole of his native land, he described it as being "quite a bit more than adequate". That made us feel great. Or at least me, the former almost Athonite. During our stay at Iveron, David's eyes had a fixed quality about them that might have made them think we had come for healing. That didn't get us a better room, either. But what could I expect? We were gawking tourists intruding on a way of life we had no intention of embracing. And we were xenoi – foreigners. Bishop Jack, by his apparent commitment to his faith (heresy though it was), was at least a distant relative. Better treat him graciously here, since it wasn't clear if they would see him up there. Quite a difference from my previous journeys, when I passed for black. If I didn't miss the life, I certainly missed the unearned perks.

There were about a dozen other guests. Before the evening meal, a monk showed us the *katholikon*, where my non-Orthodox friends could not take part in the ceremony of unveiling the relics and kissing the shiny, reputedly fragrant, bones of saints long dead. Poor them. My Orthodox union card was still good, even though I had changed crafts. I avoided having to decline the offer with word or gesture by appearing to be busy, squinting with great concentration at an icon high up on a wall while my co-religionists crossed themselves and engaged in the sacred bussing. I did pray a little. I prayed that some monk to whom relic veneration was a litmus test of one's Orthodoxy would not call me on mine. I might even have had to have dinner apart with my friends, the heretic and the heathen.

Like all of the monasteries of the new age, Iveron now had a gift shop. An elderly Greek-American monk served as host/shopkeeper. The shop had the usual paraphernalia: books, crosses, replicas of icons, incense, and prayer ropes. What I was surprised and even shocked to find in one of the display cases were elements of a monk's habit: his thick black belt and the black vest he wears at all times, inscribed in red with a cross in the middle of a tableau that reminds the monk he has died to his body. I immediately thought, Halloween. That I also found this commercialization of the sacred offensive says volumes about how little I ever had accepted the workaday Greek attitude toward monasticism, even among monks. Perhaps I was having more problems adjusting to the effects of the new economy than they were. And who knows? Calvin Klein might discover Mount Athos, and their financial worries would be another thing of the past.

The bells sounded at three A.M. It was bells because it was Sunday. Dawdling like any modern churchgoer bent on spending as little time in church as possible, I arrived at about five, in time for the final half hour of *orthros*. On entering, my senses were assaulted by present stimuli and old memories, which then made a brief two-pronged attack on my heart. Once the effect of the old, familiar smell wore off, I felt nothing special about being there. I did, however, seriously waver in my prediction that all this would eventually succumb to the relentless waves of change. It just did not seem possible that something as solid and venerable as this building, the roots of which had to be embedded in the Garden of Eden, could possibly succumb to a wrecker's ball. Outside, the church looked like a heap of expendable stones, but inside, the space it enclosed disappeared into the vaulted darkness to the limits of the known and unknown world, as indeed its unknown designer had intended. Since every day took them beyond common notions of space as well as common time, it was easy to understand why the monks might be as complacent as they appeared to be. If, as a Maronite monk is alleged once to have said, "I spend half my day praying before Holy Communion and the other half giving thanks for it," who has time to worry about such things as the possibility that someone might pull the rug out from under him? And if it happened, so what?

The Divine Liturgy followed the morning service, and I received the Eucharist even though I had done my fasting in my sleep. I don't think about Holy Communion. I do it. The priest comes out, and says "Take," and I take. It keeps me going to church whenever I want to pack it in. Do I believe it is Christ on the spoon? Is it a reminder of what I am? A habit? A sense of continuity? Depends on what day you catch me. As I left the nave, I found David and Jack in the narthex, as far as Tradition allowed them to go.

At about nine o'clock, under a leaden sky but with no rain in the forecast, David and I said goodbye to Jack and headed down the coast toward Karakkalou, where I had originally proposed we spend the next night. However, it looked to be so close on the map that we set the Great Lavra, almost twenty miles away, as our goal. No problem: I had walked it before. That should have told me something. Hearing anyone say "No problem" has put me on my guard since I first heard it uttered years ago by a Yugoslav mechanic as he hovered over my Volkswagen with his hammer. Now I had said it. Or thought it. But from what I recalled, the road was pretty flat and wouldn't amount to much more than a good, long hike. We would make a pit stop at Karakkalou. Stay there, if we took a fancy to the place.

We had been walking for about an hour when that old, Bourazerei feeling began to steal over me: half fuming at myself for getting lost, half pitying myself being lost, and half angry at Mount Athos and all the monks on it for having such lousily-posted roads. Karakkalou must be around here … somewhere. We came to a dubiously marked fork in the road. The tine that wound to our right looked as if it would take us high into the mountains, and that I did not recall. Still, it presumably was an authoritative map, and the Bourazerei business had sorely shaken my confidence in my bee-ness. We turned inland and began to ascend the omnipresent horseshoe curves. After half a sweating hour I called a halt to our folly, remembering that twenty years ago, wearing monk's loafers that were about four sizes too large for me, I had made a similar choice just outside Iveron while seeking the monastery of Philotheou. My stubbornness on that occasion had taken me four hours out of my way to the top of a mountain in logging country, all of which I had retraced on feet rubbed raw by hours of knocking about inside my holy shoes.

Even though I now was equipped with hi-tech hiking boots, I saw no spiritual or physical profit in recreating that misadventure. We turned around. We did not try to find Karakkalou – you think you can't lose a monastery? – but walked on. And on and on and on. Later, a monk told us that the missing monastery was only about a quarter of a mile off the "highway". We just hadn't seen the goat path that led to it. The sign, he consoled us, was where no one on the road could see it. With a night at Karakkalou now not even an option, our walk became a little more urgent. To our left, on the slopes leading down to the rocky shore, there were more renovated houses. Some were the size of villas, surrounded by well-kept gardens, with off-road vehicles in their driveways. Perhaps now that it was easier to keep in touch with remote places, abbots were more willing to let their monks go out from the mother house to live on their own. Perhaps they had no choice.

The road never left the coast, but it dipped inland with every valley and upward with every headland; our legs were becoming sore and our spirits low and apprehensive, when we rounded a promontory and saw – not in the distance but fifty yards ahead – the massive walls of the Great Lavra. A natural fountain gurgled out of a wall by the side of the road. I cupped my hands, made my own communion, and anointed myself. We passed through the double gates that separate the huge monastery from the world. Under the magnificent fir that spread its branches in front of the refectory stood a brand new, white, Toyota truck.

After the greeting routine and depositing our gear in the half-timbered guesthouse, David and I walked through one of the many smaller gates and found ourselves outside the monastery, overlooking a vast garden of neat fruit trees and vegetable patches. Next to us rested two expensive half-tracks. The Great Lavra is more a town than a monastery. The walls are forty feet high, and enclose an area about the size of two football fields. Except that we weren't chasing each other with bloodthirsty thoughts, as we took a late afternoon walk around the perimeter we might have been Hector and Achilles circling Troy. The ramparts, freshly sandblasted and repaired, looked as if they could still provide a formidable challenge to pirates.

Back in our quarters, I was happy to see that in the *mairos* "they" had replaced the communal urinal – a trough that, when the wind wasn't right, had given as well as it got – with individual stalls. Clean, spacious, and private. Amazingly, the doors to the stalls open outward, a sign of intelligence rarely shown in the West except at modern airports. There is no door at all at the entrance – after all, what need is there for that kind of privacy where all the facilities are monosex? There also were real showers! I never tested the temperature of the water.

The Great Lavra's refectory is the most magnificent Mount Athos has to offer. The monks and their guests sit on marble seats around horseshoe-shaped marble tables. Brilliant frescoes cover every available vertical surface of the enormous room with scenes from the life of Christ, the lives of saints, and the history of the Holy Mountain, along with vivid depictions of the hell into which one was sure to descend through the ever-hungry fires of gluttony. If it becomes the dining room of a hotel, something will simply *have* to be done about the artwork. Then again, I can't think of any time when what looked down at me from the walls had any affect on me as – in the words of Damon Runyon – I "committed eating". The food was cooked in an electric oven. I can't tell the difference. Somebody told me. David found the meal marvelous in its vegetarian simplicity, while I reverted to my monastic appreciation of God's bounty and criticized the eggplants for being too oily and overcooked.

On returning to the guesthouse, we discussed our plans for the next day with the guest master. We intended to walk across the southern tip of the peninsula, stop for a sentimental visit at Timion Prodromos, the Romanian *skiti* where the glass of tea had shattered in my hands, and proceed to Kavsokalyvia, from whence we would take a boat to the monastery of Grigoriou, the crown jewel of the Riviera. "No problem," the *archondaris* assured us. We would have plenty of time, since the boat didn't go up the coast to Dafni until one in the afternoon. The gesture that accompanied his words was the one an umpire uses to declare a runner safe. No problem, eh? I raised a mental eyebrow.

As we sat with the other visitors on the porch of the *archondariki*, enjoying cool air unmixed with white noise, something didn't sit right in my stomach, and it wasn't the oily eggplants. Then I knew what it was: if the boat was going to meet up with the large boat going to Ouranopolis, it would have to be at Dafni before noon; it must leave Kavsokalyvia about eight in the morning, not in the afternoon! How could this monk not have known this? Hmm.... I hate backtracking! Now we would have to do exactly that: retreat to

Karyes, take the bus to Dafni, and then catch the boat down the coast to Grigoriou.

At about seven in the morning, we lined up with the others, opposite the heliport, as if we were commuting to the office. A van on the side of which I pictured the logo of the Black Cab Company arrived. The image of the orderly ride-share queue immediately disappeared. This was still Greece. Before the driver could come around to our side to open the door, there was only one seat left. I pushed David into it and sat down on the floor. As we lurched along the shock-destroying road, with the eggplants threatening to give an encore, I held my camera up to the window and squeezed. The result was an astounding shot of the peak of Mount Athos illuminated by the rising sun. I also took many unastounding pictures of my fore and middle fingers.

From Karyes, I phoned and booked us a night at Grigoriou. That's the new way of doing things. While we waited for the bus to Dafni, I tried to find Father M., the monk who had told me the abbot of Konstamonitou was "a good guy". When I had told that story to Father S., I discovered that he was Father M.'s best friend! Best friend, yes. Giver of directions, no. In this regard at least, Greeks are like Italians and will tell you that some place is closer than it is to give you the courage to make your journey. Contrast this with the equally stereotyped English, who will tell you that it is *farther* just so that you will be pleasantly surprised on discovering how close it is.

Father S. had given me directions to Father M.'s house, "near" Karyes. Behind Saint Andrew's, we walked down New England lanes redolent with the quickening smells of early morning foliage. We disturbed the peace of the residents of a horse-owning *kelli* that according to my infallible sense of direction was about where Father M.'s should have been by inquiring for him. The surly brush-off we received included directions. A native might have found them crystal clear, but to me it was Peter Pan telling Wendy how to get to Never Never Land. There was a large generator in the front yard. For a moment, I wondered if they might not be growing pot. We did not find Father M.

At Dafni, we boarded the *plion* and headed south. There no longer was a stop at Simonopetra. The famous aerie was at the end of a road leading directly to Dafni, and motor vehicles had rendered the *arsanas* as obsolete as long-playing vinyl. A blue pay phone welcomed us to the quay at Grigoriou. The *kenobitic* compound is down low on the water, perched on a point that is a photographer's delight. The guesthouse was to the left, the monastery to the right. Signs indicated the hours during which visitors could visit. It was the first time I had been subjected to such a restriction. Inside the gate, beyond the beautiful flower-trellised ante court, was the noise of new construction and the sandblasting of old. From what we could see of it, the contemporary work was first-rate.

We dumped our backpacks on our beds and hurried to scale the heights behind the monastery before sunset. On the way up, we passed terraced gardens that tumbled down to the water's edge. Two monks tilled the soil with pneumatic hoes. The soft sun of the blue hour painted the monastery on the point in pastels, and an unseen finger smudged the line between stone and water. With no human visible to bring it into the present, Grigoriou looked like Camelot awaiting the arrival of a boat with a hooded man at the muffled oars, carrying a lady from across the lake.

The abbot was away, so the monks were at play. No one had to tell us he wasn't there. The monks were as lax as Konstamonitou on any ordinary day. They even allowed my friend to eat with we "saved". Evening gave way to night, and the sun sank into a sea that verily was "wine dark". On the quay, half a dozen monks outfitted a tiny *caique* for a nocturnal fishing expedition. As they yelled to each other and stepped on and off and on again, the gunwales practically dipped below the water, and lanterns rapidly traced broad arcs at both ends of the double-ended craft. When they unloosed the hawsers, five of the monks were aboard. Where they would keep their catch wasn't the question that wandered through my mind. I was looking at the single foot of freeboard that for the time being kept them out of the drink. The engine coughed to life, the last monk pushed off and leaped across the widening gap, and they were soon lost in the darkness and possibly their prayers.

As in all the monasteries we visited, the *katholikon*, the church, remained untouched by the busy-ness without. Its aging icons were of a different world from the one bustling by outside. It was there, early the next morning, that the monks atoned for their impious negligence at dinner. They banished my friend to the narthex, and I had to pass a moral security check before they allowed me to partake of the Holy Gifts. Had I been to confession? I nodded my head. "*Malista.*" Since they did not ask me when, I did not tell them. Remember, this is an apophatic church. At the *trapeza* that followed, security was once more relaxed, the monks atoned for the atonement they had made in church, and my friend again ate with the Faithful. The fare bore fragrant witness to the success of the night's sea hunt. We were treated to mounds of deep-fried *merides*, a small whitefish. And they went the whole *merida*. Fastidious as regards glazed eyeballs and tiny teeth, I left a pile of heads in my dish that would have pleased Tamerlane. The others ate with unashamed gusto. I would have liked some gusto, too, because finding the meat on the tasty, tiny carcasses was like picking lint.

Next stop, Konstamonitou. At about nine, we caught the boat back to Dafni, where we passed through Customs twice. The first time was either a dry run or a joke, because the boat we were supposed to board wasn't at the quay. Rumor had led us to join the queue and to be pushed through the unfinished Customs House like olives in a press. The second time, we simply walked through an unguarded gate. On the other side, a gendarme glanced at us, but said nothing. I could have had the "*Axion Estin*" icon rolled up in my sleeve.

On the ship from Dafni to Konstamonitou, the unshaved, portly ticket taker tried to relieve me of eight hundred drachmas – two dollars – for a ticket he had never given me for a fare that didn't exist. The usual choleric face. The indignant tone of voice. The hand chopping upward into the witnessing sky. The trapping of the unwary stranger in a position where it would be easier, even necessary, to pay if he wanted to debark. *What's two dollars to you?* He didn't have to say it. Did this petty dictator think I was Neville Chamberlain, and that the deck of this scow was Munich? I gave the cheesy entrepreneur my best impression of the Greek "You are a pig not even worth responding to" look, and left the ship with my fortune intact. The petty incident disabused me of any lingering notion I might still have had about being an insider. I was now officially a *xenos*, a red and white bull's eye emblazoned on my shirt. And to think I had once been so "in" that they'd passed me through the gate at Athens airport without a visa!

Bulldozers had leveled and widened the path that wound its way up to my old praying grounds into a legitimate two-lane road. The channels that hundreds of years of monastic feet had worn through rock were gone. As I slowly put one foot ahead of the other on the enervating incline, I had no feelings at all about returning to the monastery at which I had spent so much time. I was not a monk. If I did not have nostalgia for that life, could I have any for this monastery? I was sure it would be like looking at a light bulb with the light off. That premonition might have contributed to the weariness I felt in my legs.

Konstamonitou is the smallest monastery on the south side of The Mountain, but it looked much smaller than when it played such a large part in my life. I might have expected this, since it was no longer the chosen limit of my world. As if to emphasize this change, there was a monstrous military truck parked outside the stables. The mules were no more. I asked a monk about them, and he laughed. He gave me a Bourazereian rationale: there were not enough monks to take care of the ornery beasts. Entering the courtyard through the main gate, I looked up to the right, and saw "our" old room. Third floor. A balustraded balcony between my neighbor and me and another rickety one off to the other side where I had spent many an evening "taking the night air", my prayer rope dangling over the rail and running through my fingers. From the piles of cloth I could see through the dusty windows, I supposed "our" cell was now either a storeroom or the new occupant was a tailor. There were fewer monks than there had been, but their industry was impressive. One of them, loaded with tools and climbing among the scaffolding, looked as if he had the energy and skill to rebuild the entire monastery by himself. Nobody paid any attention to us.

The EU wasn't much in evidence. Perhaps their scouts had come to the same conclusion about the location that Athonites reached a thousand years ago. We found the *archondariki* on the third floor. Eventually, the *archondaris* appeared. Father D. was thin and slightly stooped and about forty years old. He had thick black eyebrows, a long, thin nose, and a short, neatly-trimmed beard. Two huge purple aureoles encircled his eyes. David, now fully recovered from his reaction to the sea-sickness pills, thought he looked like Igor inviting us into his castle and some as yet undetermined – but guaranteed to be horrible – end. His thick lips moved in a loose, liquid manner that did indeed suggest that something other than his jaw might be unhinged.

Father D. said he had family in Toronto and that he had lived in Detroit for a few years. Having established his pedigree, he asked if we had any American cigarettes. We shook our heads, after which the three of us proceeded to play a game of "Name the Brands". When he said "Camels", and then retracted his move, saying "No, those are Turkish cigarettes," I should have suspected the good Dr. F. had left out a few parts, but I didn't. I found him rather charming. Maybe it was his excellent English. How could anyone speak The Language – and so well! – and not be all there? David caught it, but I didn't catch the look on my friend's face as it slowly dawned on him that this friendly, talkative, almost worldly monk was also quite batty. I plowed ahead. Besides, I found a number of his other comments quite reasonable, and for a monk, rather enlightened according to my notion of enlightenment. For example, he said that the Greeks would never get back to Constantinople, and he couldn't see why non-Orthodox were excluded from Orthodox church services.

Whether Father D. qualified as a holy fool was questionable, but since he could speak English, I was satisfied with his qualifications as a commentator on the local technological scene. Did the monastery have a computer? "Yes," he answered. "Who can do without computers? It's the way of the world." Can't argue with that. Then, "We have the most advanced system, but it exploded because of our unbelief." That, I might argue with. "Or maybe it was the pirates. Yes. They've been coming here since 1451 and 1492 and 1732 – or was it 1832? Or maybe it was terrorists. All of our computers have Turks in them. They are stealing souls." The terrorists had also stolen Constantinople. "It is a dirty city. We cannot go in there because it will get to you. The City has become such an evil place that anyone who goes there has to be pure even to survive."

Okay, I got it. I fell silent. He did not. In all fairness, he could be absolutely lucid for a few seconds before entering into his own private bungalow. I asked him why he had come to this particular monastery, and he said something about "finding his status". I asked him about monastic obedience; for an answer, he gave me the etymology of five unrelated and irrelevant words. "I speak French," he continued. "*Parlez-vous français?* I spent a week in Paris. Languages are common sense. I could easily learn German." On Athonite politics: "Father A." – his abbot – "is the Supreme Head of Mount Athos. Father E. at [another monastery] is not the Big Father E., who founded two monasteries in Canada. The Father E. in America is another one. There are other Father Es." Father D. gave us our room key, and we disappeared inside, locking the door after us. Wow! This wasn't just a little carpel tunnel syndrome. If this was what technology did to monks, the situation was more serious than I had speculated.

The wood sounded for Vespers. On the way to church, I passed the padlocked workshop. Had the lethal band saw been shipped off to Madame Toussaud's to take her place alongside Jack the Ripper, or did Our Lady of Dismemberment still reside within? I entered the church that had been my church. It was the same and I wasn't. For one thing, on this day I was the only one present at a service I had almost never attended. The cumulative smell of incense, the cool, stone floor worn into undulating hollows, the pale light filtering down from the cupola, the aged icons infinitesimally more begrimed.... All the drugs were there, but I couldn't force the past through my veins. The abbot, the "good guy", was away, visiting a woman's monastery under his spiritual care. It may be a sign of the times that at none of the four monasteries we visited did we see a single abbot. If our *archondaris'* needle was stuck on the name, E., he wasn't all that far off in what he related of the overseas activities of the Athonite abbot known as Big E. (There is an abbot called Little E. in Big E.'s conglomerate.)

While we were in Thessalonica the reliable Father S. had remarked that Big E. sat at the apex of the progressive pyramid of monasteries – male and female – and had indeed founded thirteen new monastic houses in America. Along with the five monasteries under his aegis on Mount Athos, that made four to six hundred monks and nuns who owed him obedience. All eighteen establishments are *koinovia*. At the beginning of the eighties, most of the monasteries on the north coast of the Holy Mountain were *idiorrhythmic* houses where the monks walked to the beat of their own *symandron*. Today, every monastery on the Holy Mountain is a *koinovion* where the emphasis is on the common life; many of these had been joined together under one leader. Being who I am, this information made me think of Caligula's wish that all the people of Rome would have only one head, so that he could cut it off with a one stroke. I hear that Big E., himself, now lives in the American Southwest and cyber-communicates with the monks he left behind.

The Monarch of the Mohave Desert is no fool. He probably recognized that if his neo-conservative movement was to find adherents among the young, it had to be accompanied by a tacit acceptance of modern technology, although perhaps not computer games. Apparently, he has had the acumen to allow for the fact that the young, while searching for roots that technology has obscured, have known no other kind of world and are unwilling to throw away all that the modern one has to offer. Perhaps he has anticipated the coming monastic Diaspora. I don't know if he has quite reached the level of acceptance of the abbot of another monastery in Greece, whose monks published a CD of rock-Byzantine chant fusion. When the strange but recognizable music reached the ear of the Archbishop of Athens and all of Greece, His Eminence predictably demanded its immediate recall. When the album soared to the top of the pop charts, he relented and gave the entrepreneurs his blessing to cut a second disk. Some might say that this, too, was predictable.

It is also possible that the neo desert father is not exercising *oikonomia* in deference to youth but simply has no problem with the monastic world going cyber. Because the lack of technology has brought them many physical hardships in the past, it is quite likely that the majority of Greeks see modern technology as an unqualified good. Westerners who have been blessed with the technology-given time to pull finer threads from the tapestry of life, but who also may see in the love of technology the root of all modern evil, are not so likely to be as generous.

Dinner followed Vespers; once again, my friend was excluded. I sat at a table I had been responsible for cleaning twenty years before. Instead of the white, tasteless bread of my recollection, the baskets now overflowed with dark, healthy-looking stuff. Most of the monasteries now bake their own bread. Nevertheless, my experience of the meal was like eating bread without salt. Had I gone into some kind of spiritual shock? Was something confronting me that I was determined to excise from my reality? At the door to the refectory, one of the monks asked us if we had spoken to the *archondaris*. It had to be a rhetorical question. We smiled. He smiled back. "He's crazy," the monk confirmed in English. "He is okay when he takes his pills." At last, lemon juice was getting some help. After dinner, we walked outside the walls and up into the purple hills, where we found solar panels that powered the phone at the monastery. The old land line was for the small houses that dotted the sides of the valley.

That first telephone line on Mount Athos, the one that took the place of breadcrumbs for many a lost traveler, may also have been the last. Being unable to afford traditional phones has allowed Greeks and Greeks monastics to skip the wired generation. This could work to great advantage for mobile monasticism, just as it has for nations defeated in wars that blasted their antiquated industrial base to ruins and had to start over from scratch. But monks with cell phones? And pagers? What could be more foreign to the image we have of the monk living in simplicity and silence than a cell phone making sure that he can never escape from the world? But remember, that is "the" monk we know only from hearsay, literature, and our own need to define and simplify. He could turn it off, just like we can. But do we, and would he? What's next? GOD.org.? Virtual communion?

The next day was our last on the Holy Mountain. We tried to sneak away early because David thought that Father D. was quite capable of showing up at the *archondariki* with two croissants, two lattés, and a chainsaw. I went to the washroom to brush my teeth. My friend followed, still voicing his concern, when we heard the door to our room click shut. He stared at me open-mouthed. A fine conceptualist, David sometimes has trouble with details – he had left the key inside. The door had no knobs, latches, or anything else that would allow us to enter, gather our belongings, and take flight. After making a number of inquiries, it became apparent that Father D. was the only one with keys, and he was in a drugged sleep somewhere, fighting the Turks. Two hours later, which is considered being on time in Greece, our host showed up, bright-eyed, coherent, and obviously on a fresh batch of whatever had been wearing off the day before.

As we left Konstamonitou, we passed a monk who slowed his booted step and stared at me out of the corner of his eye. Clearly, he was scanning his files for some text to fit the picture. It required the skill of a sketch artist to tighten the skin and put a beard on the potato head I offered him, but he did it. He was one of the two monks left from "my" time. I had recognized him soon after our arrival, but I had no interest in waking the dead. He was a gentle soul with a face like a goateed Liberace. I think he was a cook.

We called to each other across twenty feet of fifteen years. Where had all the flowers gone? Gone to death, disillusionment, and desertion, one by one. I asked him about Father B., and he shrugged his shoulders. He didn't know where he was. He had left the monastery about ten years ago. Had he eventually succumbed to my constant badgering about what he knew about his faith until he lost it? Did he awaken one morning and say to himself, aloud, in a very calm voice, "What am I doing here?" What does it take to maintain the ritual day after day when belief has gone? When the need to believe finds nothing to believe in any more?

It's said that when God wants to laugh, he listens to our plans. Because any system, personal or institutional, religious or scientific, is a human creation, it becomes absurd when pushed to the extremes that our nature demands. That's why for humans, too, laughter *is* the only place where the constant contradictions of life make sense. Both St. Augustine and I could become priests because our baptism obliterated our many indiscretions, and canon law, like our common law, frowns on double jeopardy. But the sacrament of ordination was not a possibility for poor, possibly worthy Father B. because his lone sexual escapade came after his baptism as an non-assenting infant!

David and I walked down to the *arsanas*. We passed a monk from Konstamonitou, bulldozing earth onto the pockmarked road. Having a couple of hours before the ship was scheduled to arrive, we decided to walk to Dochiareiou and see its famous icon, the *"Gorgooepikos"* Mother of God. This walk was a snap. I'd done it before. Sound familiar? The trail hugged the shore. What could go wrong? I'll tell you what. After about twenty easy minutes, we came to the first slide, where recent rains had washed most of the path into the sea. Toes pressed against rock, we inched along, then leaped our way across the abyss. Why weren't there ...? Get real. For all its modernization, Mount Athos, as Kipling wrote about Catholicism, is still not a place "for wake souls" who expect magic coats to cover inconvenient puddles.

Two more slides, two more inchings, two more leaps, and we were at Dochiareiou. The new residential tower was still gift-wrapped in heavy polyurethane drapes. A large, well-equipped workshop at the *arsanas* sent forth the hewn and chiseled elements of the monastery's physical resurrection. Orange, lemon, and quince trees patrolled the shore below the lower walls. We entered through the double gate and made our way through narrow canyons between the church and the surrounding residential blocks. Everything of interest was off limits to us – including the allegedly "wonder-working" icon.

The ferry arrived. We shuffled off the immortal soil, traversed the gangway that ran alongside the vehicles, and ascended to the sun deck. The vessel backed her engines, turned north and rapidly took us back to the world. We made a brief stop at Konstamonitou's *arsanas*. A few pilgrims got on who hadn't been with us at "my" monastery. Zografou used the same quay. And the Bulgarians had allowed them to leave? As we headed for the promontory that in ten minutes or so would obscure the *arsanas*, I turned away from the Holy Mountain.

At Ouranopolis, the keeper of our luggage proved true to his word. It was I who had translated "*micro spiti*" to mean "shack" and failed to ask him to be more specific about where he intended to meet us. While we searched for the "little house", we missed the bus. That was all right. Only another two hours. A chance to exercise *eepomoni*, patience: the Mount Everest of all virtues from which one steps up to discernment. With the impeccable timing born of centuries of frustrating time, our host waved to us from a nearby doorway just as the bus pulled away and invited us into what was indeed his "little house" for a cup of coffee.

While we waited for the grounds to settle, he lamented on what was happening to Greece. Amid the ritual gestures of "That's life," and "What can we do?" we gulped down our thimblefuls of tepid, muddy liquid. We thanked our faithful host and had dinner at one of the empty weekend restaurants that stretched across the deserted beachfront like an unemployment line. In Ouranopolis, we heard that some monks have already left the "mountain of silence" because the din of progress is so great that it was a relief to return to the world. I, too, was glad to get back to Thessalonica, with its noise, its commerce, and its too many people. At the time, the irony was lost on me that, after my first experience at a monastery, twenty-five years earlier, even the small fishing village to which I returned had seemed impossibly busy. Now, I cannot truly focus unless things are going on around me. I do my writing at a café. I do not know I am alone unless I can hear people arguing.

For me, the magic was gone out of Mount Athos. Whether I had changed or just become more of who I am, the ever-moving water had long ago put out the fire and hardened the ashes. What concerned the monks no longer concerned me. Now it was just some beautiful old buildings in a place that was still remarkably beautiful but not uniquely so. From what I had seen, instead of a place beyond time, the Holy Mountain was in real danger of becoming a spiritual Williamsburg. Nobody walks to Williamsburg. Getting to Mount Athos now also is all too easy. The pilgrimage is gone.

When questioned about whether the very remote Giant's Causeway was worth seeing, the corpulent Doctor Johnson remarked, "Worth seeing? Yes. Worth going to see? No." I respect and even love the Great Cham, but I don't always believe him. Who he was and his prejudices invariably and wonderfully compromise the alleged objectivity of his pronouncements. I think that his dietologically swollen frame – the result of a lifetime of the suet puddings, fatty meats, and sweetened tea common to the times, which would have had a modern man in his grave before the age of thirty – simply was better suited to the cobblestoned back alleys of London than to more rugged terrain. When it is difficult to get to a place, the journey sharpens the experience. When sweat poured from my body as I trekked around the Holy Mountain from one monastic dwelling to another, I appreciated whatever hospitality awaited me at my destination. When a voyage up the coast was in a frail wooden craft, mostly alone or with silent others, I felt the isolation and remoteness of the life and lives I was bridging. And then there were the days when the weather was so bad I couldn't even get into the place and had to sit patiently like a postulant at the feet of this mysterious land until it decided the time was right; or when that isolation forced me into the company of strangers.

That time is no more. Now it is possible to get from New York to the Great Lavra without walking a single step other than the few required to get you from one means of transport to another. If you are the Archbishop of Athens and all of Greece, a helicopter will drop you at the door of your own private monastery. It is not surprising that monasteries are making outward efforts to make visitors feel they have never left home because increasingly they have not. Instead of standing apart from the crowd, I am afraid that the Holy Mountain is becoming just another easily available attraction. Subconsciously, the mind begins to categorize it as "replaceable." Did I expect things to be the same after fifteen years? It is difficult to make room for change on an altar that is crowded with idols, images, and recollections that haven't budged since the day that I put them there, dust gathering on the patina of truth.

Before visiting Mount Athos, I had spent a few weeks in Cyprus. It was seventeen years since I left the monastery above the clouds. I had phoned my Cypriot friends from the United States to tell them of my impending arrival. "Takis has a surprise for you," Lukia warned me. Had he become a monk? Takis, Lukia's husband, was the pediatrician who had treated what I'd hoped were my "stigmata" during my winter at Stavrovouni. He was curious about everything, charmingly eccentric, and a lover of life in the world. There were thousands in the city of Limassol who had traversed the first beguilingly dangerous years of life under his care. Like many Cypriots, he talked a good monastic game, but I don't think anyone ever took his threats to leave the world seriously.

I put my bags down on the marble patio that fronted their house, and Lukia led me around to the garden at the back. To "the surprise". Two years before, Takis, now in his late sixties, had taken up iconography as a hobby. In that time, he who had never so much as whitewashed a wall had covered the rear of his house with iconic murals. Iconography was now his life. He was at it fifteen hours a day, while his wife turned to soap operas for companionship. But my friend is not just the dog that talks. In an art that has strict taboos as to subject, form, line, and color, Takis produces truly brilliant, original, yet canonical icons. His labor of love reflects a life spent in the intimate company and love of people one would hope characterized every pediatrician. Once he has adorned the entire outside of his house with religious frescoes, his goal is to iconize the entire street. I have no doubt that one day his icons will be one of the reasons why tourists come to Limassol.

When I arrived, Takis was crouching at the base of a wall, paintbrush in one hand and cigarette in the other. (He was resting. He was careful to point out to me that when writing his icons, he *never* smokes.) He stared at me through the top half of his bifocals, and then stood up slowly. His mouth dropped open. "No," he said, drawing out the "o" by pursing his lower lip. Simultaneously, a question and a statement. "You can't be him," he declared. "John is thirty-five, and you are an old man!"

My reception at Stavrovouni was a bit different. A two-lane blacktop road eased the ascent. Around the unexceptional building that had stood alone against the sky for seventeen hundred years, a small village had grown inside walls whose effectiveness no longer depended on the good will of strangers. Thirty-seven young monks now surrounded their abbot, who shuffled and mumbled and blessed, apparently as oblivious to the changes as if he were still the custodian of a phantom brotherhood. I beamed when I saw him exit the church and look up at the sky as if he sensed the eyes he knew were always upon him. He greeted me warmly: *"Eh. Ioanni. Menete edhoh."* Are you staying here? In his kind of time, I hadn't aged at all.

My other experience with nostalgia again illustrated the same truths about change – that what changes is what cannot not change, while what defines us does not change at all. After our visit to the Holy Mountain, David went back to the United States, and I flew to Athens. From Piraeus, I took a sea-going ferry to Paros, the island on which I began my journey in the Orthodox Christian world twenty-five years before. I was going to see my mentor, Father G., the ex-Anglican priest, the one who hated whatever interfered with his silence and his beloved "Egyptian darkness" – who would not walk on paved roads.

Parokia, the island's capital and port, had grown far beyond the windmill from which nothing was more than a few blocks away. Queues of buses waited to take visitors to new villages. I could have taken a cab to Longovarda, but it never occurred to me. All the same, I didn't walk the six miles, as I once would have considered imperative to my *askesis* – when there was no difference between life and eternity. The local bus dropped me off at the monastery garden. I looked up at the rising landscape, its sere post-summer brown slyly creating the illusion of uniformity, and couldn't see the monastery that I knew was there. I began to climb the stony dirt road past the farmhouse; the door was sealed with an ancient padlock and the adjacent gardens looked neglected. A goat, tethered to a stubby wooden stake, eyed me with mild interest. Ten minutes on the strenuous ascent had me sweating in the old, familiar way. I took the steep short cut that monks or goatherds had pioneered centuries before and on reaching the approach road, I paused for a moment to let my legs recover their spring.

I walked on. A bend in the road suddenly gave up the monastery, and a warm smile spread across my face. It was identical to my first view of it. The horseshoe curve ended in an abrupt turn to the left like the serif on an omega. The last stretch of road to the green wooden gate was concrete and as straight and precipitous as the stairs of an Aztec temple. Thirty yards before the entrance to the 17th century compound, I passed the enormous wind-twisted eucalyptus tree under which I first talked with Father G. As on my first visit, the gate was closed and locked. Once again, I had arrived between noon and three, the Biblical "dark hours" of the day, when the sky turned dark after the Crucifixion and the monastery was closed to visitors.

Twenty-five years ago, a layman carrying a box of olives opened the monastery doors for me. And now, it happened again! Then, he had been a nonagenarian, with long white moustaches, wearing the black knickers of Old Greece, an emissary from a *metochion* of the monastery on the Peloponnesus. He had been holding a large wicker basket of olives that they sent as their yearly, very token, tribute. The 2000 incarnation emerged from a beat-up, white auto. He was forty to fifty years old with a few days' growth on his face and was clearly a local. Wearing a short sleeve white shirt and work pants, he, too, was delivering food to the monastery – not the olives of submission, however, but cans and boxes, as if to the needy.

This monastery had always been beautiful, and not merely because it occupied a special place in my journey. On this day, it looked beautiful and spotless. It wasn't that it had had a face-lift – more like a grandfather who had put on his Sunday best. The whitewash on the stone walls showed none of the accidents of use. No black rubber from the soles of monastic shoes had scuffed the flagstones, each carefully outlined with lime to light the way through lanternless nights. No monk sat in the shade, culling olives. No one was hammering iron hoops around barrel staves.

The layman went to get Father G., while I waited in the same guestroom where I had waited on my initial visit. The smells were the same. The photos on the wall were the same. The cool, northern breeze was the same one that two and a half decades before had blessed me for slogging four miles uphill on a rocky, dusty road under a late morning sun, and had spitefully turned on me in winter for my indecision. Father G. entered, appearing flummoxed – vintage Father G. At once, he began to talk to me rapidly in his signature Oxford … *Greek*! I was stunned. I interrupted him, a smile frozen on my face. Father G. reacted to my English as if a rat had dropped out of the ceiling. I had to tell him twice who I was before he accepted my language and me. His mouth opened and closed a number of times. No words came forth as he made multiple internal transitions. Finally, he managed to push a few past his toothless gums. "But you can't be him!" he cried, almost indignantly and clearly dismayed.... Alas. The heart is always young, the mind is often young, but the body never lies.

The monastery looked spotless because there was no one left to make a spot. Back in the day, it had been a community of sixteen monks, including four priests. Now, Father G. was its sole inhabitant. Alone, in his late eighties, with no teeth and a variety of ailments, he conducted as much of the grueling, daily cycle of services as his non-ordained status would allow. I awoke well before dawn the next morning to the sound of incomprehensible wailing coming from the church – the up-and-down singsong of psalms with no identifiable words. No lamps lit my descent to the courtyard, and there were no astral bodies for the whitewash to reflect. On this moonless night, Father G. had reestablished his "Egyptian darkness", which the departed "personalities" had sacrificed to convenience. Had he made a good trade? I entered the small, dark, musty church, where a familiar and beloved voice ploughed erratically through the morning service, making sounds that all came to me as wrenchingly plaintive. I stayed for as long as I could stand it.

I left later that morning, pleading the exigencies of travel. I felt terrible about leaving. Father G. obviously wanted me to stay. "You haven't fallen away from the faith," the monk said, "like..." He mentioned an Englishman who had been inquiring about Orthodoxy at the same time I began my journey. What could I say? Whether I could or could not stay, I would not. I could not pretend to be the same person who had spent many months there a long time ago. I could not use the words or express the beliefs that had once been my language and my being. And I could not face what time and circumstances do to anyone that is not myself. I had to live with this uncomfortable reality in Naousa for three more days, because already the winter winds were playing rough with the islands and temporarily left me stranded. I am not beyond believing it was a sign, though with no greater power to make me pause than a red octagonal has on a Greek motorist.

The Naousa the winter of my (eat to your heart's) content was a quiet village that existed mainly to serve its residents. Now, in early fall, the little port was dead; I imagine it comes alive only in the summer. When there were only two restaurants, both could afford to stay open year-round; with ten, none could. Nobody passed through the doors of trinket stores except the owners. The old café on the harbor – the fishermen's chat room and one-time male sanctuary – was closed. The coffee menu on the door was early Starbuck's, but you could still get Nescafé. And there was the wind.

Pity was uncomfortably woven in with the compassion I felt for my old friend. He seemed to be a man marooned. No priests, no monks, and no cook. The layman who had let me in brought him food two days a week. This was a far cry from the bounty that once allowed him to spread a bountiful welcome on the refectory table. There was no bread. There was a lock on the bakery door. Production of everything had ceased. Perhaps he inwardly rejoiced in the fact that the refrigerators were gone and he had outlasted the infernal and noisy generators, but death and desertion also had left Father G. behind, like the faithful house servant at the end of *The Cherry Orchard*, whose horrible moment of realization, "I never lived!" still raises bumps on my skin.

I did not think what he was doing was noble; neither, I would think, did he. He was simply paralyzed by his vow of obedience, even though there was no human to be obedient to. A few years before, a fire had raged across the horseshoe ridge within which the monastery nestled. At the last moment, as the firemen were giving the few monks then resident orders to evacuate, the wind changed direction and stopped the flames within a few feet of the walls. Had the wind waited a few minutes more there would have been no choice for

Father G. to make. To him it was a sign. One that, despite his long and exemplary effort to attain relative humility, did not wholly satisfy my friend's need for human companionship. "I have no regrets about coming here," Father G. said to me over and over again. "Do you think I am right to stay?"

But where could he go? By some Byzantine arrangement, control of the monastery was in the hands of a few willful men who did not want to refresh the three hundred-year old cloister with a new abbot and young monks from Mount Athos. And Father G. could not seek sanctuary on the Holy Mountain. This, despite his being an Orthodox monk for almost half a century! How could this be? As I mentioned earlier, the church allows only *one* baptism; when that baptism is a sacrament of a Trinitarian church, no matter how heretical, it cannot be repeated. Father G.'s old haunt, the Anglican Church, confesses the Holy Trinity. Theologically, therefore, Father G. could enter the Orthodox Church only by chrismation – and he had.

The gist of what the powers that be on the Holy Mountain told him was that his Anglican baptism, even though legitimized by his anointment with blessed chrism, was somehow not as good as an Orthodox one. In other words, you could be Orthodox only if you were either Greek, or if you came to Orthodoxy from a Christian sect that denied the Trinity, or if you were a lapsed heathen. (Or a Jew.) Shades of poor Father B.! I am happy to say, however, that the spirit has blown where it listeth to confute the wisdom of the wise. Half a dozen monks and their abbot are now on their way from Dochiareiou to restore life to Father G.'s home, and, incidentally, relieve his loneliness and vindicate his loyalty to the once-sacred precept: "Stay put, and your cell will teach you everything."

Tradition has it that monks are like glass tables that show every scratch, while we in the world are butcher's blocks, so scarred by life that nobody notices, not even us. When I speculate on the future of the Holy Mountain, using what I know and what I have observed, I first must answer to my internal critics. One would like to convince me that because I have disappeared from the world of

Athos, that world has no choice but to disappear. Another argues that Mount Athos is a costly illusion that the world of the spirit can no longer afford. Yet another shakes its head sadly and tells me that I am suffering from a tremendous bellyache induced by sour grapes: *Think of it – you could have been a priest by now!*

After the chattering chimps have had their say, what falls to the bottom of the barrel is the impression that Athonites are living now in a time lag between the thought and the deed. Or the deed done in other places and the deed waiting to be done there. The time when the slingshot still resists the tension – just before the release hurls the stone irrevocably toward its target. What, in the remorseless perspective of history, and all that went before history, unencumbered by a particular point of view from a particular place in a particular time, is *all* times. From what I have seen and heard, the danger that progress poses to their way of life doesn't faze many monks. They seem to believe that if the church of the monastery remains as it has been, out of bounds to temporal concerns, the past will always be present, and those who worship there will not change, no matter what forces act on them from the outside.

Yet monastics have become more aware of the value of the antiquities they have been using as doorstops for centuries, and more areas inside the walls now are off limits to strangers. When the enemy was a remote abstraction, the monks' privacy was a formality, politely requested and graciously acknowledged. No one questioned the rules of the house, and they rarely were enforced. Now, privacy is a demand reinforced by scowls and locks. The men in black shake their spears, not at pirates or heretical Franks, but vigilant to the theft of things that once hardly had mattered and wary of the world they have invited in through travel, commerce, and the Internet. After the destruction of the World Trade Center in New York, monks printed glossies from web sites and circulated them throughout the Holy Mountain. The unpredictable wild is becoming an air-conditioned sanctuary, and cloisters have already accepted their roles as museums, complete with gift shops. Electricity and oil have made it so it is no longer necessary to bear with Nature as she is.

More important, it seems that something has happened to the hospitality that has long been the hallmark of Greeks and monks alike. Money is part of the problem. Money has an effect way beyond what it can buy. "I got plenty of nothing, and nothing's plenty for me" may have been true for Porgy (Gershwin, George *Porgy and Bess*), but it is a belief that finds few subscribers where lack of material wealth equals failure. Wealth divides. Hospitality unites. While the wealthy may entertain friends and colleagues and support good causes with their wallets, true hospitality comes from a much different impulse. Deep inside us all is the fear aroused by our coming helpless into the world: that we share more than we feel comfortable imagining with the lonely, the poor, and the suffering around us. This is what the Buddha's royal father unsuccessfully tried to shield him from. True charity begins with a feeling of shared homelessness. This fear also can be the beginning of love.

The renovations on Mount Athos has resulted in the constant presence of workmen from the world and the equipment they drag in with them, while ease of access, publicity, and modern accommodations has given The Mountain a broader appeal. The increased presence of foreigners is old hat to more congested and wealthier parts of the world, but here it is new. The hospitality that people show to a lonely stranger is quite different from what they show to strang*ers* – or to a stranger who doesn't look like them – when they decide they are a threat to the citadel of their security, the *omogenia*. One beggar in the street gets the change in my pocket; four on the same block have me turning away. It doesn't take much for a host people to feel threatened by what it fears, or what it is uncomfortable with, and to activate a protective xenophobia. The surliness that sets in once foreigners become more than a few wide-eyed tourists seeking their soul or the sun has become visible on monastic faces that once were deadpan to the world. The resentment of haves that turns into lying, mischief, and thievery in the world has begun to permeate the membrane surrounding the Holy Mountain. The monk at Great Lavra who misinformed us about the boat schedule justified his promotion of the taxi to Karyes by telling us "You can afford it. Americans are rich." It was disappointing, yes, but my expectations were unreasonable. As I have insisted all along, monks are people.

Thieves have caused Greeks in the world to shut many of the family chapels that dot the countryside. The boast once was that if you dropped your wallet on a street and came back three days later, it would still be lying there with its contents intact. Not any more. Religions and states exist to protect humans from their own natural proclivities. That is why they are tolerated even when they abuse their power. With the slow collapse of mainstream religions and the world they represent, and the triumph of the laissez-faire pursuit of happiness over conventional morality, religious objects become *objets d'art* and the consequences of their theft as banal as any other theft.

I don't know which is more sinister – that there is a reason to lock doors, or that monks care about what they might lose. How different it was from my residential years, when there were only your feet and a *caique* to get you around the peninsula, and the monks were at least curious about who you were. If they ignored you then, it was because it interfered with some chore they had to do. They had time to talk because what was time, anyway? Paradoxically, as the Holy Mountain has brought the world into it, you get the feeling that your presence doesn't register any more. Everything is becoming new in a place that was born old. Like others who have welcomed conquerors, it looks as if Athonites are painting themselves into a corner and can't recognize who is holding the brush. New wine or old bottle? Is it ever possible to have both? I wonder if the Russian-American at Prophet Elijah now sells those magnificent Cossack boots with the inch-thick, virgin sheepskin lining, instead of giving them away to a stranger with aching feet.

AFTERWORD

I t's May of 2009, and Mount Athos still is. Progress continues its inexorable progress, but nothing has happened yet either to prove my suspicions unfounded or to justify them. A helicopter crashed into the sea, killing a number of prelates about a few miles away from a safe landing, but no one took that as a sign of divine retribution. The Mountain and each of the monasteries have Web sites, some more than one, and news passes in and out as readily and as tainted as any other place in the world. Vatopedi, the wealthiest monastery has been accused of using nepotism to unload some worthless property on the Greek government in exchange for blocks of flats in Athens and Thessaloniki. No government, national or international, is thus far attempting to take over the Holy Mountain, although Esphigmenou is doing its best to provoke a situation which may give someone on the outside a foot in the door.

Having labeled their spiritual leader, Bartholomew, the Ecumenical Patriarch, with the sobriquet "Black Bart", and declared him a "renegade and apostate", the monastery of the fanatically correct has been under siege and blockade for about five years. In October of 2006, "Black Bart" tried to have the ninety-three resident fanatics forcibly removed. Despite, or perhaps because of, the use of two hundred Greek police, public opinion forced him to relent. In December, the decision of the patriarch to entertain the Pope at the Phanar, in Istanbul, touched off an armed rebellion at Esphigmenou, with the dissidents wielding hammers and crowbars against the abbot— himself a fanatic but with a slightly less angry bee in his bonnet—and his small band of followers. Some said it was the abbot that attacked the monks. Others alleged that the incident took place not in the church, as the abbot claims, but in the monastery's *konak* at Karyes. "What is truth?" (John 18:38) Seven monks were hospitalized.

Unable to evict them, the patriarch has forbidden Esphigmenites to leave the Holy Mountain. One tried to escape on a tractor, took a wrong turn, and drove over a cliff. Greek courts tried nine others for trespass and gave them each two-year suspended sentences. I read that the Greek government wants to try two more monks for heresy, although I don't see how this would be possible, unless heresy has become a civil crime. This

261

situation could lead to the *Roe v. Wade* of Mount Athos. Should Mount Athos continue as a self-governing state? Can it continue in that status? Ironic, isn't it? That the self-appointed Only Defenders of the Faith, by their actions, may be the ones that open the gates to secularism and the ultimate fall of their ancient home? Are they crypto-millennialists, who, having already booked their seats on the heaven-bound train, now seek to bring on the definitive "last days"? Esphigmenou's suicidal version of Turette's Syndrome may eventually cause the Greek government to intervene: at first, temporarily, later, perhaps, permanently; for the sake of the safety of the Holy Mountain; for the sake of those who live there and of those who visit. It may even come at the behest of the ruling *Epistasia*. Sounds like the ancient Romans. Déjà vu all over again. Time and again, one side in a civil war invited the Romans in to take their part; they did and they never left, causing the historian, Livy, to remark that Rome "conquered the world in self-defense." Those who cannot remember the past ...? Until they lose their own.

Talking about the past, the Moscow Patriarchate and ROCOR have recently announced a tentative *reconciliation*, but whatever happens – and it very well could result in a split within the latter – the Church Outside of Russia apparently is here to stay. Forgive and forget, but life is too good in the West.

Updating the "woman question", since I wrote this book – though probably not because of it – women have contested the ban on a number of occasions. Some of those who dared were archaeologists, some adventurers; all were dressed in wolves' clothing. On one occasion, in 2008, a thousand women marched across the border for a distance of twenty feet to protest monastic ownership of land outside The Mountain. I wonder how many feared divine retribution is they went another step.

HINTS FOR SPEAKING WELL GREEK

In Greece, to "tchitch" with your tongue and your front teeth—the sound of a basketball hitting nothing but net—when accompanied by an upward thrust of your face usually conveys either disbelief or sympathy. To make a circular motion with your wrist, while your arm is perpendicular to your side, means either "get on with it," "that's too bad," or "no one could possibly believe *that*." When someone makes a circular motion with an apogee about mid-breast, and a perigee at mid-stomach, you are watching a Greek sign himself with the cross—or indicating that he would like some spaghetti. When he pulls on the right breast of his shirt with his thumb and index finger, he is indicating he does not think highly of you, someone is fooling around with your wife, or you are incapable of fooling around with your wife. If he makes an "o" with his forefinger and his thumb, holding the three other fingers vertical, he is commenting on your sexual orientation—unless he is a priest, in which case he is blessing you.

Add to these basics a few verbalisms: *Asta afta* (Don't give me that), *Afti ee zoee* (That's life), *Dhen birazei* (Don't mention it), *Tipote* (Nothing), *Ti na kanoumeh?* (What can we do?), *Malakha* (an observation that you probably like to have sex alone}, and *Opa!* (Zorba's favorite life-affirming expletive). Depending on the situation, Opa! can mean "Life is great!" or "I just slipped on some pumpkin seed shells!" *Takameh thalassa!* (I made a mess of it) will raise an appreciative eyebrow at how well you have learned the language. Practice *Ya soo*, an expression that establishes communication with anyone and anything (often a bottle), and *Paw paw paw*, and you will have practically every likely situation covered. *Paw paw paw* is untranslatable, and can mean anything from "That's tough" to "I don't believe a word of it"—depending on the magnitude of dolefulness in the look that accompanies it. *Siga* (slow) and *grigora* (fast) are almost always delivered as *siga siga* and *grigora grigora*, which tells you that in Greece, slow is slow slow, and fast is fast fast.

There are some aspects of the Greek language that take some getting used to besides the alphabet and the fact that when it's spoken at you it will probably be so *grigora* that you won't understand anything other than the speaker's frustration. When that happens, just smile and keep repeating "*Dhen katalavaino*"—"I don't understand." One of the hurdles facing advanced students is the apparent irony that the Greek word for "yes" is *neh* while "no" is *okhi*. Another is that when someone waves their hand as if wanting you to go away, you are being asked to come toward them. Lastly, if your experience with English tempts you to stress the first syllable of a Greek word, try putting the emphasis on the last: more often than not, you will be right. Differences in stress can be significant. For instance, with the stress on the third syllable, *evlogeia* mean "blessing;" place it on the first and it means "smallpox." The word for "thank you" is *efkaristoh*; "please" is *parakaloh*, and "toilet" is as universal a word in the global village as "Microsoft." You are now a fully qualified *andres* (man) or *yinaika* (woman) in the *odos* (street).

GLOSSARY OF WORDS AND PHRASES

Note: Much of monastic language is a patois of demotic Greek peculiar to the Holy Mountain

Afti ee zoee (aftee ee zoee´)	"That's life."
Agia Koinonia (ahgia keenonee´a)	Holy Communion
Agia Pneuma (agia pnev´ma)	The Holy Spirit
Agia trap´eza	Altar table
Agion Oros	The Holy Mountain of Athos
Agripni´a	(literally, "sleepless") A feast day service beginning with vespers and continuing unbroken through the night
Amarta´noh	To sin; literally, "to miss the mark," as with an arrow
Amarti´a	Sin
Andarte (andart´eh)	A male Communist partisan in the Greek Civil War
Andarti´na	A female Communist partisan in the Greek Civil War
Andres	Man
Antidoron (andih´dhoron)	Blessed bread, what remains of the prosphora after the Host has been removed.
Apagorevetai (ahpahgorev´iteh)	Forbidden
Apa´theia	Control of the passions
Apodeipna (apo´dheipnah)	Church service that follows dinner
Apo´stolos read during services	The book containing the epistles
Archondaris (arkhonda´ris)	Guest master
Arsanas (arsanahs´) of a monastery	Literally, a station or stop; the port
Askesis (askee´sis)	Asceticism
Asta afta (ahsta aftah´)	"Don't give me that."
A´vaton	The ban prohibiting women from entering a men's monastery
A´xion Estin´	Literally, "worthy it is:" one of the most famous icons of the Virgin Mary on the Holy Mountain

Baklava´	A fillo dough pastry made with honey and nuts
Baxmadi (paksmah´dee)	Bread rusks
Caique (cahyee´kee)	A small wooden double-ended boat
Chorta (khor´tah)	Wild greens
Chutzpah (khuts´pah)	A Yiddish word, something like hubris, but cuter
Demestica (dhemes´tica)	A Greek table wine, red or white
Demotiki (dhemotiki´)	Modern Greek
Dhen Birazei (dhen pirah´zee)	"Don't mention it; it doesn't matter."
Dhen ei´mai dho kai vlach´as	"I wasn't born yesterday"
Dhen katalavai´nou	"I don't understand"
Dhou´los	Servant or slave
Ecclesiarch (ekleez´eeark)	Monk responsible for readying church for services
Eepomonee´	Patience
Ekstasi´a	Ecstasy; going out of one's place
Eleas (elyehs´)	Olives or peace
Epikali´mon	Headgear: a short, cylinder hat and a black cloth veil
Epik´lisis	Prayer invoking Holy Spirit to consubstantiate elements
Epistasi´a	The Athonite "senate"
Epi´tropos	A monastic administrator
Esperinos´	Vespers
Evkaristoh (efkahristoh´)	Thank you
Evangel´ion	The Gospels
Evlogei´a	Blessing
Fateh (fah´teh)	"Eat!"
Flia´ria	Nonsense
Four´nos	Oven

Galatabou´reko — Custard

Gerondas (yer´ohndah) — Elder or abbot

Geshmatt´ — Yiddish for "apostate"

Grigora (gree´gora) — Quickly

Gnorizo (nawree´zo) — To know intimately

Hasid — A member of a Jewish sect obedient to a tzaddik

Hesychast (he´zikast) — A monk given to silence

Hu´bris — Overreaching pride

Hyposta´sis — Hypostasis; inside the substance; the heart of the matter

Iconostasis (ikonostah´sis) — The screen that separates nave from altar in church

Idiorrhythmic (idhiorrhyth´mic) — A monk who lives in a non-communal brotherhood

Iota (yot´a) — The seventh and tiniest letter of the Greek alphabet

Ison (ee´sohn) — Low note that supports chanter

Kafeneion (kafenay´on) — Coffee house

Kalyve (kal´eeveh) — A small house usually inhabited by a single monk

Kapneez´oh — To smoke

Kasse´ri — A hard Greek cheese

Katalav´enettai — You understand, or do you understand?

Katastima (katah´steemah) — A shop

Katharev´ousa — A kind of Greek used only in newspapers and diplomacy

Kathis´mata — Groups of psalms, each consisting of three stases (sections)

Kathol´ikon — The main church of a monastery

Kefalati´ri — Literally, head cheese

Kelli (kellee´) — A small monastic house of usually one to four monks

Koine (keen´ee)	The Greek of the New Testament
Koinonizo (keenonee´zo)	To communicate; receive Holy Communion
Koinov´ion	A monastic brotherhood
Koliva (koh´leevah)	A commemorative sweet based on boiled wheat berries
Kombologia (komboloy´)	Small string of "worry beads" (literally, "word beads")
Komboskini (komboskeen´ee)	Black woolen knotted rope used for counting prayers
Konak´	The house of a monastery's representative in Karyes
Kosmikos´	A person living in the world
Latreia (lahtree´ah)	Worship; see proskynisis
Leipsanon (lip´sahnohn)	A repository for skulls and bones
Logismoi (logizmee´)	Demonic thoughts
Mai´ros	Toilet
Ma´lista	A polite form of "yes"
Megaloschema (megaloh´skeemah)	A monk of the "great habit"
Melte´mi	Hot wind that comes north off the Sahara
Mesinik´tikon	Midnight church service
Metanoia (metan´yah)	Repentance ("change of mind") or prostration
Metochion (metokh´iaon)	A monastic dependency outside the Holy Mountain
Mezithra (mehzee´thrah)	A sweet grating cheese
Microschema (meekro´schemah)	A monk of the "little habit"
Mitzvoh (mitz´voh)	Hebrew for "good deed"
Monakhos (monakhohs´)	Monk
Monopati´	Footpath
Moussaka (moosakah´)	A layered dish featuring ground lamb and eggplant
Myste´rium	Sacrament

Nar'thex	Ante-room to the nave
Neh	Yes
O'dhos	Street
Ogdondyiatros (odhondyatros')	Dentist
Oh''pah!	Hooray! (sort of)
Oikogenia (eekoyenn'yah)	Family
Oikonomia (Eekonomee'yah)	An exception to a rule
Omogenia (omoyen'yah)	Ethnic family
Opos theleis (opos thel'ees)	"Whatever you want."
Opou theleis	"Wherever you want"
Or'thros	Matins
Ou'zo	A licorice cordial
O'khi (aw'khee)	No
Pa'raclete	The Holy Spirit
Parakaloh'	Please
Parthe'nos	Virgin or young woman
Patris (patrees')	Fatherland
Pastitsa (pahstee'tsah)	A layered macaroni dish with ground lamb
Pater Imon (patehr heemohn')	The first words of the "Our Father"—the Lord's Prayer
Paw paw paw	"Too bad"
Phanar (phanar')	The Istanbul residence of the Ecumenical Patriarch
Phia'le	The stone fountain in the courtyard of every monastery
PIrgos (pir'gos)	Tower
Plani (plah'nee)	Delusion
Plaka (plah'kah)	The district below the Acropolis in Athens
Plion (plee'ohn)	A sea-going vessel
Pneumatikos (pnevmahtikohs')	Spiritual guide
Poslush'nik	Russian believer
Pre'lest	Delusion, in Russian
Proskynisis (proskee'neesis)	Veneration

Pro'sphora	Bread used in the liturgy from which the Host is cut
Prothe'sis	The "table of preparation' within the altar
Psaltis (psal'tees)	Chanter
Raki (rahkee')	Rot-gut made from decomposing fruits and vegetables
Ram millet	Subject peoples in the Ottoman Empire
Rasaphor (rah'safor)	The lowest level of monk, after a novice
Rason (rah'sohn)	A monk's basic robe
Reb'be	Spiritual Hasidic leader, often without formal education
Retsina (retzee'nah)	A horrible wine-like beverage flavored with pine resin
Revethia (revee'thia)	A baked chickpea casserole
Rizo'gala	Rice pudding
Schnorrer	Jewish beggar with lots of chutzpah
Shabbat oy'rech	Sabbath guest
Sh'ma	The first word of the Jewish creed
Shmoo	A pear-shaped cartoon character created by Al Capp
Siga (see gah')	Slow
Skep'sis	Think (imperative)
Skiti (skee'tee)	A small dependency of a major monastery
Skufi (skoo'fee)	A monastic cap
Spanako'pita	Fillo dough pasty with spinach, eggs, and cheese
Staretz	Russian spiritual counselor
Stasida (sta si' da)	Church chair with hinged seat
Stran'nik	Russian professional pilgrim

Symandron (see´mandrohn)	Wood ecclesiarch strikes to call monks to church
Takema thalassa (ta´kehmah tha´lassah)	"I made a mess of it."
Ta´phos	Grave
Tipote (tee´poteh)	"Nothing."
Ti na kanoumeh (tee nah kah´noumeh	"What can we do?"
Theia Liturgia (thee´a liturgee´ah)	The Divine Liturgy, or mass
Theos (Theh ohs´)	God
Theo´sis	The attempt to find oneself in God
Tiro´pita	Fillo dough pasty with cheese
Tra´peza	Table; change the accent, and it means "bank"
Trapeza´rius	Steward
T'shu´vah	Turning (Hebrew)
Tzad´dik	A "righteous one;" the head of a community of Hasids
Xenos (ksen´ohs)	Stranger
Xero (kser´ro)	To know (facts)
Xerofagita (kserofagitah´)	Dry foods
Yah´soo	"Your health;" "Hello;" "Good-by"
Yinai´ka	Woman
Zacharaplastei´a	Sweet shop
Zimi´	Bread starter made from the dough of a previous bake
Zylotes (zeelotees´)	Zealot

272

A SELECT BIBLIOGRAPHY

Armstrong, Karen, *Jerusalem*. New York: Alfred A. Knopf (1996)

Brianchianinov, Ignatius, *The Arena: An Offering to Contemporary Monasticism*. Translated by Archimandrite Lazarus Moore. Jordanville: Holy Trinity Monastery (1982)

Brown, Norman O., *Life Against Death*. Wesleyan University Press; 2nd edition (1985)

Boswell, James, *The Life of Samuel Johnson LLD*. Two Volumes. Reprint. London: E. P. Dutton & Co. (1960)

Buber, Martin, *I and Thou*. New York: Charles Scribner's Sons (1958)

Buber, Martin, Tales of the Hasidim: The Early Masters. New York: Schocken Books (1961)

Buber, Martin, *Tales of the Hasidim: The Later Masters*. New York: Schocken Books (1961)

Byron, Robert, *The Station*. London: Phoenix Press. Reprint (1988)

Gibbon, Edward, *The Decline and Fall of the Roman Empire. Volumes 1-3*. New York: Everyman's Library (Random House). Boxed edition (1993)

The Holy Bible. Philadelphia: A. J. Holman Company (1902)

Johnson, Hugh, *Wine*. New York: Simon & Schuster, Inc. (1974)

Leavy, Jane, *A Lefty's Legacy*. London: Harper Perennial. Reprint edition (2003)

Kazantzakis, Nikos, *Report to Greco*. Faber and Faber; New Ed edition (2001)

The Letters of Saint Anthony the Great. Translated by Derwas J. Chitty. Oxford: SLG Press (1975)

The Little Philokalia, Volume I: St. Seraphim of Sarov. Platina: Saint Herman of Alaska Monastery Press (1978)

Lives of the Saints. I have given no specific information because there are so many saints and so many compilations, usually published in monthly collections, by every denomination that believes in saints. Until 1054, you are all right with any collection. But if you are seeking information on saints canonized after the Great Divorce, you will have to consult the publications of the particular churches.

Loch, Joice NanKivell, *A Fringe of Blue: An Autobiography*. New York: William Morrow & Company, Inc. (1968)

Melville, Herman, *Moby Dick*. New York: Bantam Classics. Reissue edition (1981)

Melville, Herman, *Billy Budd and The Piazza Tales*. Reprint. Garden City: Doubleday & Company, Inc. (1961)

Morgan, Edmund S., *The Puritan Dilemma*. Boston: Little, Brown, and Co. (1958)

Norwich, John Julius: *A Short History of Byzantium*. New York: Vintage Books (Random House). Reprint edition (1998)

Rajneesh, Bhagwan Shree, *The Mustard Seed: Discourses on the Sayings of Jesus taken from the Gospel according to Thomas*. Rajneeshpuram: Rajneesh Foundation International (1975

Sherrard, Philip: *Church, Papacy, and Schism*, Greece: Harvey (Denise) & Co. New Ed edition (1978)

Thomas A Kempis, *The Imitation of Christ*. New York: Sheed and Ward (1961)

Ware, Timothy, *The Orthodox Church*. Penguin (Non-Classics); 2 edition (1993)

The Way of a Pilgrim and The Pilgrim Continues His Way. Translated by R. M. French. New York: Seabury Press. Reprint (1980)

Writings from the Philokalia on the Prayer of the Heart. Translated by E. Kadloubovsky and G. E. H. Palmer. London: Faber and Faber (1973

ABOUT THE AUTHOR

Richard John Friedlander is a mediator who lives in the hills above Berkeley, California, with his beautiful wife, Pamela, their pet, Frank the Cat, and their anti-pet, the cat, Carlo. The Orthodox Church baptized Richard at the age of thirty-five, after which he spent more than ten years in and out of Mount Athos, leading a self-regulated, monastic life, free of vows. The Church gave him the name, John, but he will answer to whatever makes you comfortable – proof he does indeed have a degree from Yale Law School. He is the author of seven plays from his pre-monastic days, but upon donning the black, he burned his work in a dramatic auto de fe attended only by himself. True to form, he had back-pocketed a full set and entrusted them to a good friend; in his absence the friend moved, the plays vanished, and the world will never know what it lost. More recently, he has written a children's book about otters, called *An Otterian Quartet*, and a novel entitled *Stranger on the Earth* – the true story of *Paradise Besieged*.